SIMPLIFIED CHARACTER VERS

Chinese Link

中 文 天 地

Zhōng Wén Tiān Dì

Elementary Chinese

Level 1	Part 2

吴素美 Sue-mei Wu
于月明 Yueming Yu
张燕辉 Yanhui Zhang
田维忠 Weizhong Tian

Carnegie Mellon University

PEARSON Prentice Hall
world Languages
Upper Saddle River, New Jersey 07458

Library of Congress Cataloging-in-Publication Data

Chinese link : Zhong wen tian di : elementary Chinese / Sue-mei Wu ... [et al]—Simplified character version.
p. cm.
ISBN 0-13-242977-2 (alk. paper)
1. Chinese language—Textbooks for foreign speakers—English. I. Title: Elementary Chinese. II. Wu, Sue-mei, 1968–

PL1129.E5C418 2006
495.1'82421—dc22

2005050939

Acquisitions Editor: Rachel McCoy
Publishing Coordinator: Claudia Fernandes
Executive Director of Market Development: Kristine Suárez
Director of Editorial Development: Julia Caballero
Production Supervision: Nancy Stevenson
Project Manager: Margaret Chan, Graphicraft
Assistant Director of Production: Mary Rottino
Supplements Editor: Meriel Martínez Moctezuma
Media Editor: Samantha Alducin
Media Production Manager: Roberto Fernandez
Prepress and Manufacturing Buyer: Brian Mackey
Prepress and Manufacturing Manager: Nick Sklitsis
Interior and Cover Design: Wanda España/Wee Design Group
Director, Image Resource Center: Melinda Reo
Interior Image Specialist: Beth Boyd Brenzel
Manager, Rights & Permissions IRC: Zina Arabia
Senior Marketing Manager: Jacquelyn Zautner
Marketing Assistant: William J. Bliss
Publisher: Phil Miller
Cover image: Jerry Darvin

This book was set in 12/15 Sabon by Graphicraft Ltd., Hong Kong, and was printed and bound by Courier – Westford. The cover was printed by Phoenix Color Corp.

PEARSON Prentice Hall

Printed in the United States of America
10 9 8 7 6 5

ISBN 0-13-242977-2

Pearson Education Ltd., *London*
Pearson Education Australia Pty, Limited, *Sydney*
Pearson Education Singapore Pte. Ltd.
Pearson Education North Asia Ltd., *Hong Kong*
Pearson Education Canada, Ltd., *Toronto*
Pearson Educación de México, S.A. de C.V.
Pearson Education – Japan, *Tokyo*
Pearson Education Malaysia Pte. Ltd.
Pearson Education, *Upper Saddle River,* New Jersey

目录 CONTENTS

范围和顺序　Scope and Sequence

Foundation

Introduction to Chinese *p. xix*
Pinyin Foundation and Exercises *p. F-1*
The Chinese Writing System *p. F-26*
Classroom Expressions and Exercises *p. F-33*
Abbreviations of Parts of Speech *p. F-37*

Lessons & Topics	Objectives & Communications	Grammar	Culture Link
11 Do You Want Black Tea or Green Tea? 你要红茶还是绿茶? *p. 169*	■ Order food at a restaurant ■ Present/choose from alternatives ■ Ask what someone wants ■ Tell someone what you want	1. 还是 2. 量词 (Measure Words/Classifiers) (3)	**Culture Notes:** Chinese Food 中国菜系介绍 **Fun With Chinese:** Slang: 饭后百步走，活到九十九。 **Let's Go:** Chinese Snacks 小吃
12 May I Borrow Your Car? 我可以借你的车吗? *p. 187*	■ Make a request ■ Express wishes, obligations, capabilities, possibilities, or permissions	1. Optative Verbs (能愿动词): 要, 想, 应该, 得, 能, 可以, 会 2. 从 ... 去(到) ... 3. 多 VP (学习, 练习)	**Culture Notes:** China's Auto Industry 中国的汽车工业 **Fun With Chinese:** Slang: 有借有还，再借不难。 **Let's Go:** Parking Sign and Car for Sale 停车标志和汽车出售

Lessons & Topics	Objectives & Communications	Grammar	Culture Link
13 I Want to Buy a Shirt 我想买一件衬衫 *p. 203*	■ Go shopping ■ Talk about clothing, colors, and prices ■ Provide opinions	1. Conjunction 或者 2. 量词 (Measure Words/Classifiers) (4): 件，条，张 3. Duplication of Verbs	**Culture Notes:** Chinese Traditional Dress 中国的传统服饰 **Fun With Chinese:** Slang: 情人眼里出西施。 **Let's Go:** Shopping: Bill, Receipt, and Invoice 购物：钱币，收据和发票
14 I Am 20 This Year 我今年二十岁 *p. 227*	■ Say the days of the week ■ Extend/accept an invitation ■ Talk about people's birthdays	1. Days of the Week 2. Expressing Dates, Year, Month, and Days of the Week 3. Preposition 为	**Culture Notes:** Chinese Zodiac 十二生肖 **Fun With Chinese:** Slang: 女大十八变。 **Let's Go:** Common Phrases for Congratulations and Best Wishes 庆祝贺词
15 The Library Is in Front of the Dorm 图书馆在宿舍前边 *p. 243*	■ Show people around ■ Ask where something is located ■ Explain where something is located	1. Position Words 2. Sentences Expressing Location and Existence with 在, 有, and 是	**Culture Notes:** The Chinese Art of Placement 风水 **Fun With Chinese:** Slang: 有缘千里来相会，无缘对面不相识。 **Let's Go:** Scenic Spots in Beijing 北京观光景点

Lessons & Topics	Objectives & Communications	Grammar	Culture Link
16 She Plays Basketball Very Well 她打篮球打得很好 *p. 259*	■ Describe how an action is performed ■ Talk about hobbies and exercises	1. Degree of Complement Sentences	**Culture Notes:** Chinese Sport 中国体育 **Fun With Chinese:** Slang: 临时抱佛脚 **Let's Go:** Announcements and Notifications 公布告示
17 Spring Is Coming Soon 春天就要来了 *p. 277*	■ Talk about the four seasons ■ Describe the weather ■ Express that something will happen in the near future	1. 就/快要... 了 2. 最 3. Adj. + 极了	**Culture Notes:** The Three Main Chinese Festivals 中国的主要节庆 **Fun With Chinese:** Slang: 热锅上的蚂蚁 **Let's Go:** Weather Forecast 天气预报
18 We Are Going to Take a Train Trip 我们要坐火车去旅行 *p. 293*	■ Describe means of transportation ■ Talk about travel plans	1. 离 2. 先……(再)……然后…… 3. 坐, 骑 and 开	**Culture Notes:** Traffic Signs and Rules in China 中国的交通标志与规则 **Fun With Chinese:** Proverb: 读万卷书，行万里路。 **Let's Go:** Train and Airplane Tickets 火车和飞机票

Lessons & Topics	Objectives & Communications	Grammar	Culture Link
19 I Caught a Cold 我感冒了 *p. 313*	■ Describe the symptoms of an illness ■ Describe something that has happened	1. The Aspect Particle 了 2. 的, 得, and 地	**Culture Notes:** Traditional Chinese Medicine and Pharmacology 中医中药 **Fun With Chinese:** Proverb: 良药苦口，忠言逆耳。 **Let's Go:** Watermelon Frost Throat Lozenges 西瓜霜润喉片
20 I've Brought Xiao Xie Over . . . 我把小谢带来了... *p. 331*	■ Rent an apartment ■ Indicate the direction of a movement ■ Describe an event and its cause	1. Directional Complement 趋向补语 (DC) 2. 把 Sentences 3. 把 Sentences and the Directional Complement 4. 把 Construction	**Culture Notes:** Housing Reform in China 中国的住房改革 **Fun With Chinese:** Proverb: 秀才不出门，能知天下事。 **Let's Go:** Houses for Rent and Houses for Sale 出租和出售房子
21 What Will You Do During the Summer Vacation? 暑假你要做什么? *p. 355*	■ Talk about plans ■ Express blessings and wishes	1. 一面……一面…… 2. 语法总复习 (1): Summary of the Aspects of Verbs	**Culture Notes:** Travel in China 中国的旅游业 **Fun With Chinese:** Slang: 活到老，学到老。 **Let's Go:** Receipt for Transcript Printing 申请成绩单的发票

Lessons & Topics	Objectives & Communications	Grammar	Culture Link
22 I Have Arrived in Shanghai 我到上海了 *p. 371*	■ Exchange e-mails ■ Describe your current situation	1. 比如 2. Summary of Measure Words in Chinese 3. Summary of Conjunctions in Chinese	**Culture Notes:** Peking Opera; Chinese Calligraphy 京剧；书法 **Fun With Chinese:** Idiom: 心想事成 **Let's Go:** Slogan 标语

Appendices

前言 PREFACE

Recognizing that the world is becoming increasingly interlinked and globalized, the goal of the **CHINESE LINK: Zhongwen Tiandi 中文天地** (**Elementary Chinese**) project has been to integrate the "5Cs" principles of the National Standards for Foreign Language Education — Communication, Cultures, Comparisons, Connections, and Communities — throughout the program in order to provide a new approach for the teaching and learning of Chinese language in the 21st century. The program aims to help beginners develop their communicative competence in the four basic skills of listening, speaking, reading, and writing, while gaining competence in Chinese culture, exercising their ability to compare aspects of different cultures, making connections to their daily life, and building links among communities.

A language curriculum should be attractive to both students and instructors, therefore the authors provide a practical, learner-centered, and enjoyable language and culture learning experience for beginning students of Chinese, as well as an efficient and comprehensive teaching resource for instructors.

Proficiency in a language involves knowing both the structural forms of the language and their appropriate use in different cultural contexts. Care has been taken to introduce and explain grammar points clearly and systematically, yet not in a fashion that would be overwhelming to beginners. In keeping with the communicative focus of the text, grammar points are related to communicative, task-oriented content.

Each version of the text (Traditional and Simplified) presents both traditional and simplified versions of Chinese characters, since it is likely that students will encounter both forms. Similarly, care has been taken to present both Taiwan and Mainland China usage where they differ, and to incorporate new vocabulary items, such as "Internet," "cell phone," and "VCD." Culture notes at the end of each lesson are designed to catch the interest of the beginning learner and to explain important features of Chinese culture. Photographs and drawings are provided to make the text vivid and eye-catching, and to provide visual cues to aid in communicative exercises and activities.

Features of CHINESE LINK: Zhongwen Tiandi 中文天地 (Elementary Chinese)

- A clear and organized **Scope and Sequence** of the textbook is presented that provides an overview of the entire textbook, listing each lesson and its objectives, as well as the contents of the lesson's subsections. The **Scope and Sequence** lists the contents of four major sub-sections of each lesson: Grammar, Culture Notes, Fun with Chinese, and Let's Go!
- The **5Cs** (**National Standards**) are blended consistently throughout the content and exercises in the program.
- The **Foundation** unit introduces important background information on Chinese language, useful classroom expressions, and a complete introduction to Pinyin and pronunciation.
- From the beginning of the text, we help students build from words and phrases to sentences and cohesive passages and then to application in **communicative tasks**.
- The textbook contains many **drawings** and **authentic photographs**, and utilizes a clear, attractive layout.

- **Grammar** points are introduced systematically and with a writing style that attempts to avoid excessive linguistic jargon. Grammar points include many examples.
- **Pronunciation and Pinyin** exercises are consistently emphasized throughout the entire text.
- **Both Traditional and Simplified character forms** are listed for every **vocabulary** item. When students see the two forms side by side it helps them to make an association between the two.
- **In-class exercises** are included in the main text as handy teaching aids and guidelines for instructors.
- Each lesson consists of **four types of exercises:** Pinyin, character, grammar, and communicative tasks. The exercises progress from drills and practice to content-based communicative tasks.
- Differences in usage between **Mainland China and Taiwan** are consistently identified.
- Interesting **cultural notes** are included in each lesson and supplemented with authentic photographs from Mainland China, Taiwan, and Hong Kong.

Organization of the Textbook

The textbook is divided into three main parts: **Foundation, core lessons,** and **Appendices.** The flexible design of the text allows instructors to use it in varying ways, depending on the number of contact hours per week and whether a school is on the semester or quarter system. Sample syllabi are available in the Instructor's Resource Manual.

Foundation:

The **Foundation** module provides fundamental knowledge about Chinese and learning Chinese that is useful for beginning students. It contains linguistic as well as cultural background material. Following are the major sections of the **Foundation** unit:

- **Introduction to Chinese:** This section briefly introduces some characteristics of Chinese language such as tones, the importance of word order, pictographic characters and its history and development.
- **Pinyin Foundation and Exercises:** Pinyin is the most widely used phonetic transliteration system to be introduced as a tool for representing the sounds of Chinese. This section introduces the Pinyin system as well as the structural components of Chinese syllables: initials, finals, and tones. There are many Pinyin exercises. Tongue twisters are introduced to show different aspects of rhythm and rhyme and the sounds of Chinese.
- **The Chinese Writing System:** This section discusses the formation of Chinese characters. It introduces the common components, radicals, and the structure of Chinese characters. Exercises are included.
- **Classroom Expressions and Exercises:** This section introduces the most useful and common phrases encountered in the Chinese classroom. Introducing these phrases early helps the instructors to limit use of English in the classroom. It also allows students to learn some phrases that they can make use of right away.

- **Abbreviations of Parts of Speech:** This section lists the abbreviations used later in the grammar notes and vocabulary sections.

Core Lessons:
The content of the 22 lessons is selected to meet the practical needs and interests of students. The focus of the content begins with individual, family, and school activities, then gradually expands to include wider social occasions and societal contact. Great care has been taken to clearly and systematically present and practice the core vocabulary and grammatical expressions of elementary Chinese.

The major sections of each lesson are described below:

- **Core Vocabulary:** Core vocabulary terms, which appear in the **Language Link** section, are introduced here. For each vocabulary item, traditional and simplified character forms are presented along with Pinyin pronunciation, grammatical function, and English meaning. This section also points out differences between Mainland China and Taiwan usage.
- **Language Link:** This section contains situations that incorporate the lesson's core vocabulary and grammar points. It is accompanied by an art program that adds context and makes the lesson more interesting. **Language Link** serves as a model of the correct usage of the vocabulary and grammar points introduced in the lesson. Notes are provided to further explain the text. For most of the lessons, **Language Link** includes dialogues; for some selections it includes essays, diaries, e-mail, and letters. The length of **Language Link** is carefully controlled, and gradually increases to provide pedagogical sufficiency and challenge.
- **Grammar:** Core grammar points from **Language Link** are explained in this section. We adopt the pedagogical grammar approach to better fit with the communicative approach to language learning. Grammar explanations are supplemented with examples that use vocabulary items previously covered in the textbook. We have tried to avoid linguistics jargon, with the exception of such commonly used terms as *syntax*, *sentence*, *clause*, *subject*, *predicate*, *object*, *modifier*, etc. For review and consolidation, the communicative exercises of each lesson are designed to elicit the use of grammatical structures introduced in the lesson.
- **Supplementary Practice:** Each lesson has a **Supplementary Practice** section with themes, vocabulary, and grammar similar to those found in **Language Link**. This allows students to practice immediately what they have learned from their study of the main text. Care has been taken to use a different format from that found in **Language Link**. For example, if **Language Link** contains a dialogue, **Supplementary Practice** will include a prose format, and vice versa. The pedagogical purpose is to help students learn to use vocabulary and grammar structures in varying forms of communication.
- **Activities:** This section is designed primarily for classroom use. Listening, character, grammar, and communicative exercises are included throughout the text. Care has been taken to provide balance between structural drills and real-life communicative tasks. The exercises integrate with the grammar points to provide a systematic extension of usage skills from vocabulary-item level to sentence level and on to discourse-level narration and description. Since these exercises are for class meeting time, they are designed to be dynamic and interactive. Most involve interaction between instructor and students,

student and student, or group and group. Communicative activities are based on situations designed to elicit the grammar points and vocabulary students have learned in the lesson and in prior lessons. Visual aids are provided to help set the context for the communicative activities. Our goal in providing classroom exercises is to help save instructor time, which makes the text convenient and efficient for instructors to use.

- **Culture Link:** This section contains three components:
  - **Culture Notes:** The topics of the **Culture Notes** are carefully chosen to relate to those of the core lessons. It is hoped that the **Culture Notes** will help students to better understand Chinese societies, as well as how language reflects culture. Authentic photos are provided to create a vivid and interesting learning experience. The discussion questions are designed to encourage students to discuss and compare cultural differences by helping them to be aware of the features of their own culture and to be more understanding and tolerant toward other cultures.
  - **Fun with Chinese:** This section introduces a common slang expression, an idiom, or a motto that either utilizes new vocabulary presented in the lesson or is closely related to the theme of the lesson. Drawings are included to help make this section more fun and eye-catching. Discussion questions are provided to offer another fun way to relate the common Chinese expressions to the theme of the lesson.
  - **Let's Go!:** This section gives students an opportunity to interact with Chinese in an authentic context. It assists the students to connect themselves to authentic Chinese societies and communities. This section promotes students' motivation and helps them develop survival skills for life in authentic Chinese societies.

Appendices: The appendices serve as a learning resource for both students and instructors. It can also be used for review exercises in class or for self-study. The Appendices include the following:

- Vocabulary List
- Simplified/Traditional Character Table
- Chinese Transcriptions of **Language in Use**
- English Transcriptions of **Language in Use:** These can be used for translation or interpretation practice, for self-study or in-class review.
- Index (Pinyin and English)
- Characters in The Character Book

Other Program Components

Workbook: Homework and Character Book

The **Homework** portion contains a homework assignment for each lesson in the main textbook. A typical assignment is 3–4 pages, including space for students to write their responses. Homework activities are divided among listening, character recognition and writing, grammar exercises, and communicative tasks.

The **Character** portion provides the Chinese characters for the core vocabulary in every lesson. It shows the following for each character:

1. Character with its stroke order indicated by numbers
2. Simplified form of the character
3. Traditional form of the character
4. Pinyin pronunciation, grammatical usage, and sample sentences or phrases
5. Stroke order illustrated by writing the character progressively
6. Radical of the character with its Pinyin pronunciation and meaning
7. Ghosted images for students to trace over
8. Dotted graph lines to aid students' practice

Blank boxes are also included for students to practice writing the character. As a handy reference, three types of indices are provided in the Character Book: (1) By number of strokes; (2) By Lesson number; (3) Alphabetic by Pinyin.

Instructor's Resource Manual

The **Instructor's Resource Manual** provides sample syllabi, daily schedules, the answer key for in-class and homework exercises, and sample test questions.

Audio Materials

The audio files for all the lesson texts, vocabulary, listening exercises, tongue twisters, and poems in the textbook, as well as the listening exercises in the **Homework Portion of the Workbook** are provided on audio CDs.

Companion Website, <www.prenhall.com/chineselink>

This open-access Web site will provide useful tools that will allow students to further their learning of the Chinese language and culture.

致谢 ACKNOWLEDGMENTS

While we have a sense of accomplishment for completing this project, we are also keenly aware and appreciative of the support and encouragement we have received from the many individuals who contributed. We would like to express our gratitude to everyone who offered us support, suggestions, and encouragement.

We would like to thank Mark Haney for his assistance with English proofreading of the manuscript during many different stages of its preparation. We also owe our thanks to Denny Chen for his delicate skills in tracing the stroke order of most of the Chinese characters in the character book manuscript. With Mark and Denny's devotion and patience, the **Chinese Link** project moved along smoothly and well.

We sincerely appreciate the illustrators for our manuscript and the custom copy, Chi-chen Wu, Chung-ning Lu, and Yi-ju Chen. Their wonderful line art with Chinese flavor helped the manuscript to be more vivid and pleasing. Their line art also provided good models for this project.

Thanks to our loving families in Taiwan and Mainland China and the sincere friends who served as our photographers and photo providers: Vincent Sha, Mark Shope, Wenze Hu, Su-ying Wu, Tsan-lung Wu, Su-yueh Wu, Yi-ching Liu, and Mark Haney. Their artistic and authentic photos bring our project to a professional level.

We would like to express our gratitude to the Elementary Chinese instructors and students at Carnegie Mellon University and St. Vincent College in 2003–2004 and 2004–2005 who took the time to assist us with comments and suggestions during the course of our revision of the manuscript. Thanks also go to our colleagues in the Department of Modern Languages at CMU for their consistent encouragement. Special thanks to our department head, Professor Richard Tucker, for his warm support, and to Dean Gary Quinlivan of St. Vincent College for his enthusiasm and promotion of Chinese Link.

We would like to give our sincerest thanks to the folks at Prentice Hall for bringing their talent and professional publishing experience to this project. Many thanks go to Rachel McCoy, Acquisitions Editor, for her enthusiasm, sincere dedication, and professional guidance. Many thanks also go to Nancy Stevenson, Senior Production Editor, and Mary Rottino, Assistant Director of Production, for their patient and detailed instructions and guidelines about production procedures. We would also like to thank Meriel Martínez Moctezuma, Supplements Editor, for carefully overseeing the production of the Instructor's Resource Manual, Workbook, and Audio program. Thanks to Claudia Fernandes, Publishing Coordinator, for handling the mail and details in a timely fashion. Thanks to Phil Miller for his faith and commitment to this project, and to Wanda España, Weedesign, whose creativity resulted in a wonderful design for this project.

Many thanks to Margaret Chan, Project Manager, and her Graphicraft team members. Their prompt communication and hard work helped this project to reach the production stage.

We would like to conclude by thanking our families, without whose love and support this project would not have been possible. Many thanks to our husbands, Mark, Denny, Dejun, and Jinghong, for enduring our long hours. Special thanks to our children, Carrie, Marion, Sara, and Ryan, for giving up a lot of time with their moms so that this project could be completed.

We extend our sincere thanks and appreciation to the colleagues who reviewed the manuscript and provided valuable input. Their detailed comments and insightful suggestions helped us to further refine our manuscript.

Gary Quinlivan, Saint Vincent College, PA
Xiaohong Wen, University of Houston, TX
Wenze Hu, Harvard University, MA
Weijia Huang, Brown University, RI
Mingjung Chen, De Anza College, CA
Dana Scott Bourgerie, Brigham Young University, UT
Zheng-sheng Zhang, San Diego State University, CA
Jun Yang, University of Chicago, IL
Jean Yu, The Hotchkiss School, CT

Sue-mei Wu
Yueming Yu
Yanhui Zhang
Weizhong Tian

中国地图 MAP OF CHINA

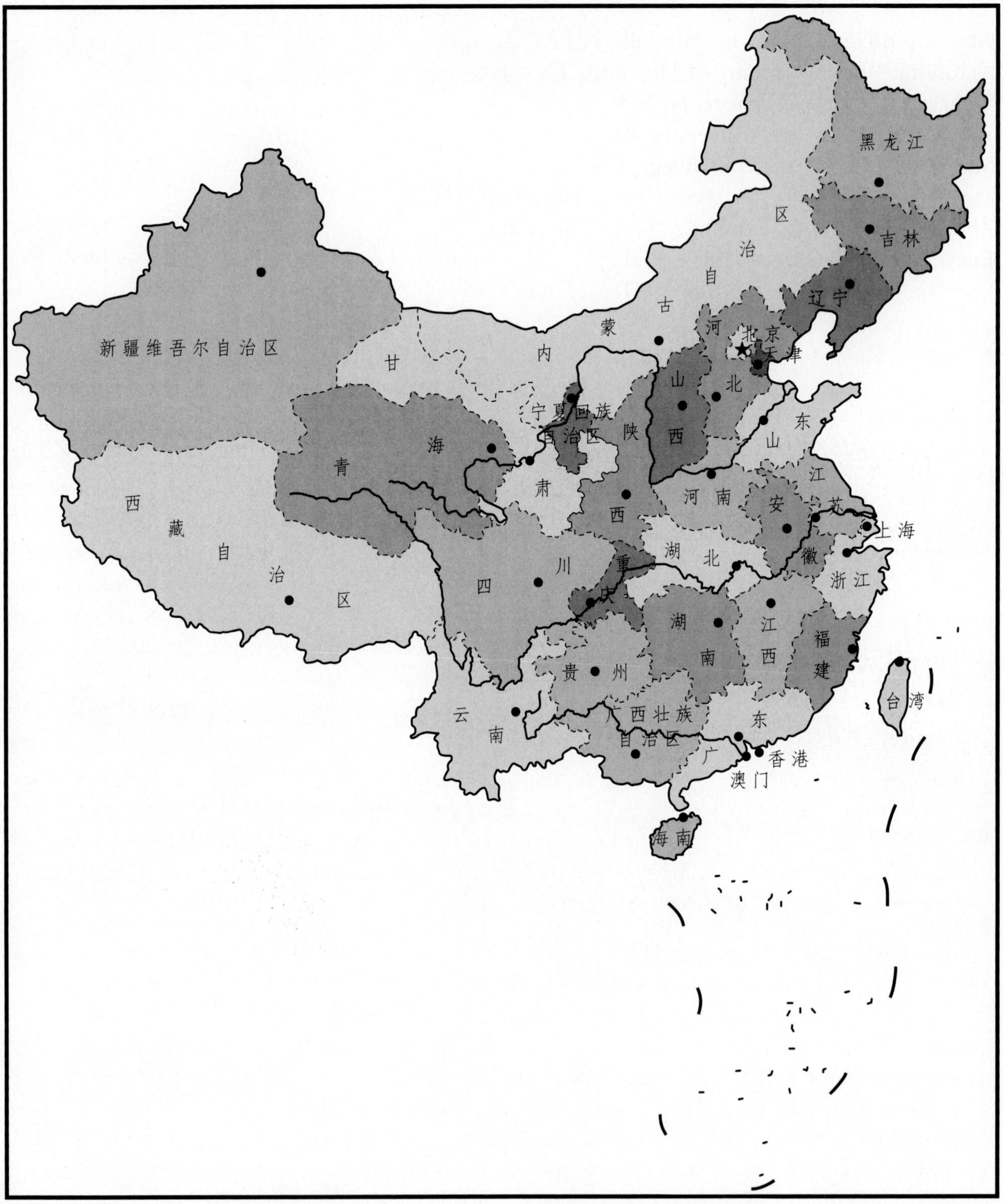

中文简介 INTRODUCTION TO CHINESE

Chinese is a language spoken by about a quarter of the world's population. It is also one of the six working languages of the United Nations. It is called 汉语 [Hànyǔ] (Hanyu) in Chinese because it is spoken by the Han people, the largest ethnic group in China.

A member of the Sino-Tibetan language family, Chinese differs from other languages in many respects. Following are a few of its distinctive characteristics:

- It has no inflection of words to indicate person, gender, number, tense, or mood. The meaning of a sentence relies heavily on the context and word order.
- It is a tonal language. There are many Chinese words whose meanings are differentiated solely by which of the four tones is assigned to them.
- It comprises a large number of dialects, which share the same written form but can be mutually unintelligible when spoken. The Chinese dialects are generally categorized into eight groups: Mandarin (Northern), Northern Min (Northern Fujian), Southern Min (Southern Fujian, Taiwan), Xiang (Hunan), Gan (Jiangxi), Wu (Jiangsu and Zhejiang), Hakka (Guangdong, Guangxi), and Yue (Guangdong).
- The written form of the language consists of roughly square-shaped characters, each of which are formed by a number of strokes. The number of Chinese characters keeps growing. Scholars believe that 3,000 years ago there were around 4,500 characters in use. More recently the Kangxi Dictionary, compiled in 1710, lists about 48,000 characters. A dictionary published in 1994 lists around 86,000 characters! But don't let the sheer number of characters scare you away from studying Chinese. According to a list of commonly used Chinese characters published by China's Education Commission, only 3,500 characters are commonly used in daily life. It is generally acknowledged that a well-educated Chinese person has mastered 6,000 to 7,000 characters.
- Radicals often provide clues to the meaning of the character. The radical is also important for ordering and grouping characters. For example, dictionaries often have characters grouped by radical, and then by the number of strokes required to write the character. According to Chinese linguists, there are approximately 1,500 radicals in total, but most modern Chinese dictionaries only include 214.

About 400 years ago, a unified system of pronunciation for Chinese began to be established, which would be intelligible to everybody in the country. These efforts continued up until the beginning of the 20th century. As a result, *Guoyu* (the National Language) developed and became the language for all official communication. *Guoyu* takes Beijing Dialect as the standard for pronunciation and is based on dialects used in the northern part of the country. It also incorporates some language features of other dialects.

After the People's Republic of China was founded in 1949, some changes in the pronunciation of *Guoyu* were made and its name was changed to *Putonghua*, which means "Common Language." *Putonghua* has been the official language in Mainland China ever since, while *Guoyu* is still being used in Taiwan. In Singapore, Chinese is referred to locally as *Huawen*. In the West, "Mandarin Chinese" is the common term for Chinese.

Phonetic Transliteration Systems

In the last few centuries there have been efforts to develop a method of representing the Chinese language using the Latin alphabet. The most widely used system is called the *Pinyin* system. It was developed in Mainland China in the 1950s and officially adopted in 1979. *Pinyin*, which literally means "spell the sounds," is used to help people learn the pronunciation of characters or to look up words in dictionaries. The "Pinyin Foundation" section of this textbook gives you a more detailed introduction to this phonetic system.

Characters

Legend says that Chinese characters were created by Cang Jie, an official recorder of the Yellow Emperor, over 5,000 years ago. But the earliest use of a fully developed form of Chinese characters can be traced back to around 3,300 years ago in the Shang Dynasty. These writings, called the "Oracle Bone Scripts," consist of characters carved on ox bones or tortoise shells. Scholars believe that Chinese characters originally were pictographs that represented objects in the real world. Recent archeological discoveries also show that character-like pictographs existed as far back as 7,000 years ago. Xu Shen (58–147), a well-known linguist of the Eastern Han Dynasty (25–220 A.D.), analyzed the existing characters, examined their shapes, pronunciations and meanings, traced their roots, and finally compiled the first ever Chinese dictionary in history — *Shuo Wen Jie Zi* 《说文解字》— in which he collected over 9,000 characters categorized under 540 radicals. He concluded that Chinese characters were basically formed in six forms, called *Liu Shu* (the six writings):

- *Xiang xing* (Pictographs to represent real objects): e.g., 木、月、女,
- *Zhi shi* (Pictographs with an indicative sign; indirect symbols): e.g., 上、下、本,
- *Hui yi* (Meeting of ideas; compound characters): e.g., 明、休、好,
- *Xing sheng* (Picture and sound; semantic-phonetic combinations): e.g., 想、清、爸,
- *Zhuanzhu* (Transferable meaning; transformed characters): e.g., 考、老,
- *Jiajie* (Borrowed or loaned characters): e.g., 莫、其.

Shuo Wen Jie Zi is not only the first dictionary in Chinese history, it is also a scholarly masterpiece with great theoretical and practical value. Xu Shen's analysis of "Liu Shu" has been followed by scholars in China and other East Asian countries as well.

The section "The Chinese Writing System" provides a more detailed introduction on the rules for writing Chinese characters.

Simplification of Characters

Because of a belief that the complexity of Chinese characters constituted an obstacle to raising the nation's literacy level, and also to learning of the language by non-Chinese, efforts to simplify the characters began in the 19th century. In the 1950s, a simplified system of characters was promulgated in Mainland China. This system eliminated 1,053 variant characters and reduced the number of strokes for many other characters. The "Complete List of Simplified Characters" published in May 1964 listed 2,236 simplified characters. This system of simplified characters has become the major writing system used in Mainland China and Singapore. The traditional forms are still the standard way of writing in Taiwan and many overseas Chinese communities.

China has a history of several thousand years. In spite of periods of unity and disunity, China has remained intact as a country and is one of the only ancient civilizations that still exists today. It is believed that the Chinese writing system has played a crucial role by serving as an important binding factor in the cohesiveness of the country.

拼音基础 PINYIN FOUNDATION

I.

The Pinyin system is a tool used by native Chinese speakers in Mainland China to learn the sounds of Chinese, or to look up unknown characters in dictionaries. It uses the 26 letters of the Latin alphabet to represent the sounds of Chinese. Many of the letters are pronounced in a similar way to their English pronunciation, but not all of them. Some are, in fact, pronounced quite differently from what an English speaker might expect. In this section, for many of the Chinese sounds we have pointed out similar sounds in English for students to use as a reference point. However, it is very important to imitate your instructors and recordings of native speakers so that you learn standard Mandarin pronunciation.

II. Structure of Chinese Syllables

A Chinese syllable consists of three elements: initial, final, and tone.

TONE			
INITIAL	FINAL		
(Consonant)	(y/w) (i u ü medial)	Vowel (a e o i u ü)	(Ending) (n ng)

For example,

Character	Meaning	Pinyin	Initial	Final			Type of final
1. 八	eight	bā	**b**	**a** (vowel)			simple final (a simple vowel)
2. 好	good	hǎo	**h**	**a** (vowel)	**o** (vowel)		compound final (a compound vowel)
3. 班	class	bān	**b**	**a** (vowel)	**n** (ending)		a nasal final
4. 忙	busy	máng	**m**	**a** (vowel)	**ng** (ending)		a nasal final
5. 也	also	yě		**y**	**e** (vowel)		final (with -y)
6. 我	I, me	wǒ		**w**	**o** (vowel)		final (with -w)
7. 亮	bright	liàng	**l**	**i** (medial)	**a** (vowel)	**ng** (ending)	a nasal final (with medial -i)
8. 国	country	guó	**g**	**u** (medial)	**o** (vowel)		double final (with medial -u)
9. 略	brief	lüè	**l**	**ü** (medial)	**e** (vowel)		double final (with medial -u (ü sound))

Notes:

1. There are four basic tones, which are indicated by marks placed over a vowel.
   For example, **bā bá bǎ bà**
2. In modern Chinese, there are 21 initials and 38 finals altogether. In a Chinese syllable, the vowel has to be present. Other components such as an initial or ending are optional.
3. The initial, if present, is always a consonant.
4. The final always contains a vowel. The final may be a simple final (a simple vowel, e.g., **bā**); a compound final (a compound vowel, e.g., **hǎo**; note that the tone mark is placed over the first vowel), or a nasal final, e.g., **bān** (vowel followed by a nasal consonant).
5. When -i-, -u-, and -ü- are not preceded by any initials, their Pinyin presentations are **y**, **w**, and **y**, respectively, e.g., yě, wǒ, and yǔ. If they are preceded by an initial, they are presented as **i**, **u**, and **ü** (as medial element, not the main vowel), e.g., liàng, guó, and lüè.

   There are three medials: **i**, **u**, and **ü**. They serve as transitional sounds, not as main vowels. For example, in liàng, guó, and lüè, **i**, **u**, and **ü** are the medial elements. **à**, **ó**, and **è** are the main vowels. Note that the tone marks are placed over the main vowels rather than over the medials.

III. Tones and Tone Marks

Chinese is a tonal language. This means different levels of pitch and the contour of its pronunciation are capable of differentiating meanings. There are four basic tones: the first tone, the second tone, the third tone, and the fourth tone.

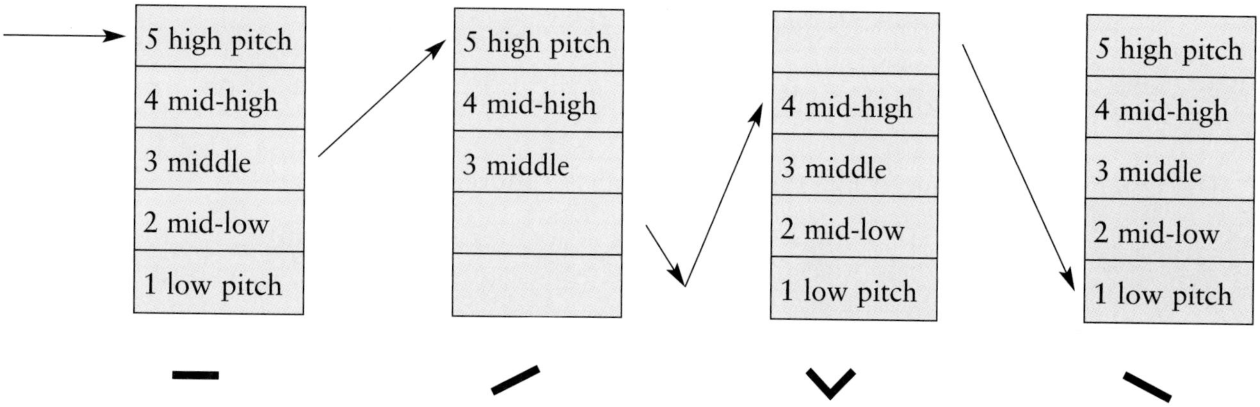

(1st tone)	(2nd tone)	(3rd tone)	(4th tone)
(5 → 5)	(3 → 5)	(2 → 1 → 4)	(5 → 1)
high and level	rising from middle to high	first falling then rising	falling from high

Examples:

1.	PINYIN	bā	bá	bǎ	bà
	CHARACTER	八	拔	靶	爸
	MEANING	eight	to pull out	target	dad
2.	PINYIN	mā	má	mǎ	mà
	CHARACTER	妈	麻	马	骂
	MEANING	mom	hemp	horse	to scold
3.	PINYIN	bō	bó	bǒ	bò
	CHARACTER	波	伯	跛	擘
	MEANING	wave	uncle	lame	thumb
4.	PINYIN	dā	dá	dǎ	dà
	CHARACTER	搭	答	打	大
	MEANING	to build up	to answer	to hit	big

IV. Vowels/Simple Finals

a o e i u ü

- The letter **a** is pronounced like the "a" in English "father."

PRACTICE			
(repeat after your teacher):	ba	ma	pa

- The letter **o** is pronounced like the "o" in English "more."

PRACTICE			
(repeat after your teacher):	bo	po	mo

- The letter **e** sounds very similar to the "u" in English "bud."

PRACTICE			
(repeat after your teacher):	de	ke	ne

- The letter **i** is pronounced like the "ee" in English "bee."
(except after the initials: z c s, zh ch sh r, details later).

PRACTICE			
(repeat after your teacher):	mi	pi	li

- The letter **u** is pronounced like the "ue" in "**true**" or "oe" in "**shoe**" in English.

PRACTICE			
(repeat after your teacher):	gu	ku	lu

- The letter **ü** is pronounced like the [u] in French "**tu.**" This sound is produced by first preparing to pronounce a long [i] sound, then holding that mouth position and rounding your lips as if to pronounce [**u**].

PRACTICE			
(repeat after your teacher):	ju	qu	xu

V. Initials

There are 21 initials. They can be categorized into six groups (labials, velars, palatals, alveolars, dental sibilants, and retroflex) as illustrated below:

	Unaspirated	Aspirated[8]	Nasal	Fricative[9]	Voiced[10]
1. Labial[1]	b	p	m	f	
2. Alveolar[2]	d	t	n		l
3. Velar[3]	g	k		h	
4. Palatal[4]	j	q		x	
5. Dental[5] sibilant[6]	z	c		s	
6. Retroflex[7]	zh	ch		sh	r

Notes:

1. Labial: (speech sound) made using one or both lips.
2. Alveolar: (speech sound) made by putting the end of the tongue at the top of the mouth just behind the upper front teeth.
3. Velar: (speech sound) made with the back of the tongue against or near the soft part of the top of the mouth.
4. Palatal: (speech sound) made by putting the tongue against or near the hard palate. (Palate: the top inside part of the mouth)
5. Dental: (speech sound) made by putting the end of the tongue against the upper front teeth.
6. Sibilant: (speech sound) made by forcing air through a constricted passage.
7. Retroflex: (speech sound) made with the tip of the tongue curled upwards and backwards.
8. Aspirated: (speech sound) made with audible breath accompanying the articulation of the sound.
9. Fricative: (speech sound) made by impeding the flow of air through a narrow channel at the place of articulation.
10. Voiced: (speech sound) made when the vocal cords vibrate.

The following two groups are pronounced like their English counterparts.

1. Labials: b p m f

PRACTICE
ba bi bo bu pa pi po pu ma mi mo mu me fa fo fu

2. Alveolars: d t n l

PRACTICE
da de du ta ti te tu na ni ne nu la li le lu

Note: To practice what has been presented above, please see Pinyin Exercises, In-class Practice I.

3. Velars: g k h

The letter **g** sounds similar to the "g" in "**g**o."
The letter **k** sounds similar to the "k" in "**k**ing."
The letter **h** sounds similar to the "h" in "**h**appy."

Note that **g**, **k**, and **h** are never followed by the [i] sound.

PRACTICE
ge gu ka ke ku ha he hu

The sounds in groups 4, 5, and 6 below are some of the most challenging for learners of Chinese. Please note that the English counterpart sounds are listed here only as a rough approximation of the Chinese sounds. To pronounce these sounds correctly, it is very important to imitate your instructors and the recordings.

4. Palatals: j q x

The letter **j** sounds somewhat like the "g" in English "**g**esture" or the "j" in "**j**eep."
The letter **q** is formed like j above, but j is unaspirated, while q is aspirated. It sounds like "ch" in English "**ch**eap."
The letter **x** sounds somewhat like "sh" in English "**sh**eep."
Note that **j**, **q**, and **x** are never followed by the [u] sound.

PRACTICE
ji qi xi

5. Dental sibilants: z c s

The letter **z** sounds like "ds" in English "la**ds**."
The letter **c** is formed in the same way as "z" above but is aspirated while "z" is unaspirated. It sounds like "ts" in English "ca**ts**."
The letter **s** is very similar to "s" in English "**s**on."

PRACTICE
za ze zu zi ca ce cu ci sa se su si

Note that with zi, ci, and si, the vowel [i] acquires a special sound quality. It is pronounced as [ɿ] (blade-alveolar vowel), a continuation of a [z] sound. The tongue is kept still. Be aware that it must not be pronounced like the simple final [i] (as in "bi," "pi," "mi," and "di").

6. Retroflexes: zh ch sh r

This group is pronounced by curling the tip of the tongue to touch the front of the hard palate, leaving a narrow opening between the tongue and roof of the mouth to allow some air to flow through.

zh sounds like "g" in English "**g**erm."
ch sounds like "ch" in English "**ch**urch."
sh sounds like "sh" in English "**sh**irt."
r is pronounced like the "r" sound in English "plea**sure**," "trea**sure**," and "lei**sure**."

PRACTICE

zha	zhe	zhu	zhi	cha	che	chu	chi
sha	she	shu	shi	re	ru	ri	

Note that as with the [i] sound in "zi," "ci," and "si" above, in "zhi," "chi," "shi," and "ri" the vowel [i] also acquires a special sound quality. It is pronounced as [ʃ] (blade-palatal vowel), a continuation of a [zh] sound.

Summary: the pronunciation of -i sound

- pronounced as [i] in **bi pi mi di ti**
- pronounced as [ʅ] (blade-alveolar vowel) in **zi ci si**
- pronounced as [ʃ] (blade-palatal vowel) in **zhi chi shi and ri**

Note: To practice what has been presented in points 3 to 6 (gkh; jqx; zcs; zh; ch; sh; r), please see Pinyin Exercises, In-class Practice II.

VI. Compound Finals

Compound finals comprise a main vowel and a secondary vowel. There are four types as illustrated below.

1. main vowel + secondary vowel	**ai**	**ei**	**ao**	**ou**
2. medial i + main vowel	**ia**	**iao**	**ie**	**iu (iou)#**
3. medial u + main vowel	**ua**	**uo**	**uai**	**ui (uei)##**
4. medial ü + main vowel	**üe/yue###**			

Note: #Please see IX. Special Pinyin Rules for details (#rule 3; ##rule 2; ###rule 1: ü → y).

In group (1), the first vowel is the main vowel (and the tone mark is placed over it). It is stressed, and is the longer of the two vowel sounds. The following vowel is soft and brief. For example, "ai" is pronounced beginning with the [a] sound then gliding into the direction of the [i] sound. Groups (2), (3), and (4) are compound finals that begin with medials (transitional sounds) followed by main vowels.

PRACTICE

bai	pei	mao	dou	jia	jiao	jie	jiu
zhua	zhuo	shuai	rui				

Note: To practice VI Compound Finals, please see Pinyin Exercises, In-class Practice III.

VII. Nasal Finals

Finals ending with "**n**" are called front nasals, and finals ending with "**ng**" [ŋ] are called back nasals.

1. Front nasals (+ n):

vowel + n	**an**	**en**
medial i + main vowel + n	**ian**	**in**
medial u + main vowel + n	**uan**	**un (uen)**#
medial ü + main vowel + n	**üan**	**ün (üen)**##

Note: Please see IX. Special Pinyin Rules for details (#rule 4; ##rule 1).

To produce the front nasal final, first form the final vowel sound. Then, without stopping the air flow, form the ending "**n.**" The [n] sound is pronounced similarly to "n" in the English "**in**" and "noon."

PRACTICE

ban	pan	man	fan	gen	ken	hen
jian	qian	xian		jin	qin	xin
gun	kun	hun	wen (uen)#	huan	guan	kuan ([u] sound)
jun	qun	xun	([ü] sound)##	juan	quan	xuan ([ü] sound)

Notes: # Please see IX. Special Pinyin Rules for details (#rule 1).
Note that "j q x" can be followed by the [i] and [ü] sounds, but never by the [u] sound. So the umlaut (two dots) is omitted over the [ü] sound (##rule 5).

2. Back nasals (+ ng)

vowel + ng [ŋ]	**ang**	**eng**	**ong**
medial i + main vowel + ng	**iang**	**ing**	**iong**
	(yang)#	(ying)#	(yong)#
medial u + main vowel + ng	**uang**	**ueng**	
	(wang)##	(weng)##	

Note: #Please see IX. Special Pinyin Rules for details (#rule 1; ##rule 1).

To produce a back nasal final, form the final vowel sound. Then, without stopping the air flow, follow it with the nasal "ng."

PRACTICE

bang	pang			deng	neng	feng		dong	long	kong
jiang	qiang	xiang	yang	jing	qing	xing	ying	jiong	qiong	xiong
wang	weng									

Note: To practice Nasal Finals, please see Pinyin Exercises, In-class Practice IV.

VIII. Summary of Finals

Simple finals	a o e i u ü
Compound finals	ai ei ao ou ia iao ie iu (iou) ua uo uai ui (uei) üe/yue
Nasal finals	an en ang eng ong ian in iang ing iong uan un (uen) uang ueng üan ün (üen)

IX. Special Pinyin Rules

1. i u ü without initial consonant.

   i → y e.g., ya ye yao yan yong you yi yin ying
   u → w e.g., wa wo wai wang wu wei wen
   ü → y e.g., yu yue yuan yun

2. When the final "uei" has an initial, it is written as "ui."

   uei → ui e.g., dui tui gui kui hui

3. When the final "iou" has an initial, it is written as "iu."

   iou → iu e.g., liu niu jiu qiu xiu

4. When the final "uen" has an initial, it is written as "un" e.g., sun.

   uen → un e.g., zun cun sun zhun chun shun

5. The initials **j q x** are only followed by -i and -ü. They are never followed by -u. Therefore, when j q x are followed by the ü sound, the umlaut (two dots) above the u is omitted.

   e.g., ju qu xu juan quan xuan jun qun xun

6. Initials **z c s** and **zh ch sh r** are only followed by -i and -u. They are never followed by the -ü sound.

7. When the initials are l and n, the two dots on the ü sound have to be present in order to differentiate it from the u sound.

   e.g., lǜ 绿 "green" lù 路 "road"
   nǚ 女 "female" nǔ 努 "diligent"

8. Neutral tone: Some syllables are unstressed; this is known as the neutral tone. There is no need to place a tone mark over neutral tone syllables.

PRACTICE	
bàba 爸爸 (Dad)	māma 妈妈 (Mom)
gēge 哥哥 (older brother)	jiějie 姐姐 (older sister)

9. Retroflex final -er: In Mandarin Chinese, sometimes we can see a final [**er**] attached to another final to form a retroflex final. There are some special rules for the spelling as illustrated below. These rules are listed here only as a reference. Note that the final [**er**] sound occurs more frequently in northern China.

- When -er attaches to another final:

a. In general, add only **-r**:

huār	花儿	(flower)	(huā + ér → huār)
hàomǎr	号码儿	(number)	(hàomǎ + ér → hàomǎr)
zhèr	这儿	(here)	(zhè + ér → zhèr)
yíxiàr	一下儿	(one time)	(yíxià + ér → yíxiàr)

b. with **-ai -ei -an -en**, drop the last letter and add **-r**:

nánhár	男孩儿	(boy)	(nánhái + ér → nánhár)
yíkuàr	一块儿	(together)	(yíkuài + ér → yíkuàr)
wár	玩儿	(play)	(wán + ér → wár)
yìdiǎr	一点儿	(a little)	(yìdiǎn + ér → yìdiǎr)
shùgēr	树根儿	(root)	(shùgēn + ér → shùgēr)

c. with **zhi chi shi ri**, drop **-i** and add **-er**.

shùzhēr	树枝儿	(branch)	(shùzhī + ér → shùzhēr)
shèr	事儿	(matter)	(shì + ér → shèr)

d. with **-in**, drop **-n** and add **-er**

xìer	信儿	(message)	(xìn + ér → xìer)

e. with **-ng** endings, drop **-ng** and add only **-r**.

dàshēr	大声儿	(louder)	(dàshēng + ér → dàshēr)
bǎndèr	板凳儿	(stool)	(bǎndèng + ér → bǎndèr)

10. When two syllables come together to form a word and the second syllable begins with a vowel, they are sometimes separated with an apostrophe " ' ":

xī ān	西安 (a city in China)	→ xī'ān
xiāng ài	相爱 (love each other)	→ xiāng'ài

Without an apostrophe, [xī'ān] 西安 and [xiāng'ài] 相爱 may be misread as [xiān] 先 (first) and [xiān gài] 先盖 (to build first).

X. Special Tone Rules

1. Tone change for 3rd tone:

- 3rd tone is pronounced as a full 3rd tone when it occurs alone.

e.g.,	nǐ 你 (you)	hǎo 好 (good)	hěn 很 (very)	hǎo 好 (good)
	yǔ 语 (language)	fǎ 法 (rule)	biǎo 表 (surface)	yǎn 演 (perform)

- When two 3rd tones co-occur, the first 3rd tone will be pronounced as the 2nd tone, but with its tone mark unchanged.

$3 + 3 \rightarrow 2 + 3$

e.g.,	nǐhǎo 你好 (hello)	(pronounced as níhǎo)
	hěnhǎo 很好 (very good)	(pronounced as hénhǎo)
	yǔfǎ 语法 (grammar)	(pronounced as yúfǎ)
	biǎoyǎn 表演 (perform)	(pronounced as biáoyǎn)

- Half 3rd tone[#]: 3rd tone + the 1st, 2nd, 4th tone or most neutral tones.

nǐtīng 你听 (you listen)	nǐshuō 你说 (you speak)	nǐlái 你来 (you come)
nǐkàn 你看 (you see)	hěnmáng 很忙 (very busy)	jiějie 姐姐 (older sister)

Note: [#]Half 3rd tone: The rising part of the tone is curtailed. This results in a half-finished 3rd tone.

2. Conditional tone change for "一":

- When "一" stands alone, it is pronounced as 1st tone [**yī**].
- When "一" + the 1st, 2nd, or 3rd tones, it is pronounced as the 4th tone [**yì**].

yì + 1st tone	yìtiān	一天 (one day)
yì + 2nd tone	yìtóng	一同 (together)
yì + 3rd tone	yìqǐ	一起 (together)

- When "一" + the 4th tone, it is pronounced as the 2nd tone [**yí**].

yímiàn 一面 (at the same time)　　yíjiàn 一件 (one piece of <e.g., clothing>)

3. Conditional tone change for "不":

- When "不" stands alone, or is followed by a 1st, 2nd, or 3rd tone, it is pronounced as the 4th tone [**bù**].

bùmáng 不忙 (not busy)　　bùhǎo 不好 (not good)

- When "不" + the 4th tone, it is pronounced as the 2nd tone [**bú**].

búshì 不是 (is not)　　búduì 不对 (incorrect)　　búkàn 不看 (not see)

Notes: 1. To practice IX. Special Pinyin Rules and X. Special Tonal Rules, please see Pinyin Exercises, In-class Practice V.
2. To review the Pinyin Foundation, please see Pinyin Exercises, In-class Practice VI.

拼音表 PINYIN TABLE

	Initials/Finals	_	b	p	m	f	d	t	n	l	g	k	h	j	q	x	zh	ch	sh	r	z	c	s
1	a	a	ba	pa	ma	fa	da	ta	na	la	ga	ka	ha	_	_	_	zha	cha	sha	_	za	ca	sa
2	o	o	bo	po	mo	fo	_	_	_	_	_	_	_	_	_	_	_	_	_	_	_	_	_
3	e	e	_	_	me	_	de	te	ne	le	ge	ke	he	_	_	_	zhe	che	she	re	ze	ce	se
4	ê																						
5	ai	ai	bai	pai	mai	_	dai	tai	nai	lai	gai	kai	hai	_	_	_	zhai	chai	shai	_	zai	cai	sai
6	ei	ei	bei	pei	mei	fei	dei	_	nei	lei	gei	kei	hei	_	_	_	zhei	_	_	_	zei	_	_
7	ao	ao	bao	pao	mao	_	dao	tao	nao	lao	gao	kao	hao	_	_	_	zhao	chao	shao	rao	zao	cao	sao
8	ou	ou	_	_	mou	fou	dou	tou	nou	lou	gou	kou	hou	_	_	_	zhou	chou	shou	rou	zou	cou	sou
9	an	an	ban	pan	man	fan	dan	tan	nan	lan	gan	kan	han	_	_	_	zhan	chan	shan	ran	zan	can	san
10	en	en	ben	pen	men	fen	_	_	nen	_	gen	ken	hen	_	_	_	zhen	chen	shen	ren	zen	cen	sen
11	ang	ang	bang	pang	mang	fang	dang	tang	nang	lang	gang	kang	hang	_	_	_	zhang	chang	shang	rang	zang	cang	sang
12	eng	eng	beng	peng	meng	feng	deng	teng	neng	leng	geng	keng	heng	_	_	_	zheng	cheng	sheng	reng	zeng	ceng	seng
13	ong	ong	_	_	_	_	dong	tong	nong	long	gong	kong	hong	_	_	_	zhong	chong	_	rong	zong	cong	song
14	er	er	_	_	_	_	_	_	_	_	_	_	_	_	_	_	_	_	_	_	_	_	_
15	i	yi	bi	pi	mi	_	di	ti	ni	li	_	_	_	ji	qi	xi	_	_	_	_	_	_	_
16	-i	_	_	_	_	_	_	_	_	_	_	_	_	_	_	_	zhi	chi	shi	ri	zi	ci	si
17	ia	ya	_	_	_	_	_	_	_	_	_	_	_	jia	qia	xia	_	_	_	_	_	_	_
18	iao	yao	biao	piao	miao	_	diao	tiao	niao	liao	_	_	_	jiao	qiao	xiao	_	_	_	_	_	_	_
19	ie	ye	bie	pie	mie	_	die	tie	nie	lie	_	_	_	jie	qie	xie	_	_	_	_	_	_	_
20	iu (iou)	you	_	_	miu	_	diu	_	niu	liu	_	_	_	jiu	qiu	xiu	_	_	_	_	_	_	_
21	ian	yan	bian	pian	mian	_	dian	tian	nian	lian	_	_	_	jian	qian	xian	_	_	_	_	_	_	_
22	in	yin	bin	pin	min	_	_	_	nin	lin	_	_	_	jin	qin	xin	_	_	_	_	_	_	_
23	iang	yang	_	_	_	_	_	_	niang	liang	_	_	_	jiang	qiang	xiang	_	_	_	_	_	_	_
24	ing	ying	bing	ping	ming	_	ding	ting	ning	ling	_	_	_	jing	qing	xing	_	_	_	_	_	_	_
25	iong	yong	_	_	_	_	_	_	_	_	_	_	_	jiong	qiong	xiong	_	_	_	_	_	_	_
26	u	wu	bu	pu	mu	fu	du	tu	nu	lu	gu	ku	hu	_	_	_	zhu	chu	shu	ru	zu	cu	su
27	ua	wa	_	_	_	_	_	_	_	_	gua	kua	hua	_	_	_	zhua	chua	shua	_	_	_	_
28	uo	wo	_	_	_	_	duo	tuo	nuo	luo	guo	kuo	huo	_	_	_	zhuo	chuo	shuo	ruo	zuo	cuo	suo
29	uai	wai	_	_	_	_	_	_	_	_	guai	kuai	huai	_	_	_	zhuai	chuai	shuai	_	_	_	_
30	ui (uei)	wei	_	_	_	_	dui	tui	_	_	gui	kui	hui	_	_	_	zhui	chui	shui	rui	zui	cui	sui
31	uan	wan	_	_	_	_	duan	tuan	nuan	luan	guan	kuan	huan	_	_	_	zhuan	chuan	shuan	ruan	zuan	cuan	suan
32	un (uen)	wen	_	_	_	_	dun	tun	_	lun	gun	kun	hun	_	_	_	zhun	chun	shun	run	zun	cun	sun
33	uang	wang	_	_	_	_	_	_	_	_	guang	kuang	huang	_	_	_	zhuang	chuang	shuang	_	_	_	_
34	ueng	weng	_	_	_	_	_	_	_	_	_	_	_	_	_	_	_	_	_	_	_	_	_
35	ü	yu	_	_	_	_	_	_	nü	lü	_	_	_	ju	qu	xu	_	_	_	_	_	_	_
36	üe	yue	_	_	_	_	_	_	nüe	lüe	_	_	_	jue	que	xue	_	_	_	_	_	_	_
37	üan	yuan	_	_	_	_	_	_	_	_	_	_	_	juan	quan	xuan	_	_	_	_	_	_	_
38	ün(üen)	yun	_	_	_	_	_	_	_	_	_	_	_	jun	qun	xun	_	_	_	_	_	_	_

拼音练习 PINYIN EXERCISES

In-class Practice I

Simple finals: a o e i u ü *Labial initials: b p m f* *Alveolar initials: d t n l*

USEFUL CLASSROOM EXPRESSIONS:

请你再说一遍。	Qǐng nǐ zài shuō yí biàn.	Please say it again.
对(了)。	Duì(le).	Correct.
不对。	Bú duì.	Incorrect.
第几声?	Dì jǐ shēng?	Which tone?
第一声	dì yī shēng	the first tone
第二声	dì èr shēng	the second tone
第三声	dì sān shēng	the third tone
第四声	dì sì shēng	the fourth tone
轻声	qīng shēng	neutral tone

F-1 Repeat after the instructor:

1. bā bá bǎ bà
2. mī mí mǐ mì
3. dē dé dě dè
4. nū nú nǔ nù
5. pō pó pǒ pò
6. fā fá fǎ fà
7. tī tí tǐ tì
8. lǖ lǘ lǚ lǜ

F-2 In each group, circle the syllable your instructor pronounces:

1. mū mú mǔ mù
2. mō mó mǒ mò
3. lī lí lǐ lì
4. lǖ lǘ lǚ lǜ
5. tū tú tǔ tù
6. dū dú dǔ dù
7. nā ná nǎ nà
8. pō pó pǒ pò

F-3 Read aloud the following syllables:

1. pá bá
2. bó pó
3. mǔ nǔ
4. lù nù
5. lú lǘ
6. dī tī
7. lǔ nǚ
8. tā tē
9. mō mū

F-4 Read aloud the following words or phrases:

1.	lùdì	land	陆地	11.	bìmá	castor oil plant	蓖麻
2.	báhé	tug-of-war	拔河	12.	mǎlù	road, street	马路
3.	pífū	skin	皮肤	13.	dútè	unique	独特
4.	tèlì	special case	特例	14.	púfú	crawl	匍匐
5.	lǚbó	aluminum foil	铝箔	15.	fābù	issue, release	发布
6.	mùmǎ	wooden horse	木马	16.	mābù	rag	抹布
7.	bófù	uncle	伯父	17.	tūpò	break through	突破
8.	dìtú	map	地图	18.	dībà	dam	堤坝
9.	lǐfà	haircut	理发	19.	làbǐ	crayon	蜡笔
10.	tǐlì	physical strength	体力	20.	fùmǔ	parents	父母

F-5 In each pair, circle the one your instructor pronounces:

1. lǚ nǚ
2. mā mō
3. lù nù
4. mò mù
5. dū dē
6. tā tē

F-6 Fun with Pinyin

Read the following ràokǒulìng (tongue twister):

bóbo	伯伯	uncle
bàba	爸爸	dad
mǎ	马	horse
pá	爬	to climb
dǎ	打	to hit, play
tǔpō	土坡	muddy slope
lǜbō	绿波	green water

Bóbo de mǎ,	伯伯的马，	Uncle's horse,
Bàba de é.	爸爸的鹅。	Father's goose.
Mǎ pá tǔpō,	马爬土坡，	The horse is climbing a muddy slope,
É dǎ lǜbō.	鹅打绿波。	The goose is playing in the green water.

In-class Practice II

Velar initials: g k h *Palatal initials: j q x*
Dental sibilant initials: z c s *Retroflex initials: zh ch sh r*

USEFUL CLASSROOM EXPRESSIONS:

请你再说一遍。	Qǐng nǐ zài shuō yí biàn.	Please say it again.
对(了)。	Duì(le).	Correct.
不对。	Bú duì.	Incorrect.
第几声?	Dì jǐ shēng?	Which tone?
第一声	dì yī shēng	the first tone
第二声	dì èr shēng	the second tone
第三声	dì sān shēng	the third tone
第四声	dì sì shēng	the fourth tone
轻声	qīng shēng	neutral tone

F-7 Repeat after the instructor:

1. shā shá shǎ shà
2. chū chú chǔ chù
3. sū sú sǔ sù
4. jī jí jǐ jì
5. xī xí xǐ xì
6. zū zú zǔ zù
7. zhē zhé zhě zhè
8. rū rú rǔ rù
9. qī qí qǐ qì
10. cū cú cǔ cù

F-8 Read the following words or phrases. Pay attention to the initials "j, q, x" and "z, c, s."

1.	qìxī	breath	气息
2.	xīqǔ	absorb	吸取
3.	qìjù	utensil	器具
4.	jīxù	savings	积蓄
5.	qícì	secondly	其次
6.	jīqì	machine	机器
7.	qízǐ	chess piece	棋子
8.	zìjǐ	oneself	自己
9.	sījī	driver	司机
10.	xíjī	raid	袭击
11.	zájì	acrobatics	杂技
12.	zǐxì	attentively	仔细
13.	cíqì	porcelain	瓷器
14.	cíxù	word order	词序
15.	zìjù	written pledge	字据
16.	cūsú	vulgar	粗俗
17.	jìcè	stratagem	计策
18.	qǐsù	sue	起诉
19.	xìjù	drama	戏剧
20.	zìsī	selfish	自私

F-9 Read the following words or phrases. Pay attention to the initials "j, q, x" and "zh, ch, sh, r."

1.	chúxī	New Year's Eve	除夕
2.	rèqì	heat	热气
3.	xīshì	Western style	西式
4.	xùshì	narrate	叙事
5.	qìzhì	temperament	气质
6.	qūshǐ	spur on	驱使
7.	qízhì	flag	旗帜
8.	jīzhì	quick-witted	机智
9.	jīchǔ	foundation	基础
10.	jùchǐ	sawtooth	锯齿
11.	zhàqǔ	extort	榨取
12.	zhījǐ	intimate	知己
13.	zhìxù	order	秩序
14.	zhúzì	word for word	逐字
15.	zhǔxí	chairman	主席
16.	chājù	gap	差距
17.	chíxù	continue	持续
18.	shíjī	opportunity	时机
19.	shìqì	morality	士气
20.	rúqī	on schedule	如期

F-10 Read the following words or phrases. Pay attention to the initials "z, c, s" and "zh, ch, sh, r."

1.	zǔzhī	organize	组织
2.	sīshì	personal affairs	私事
3.	zīzhù	subsidize	资助
4.	zhízé	duty	职责
5.	qìchē	car	汽车
6.	chìzì	deficit	赤字
7.	zhīchí	support	支持
8.	zhùcí	congratulatory speech	祝词
9.	shísù	board and lodging	食宿
10.	shǐcè	annals	史册
11.	chúshī	chef	厨师
12.	shìsú	secular	世俗
13.	shùzì	figure	数字
14.	chūrù	discrepancy	出入
15.	rúcǐ	in this way	如此
16.	rǔzhī	milk	乳汁
17.	shízǐ	cobble	石子
18.	shízì	learn to read	识字
19.	chìrè	blazing	炽热
20.	chūcì	the first time	初次

F-11 In each pair, circle the one your instructor pronounces:

1. rì shì	4. shī sī	7. zhà chà	10. cā zā
2. xī sī	5. qì xì	8. shú chú	11. zǔ sǔ
3. zhè zè	6. xì shì	9. jǐ xǐ	12. cè chè

F-12 Listen to the instructor pronounce each syllable, then fill in the initials:

Part I:

1. ____ē	4. ____í	7. ____à
2. ____ī	5. ____ù	8. ____ú
3. ____è	6. ____ì	9. ____ǐ

Part II:

10. ____è	13. ____ù	16. ____ā
11. ____ù	14. ____á	17. ____ì
12. ____é	15. ____ě	18. ____ǔ

F-13 Fun with Pinyin

Read the following ràokǒulìng (tongue twister):

shí shīzi	石狮子	stone lion
shī shīzi	湿狮子	wet lion
sǐ shīzi	死狮子	dead lion
sī shīzi	丝狮子	silk lion
chī shīzi	吃狮子	eat lion
cí shīzi	瓷狮子	porcelain lion

Sì zhī shí shīzi,	四只石狮子，	Four stone lions,
Shí zhī zhǐ shīzi.	十只纸狮子。	Ten paper lions.
Zhǐ shīzi bù kě chī,	纸狮子不可吃，	Paper lions cannot be eaten,
Shí shīzi bù kě sī.	石狮子不可撕。	Stone lions cannot be torn.

In-class Practice III

Compound finals: ai ei ao ou   ia iao ie iu   ua uo uai ui üe

USEFUL CLASSROOM EXPRESSIONS:

请你再说一遍。	Qǐng nǐ zài shuō yí biàn.	Please say it again.
对(了)。	Duì(le).	Correct.
不对。	Bú duì.	Incorrect.
第几声?	Dì jǐ shēng?	Which tone?
第一声	dì yī shēng	the first tone
第二声	dì èr shēng	the second tone
第三声	dì sān shēng	the third tone
第四声	dì sì shēng	the fourth tone
轻声	qīng shēng	neutral tone

F-14 Repeat after the instructor:

1. juē jué juě juè
2. jiā jiá jiǎ jià
3. tuī tuí tuǐ tuì
4. zhōu zhóu zhǒu zhòu
5. fēi féi fěi fèi
6. qiāo qiáo qiǎo qiào
7. xiē xié xiě xiè
8. niū niú niǔ niù
9. zāo záo zǎo zào
10. duō duó duǒ duò

F-15 Listen to the instructor pronounce each syllable, then add the correct tone mark:

1. bie
2. shuai
3. zhou
4. hua
5. biao
6. liu
7. mao
8. tou
9. cui
10. zhua
11. nuo
12. ren
13. shuo
14. lüe
15. pei

F-16 Read aloud the following syllables:

1. huó hóu
2. diū duī
3. rào ròu
4. bǎo biǎo
5. jué xué
6. lüè nüè
7. luó lóu
8. chāo qiāo
9. chóu zhóu
10. shāo xiāo
11. lín liú
12. xuē xiū

F-17 Read aloud the following words or phrases:

1.	báicài	Chinese cabbage	白菜	11.	nǎilào	cheese	奶酪
2.	cáixué	scholarship	才学	12.	páiliè	put in order	排列
3.	còuqiǎo	luckily	凑巧	13.	quèqiè	exact	确切
4.	dàotuì	go backwards	倒退	14.	róudào	judo	柔道
5.	fēikuài	very fast	飞快	15.	sǎomiáo	scan	扫描
6.	gàobié	bid farewell to	告别	16.	shōuhuò	harvest	收获
7.	huàxué	chemistry	化学	17.	táoshuì	evade a tax	逃税
8.	jiézòu	rhythm	节奏	18.	tuóniǎo	ostrich	驼鸟
9.	liúxué	study abroad	留学	19.	wèilái	future	未来
10.	měimiào	wonderful	美妙	20.	zuòjiā	writer	作家

F-18 In each pair, circle the one your instructor pronounces:

1. jué	xué		3. huó	hóu		5. guò	gòu		7. jiǔ	xiǔ
2. lüè	nüè		4. xuē	xiū		6. shāo	xiāo		8. rào	ròu

F-19 Fun with Pinyin

Read the following ràokǒulìng (tongue twister):

huīmāo 灰猫 gray cat
huāniǎo 花鸟 spotted bird
táopǎo 逃跑 to run away

Huīmāo zhuī huāniǎo

Huīmāo tiào, huāniǎo jiào,
Huīmāo tiào qǐ zhuā huāniǎo.
Huāniǎo pà huīmāo,
Bátuǐ jiù táopǎo.

灰猫追花鸟

灰猫跳，花鸟叫，
灰猫跳起抓花鸟。
花鸟怕灰猫，
拔腿就逃跑。

The Gray Cat Chases the Spotted Bird

The gray cat leaps, the spotted bird cries,
The gray cat leaps up to catch the spotted bird.
The spotted bird is afraid of the gray cat,
It flies away quickly.

In-class Practice IV

Nasal finals: *an en* *ian in* *uan un* *ang eng ong* *iang ing iong* *uang*

USEFUL CLASSROOM EXPRESSIONS:

请你再说一遍。	Qǐng nǐ zài shuō yí biàn.	Please say it again.
对(了)。	Duì(le).	Correct.
不对。	Bú duì.	Incorrect.
第几声?	Dì jǐ shēng?	Which tone?
第一声	dì yī shēng	the first tone
第二声	dì èr shēng	the second tone
第三声	dì sān shēng	the third tone
第四声	dì sì shēng	the fourth tone
轻声	qīng shēng	neutral tone

F-20 Repeat after the instructor:

1. liān lián liǎn liàn
2. guān guán guǎn guàn
3. kūn kún kǔn kùn
4. mēng méng měng mèng
5. tōng tóng tǒng tòng
6. qiāng qiáng qiǎng qiàng
7. xīng xíng xǐng xìng
8. jiōng jióng jiǒng jiòng

F-21 Listen to the instructor pronounce each syllable, and then add the correct tone mark:

1. mian
2. ling
3. zhun
4. hen
5. zhuang
6. qiang
7. lun
8. rong

F-22 Read aloud the following syllables:

1. jūn qūn
2. cóng chóng
3. huán huáng
4. zhàn zhèn
5. juān jūn
6. tūn tuān
7. xūn sūn
8. xiàng xuàn
9. qiáng qióng
10. zhāng jiāng
11. rǎn zhǎn
12. kěn kǔn

F-23 Read aloud the following words or phrases:

1.	ānjìng	quiet	安静	11.	miànfěn	flour	面粉
2.	bàngwǎn	at dusk	傍晚	12.	niánqīng	young	年轻
3.	Chángchéng	the Great Wall	长城	13.	píngjūn	average	平均
4.	diànyǐng	movie	电影	14.	qiānzhèng	visa	签证
5.	fāngbiàn	convenient	方便	15.	ruǎnjiàn	software	软件
6.	guāngxiàn	ray	光线	16.	sēnlín	forest	森林
7.	hǎnjiàn	rare	罕见	17.	tiānrán	natural	天然
8.	jǐnzhāng	nervous	紧张	18.	xiāngcūn	village	乡村
9.	kěndìng	affirm	肯定	19.	zhèngcháng	normal	正常
10.	línggǎn	inspiration	灵感	20.	huánjìng	environment	环境

F-24 In each pair, circle the one your instructor pronounces:

1.	zhèn	shè	5.	xūn	sūn	9.	jūn	qūn	13.	háng	huáng
2.	zhàn	zhèn	6.	qiáng	qióng	10.	kàn	kèn	14.	rēng	zhēng
3.	lín	líng	7.	tūn	tuān	11.	xiàng	xuàn	15.	shāo	shōu
4.	juān	jūn	8.	huán	huáng	12.	zhāng	jiāng	16.	shùn	shèn

F-25 Listen to the instructor pronounce each syllable, then fill in the blank with the correct final:

1. k ____________	5. x ____________	9. r ____________
2. h ____________	6. zh ____________	10. z ____________
3. j ____________	7. ch ____________	11. c ____________
4. q ____________	8. sh ____________	12. s ____________

F-26 Fun with Pinyin:

Read the following ràokǒulìng (tongue twister):

dēngshān:	登山	to climb a mountain
Xiǎosān:	小三	Little San (name of a person)
sān lǐ sān:	三里三	three miles plus three feet
sān jiàn shān:	三件衫	three shirts

Dēngshān	登山	Climb the Mountain
Xiǎosān qù dēngshān,	小三去登山，	Little San went to climb a mountain,
Pǎo le sān lǐ sān.	跑了三里三。	He ran for three miles plus three feet.
Chū le yì shēn hàn,	出了一身汗，	He was sweaty all over,
Shī le sān jiàn shān.	湿了三件衫。	Three of his shirts were wet.

In-class Practice V

Special Pinyin and tonal rules

F-27 Listen to the instructor pronounce each syllable, then fill in the blank with the correct tone and final:

1. y ____	5. m ____	9. j ____	13. l ____
2. y ____	6. n ____	10. q ____	14. n ____
3. h ____	7. s ____	11. zh ____	15. b ____
4. zh ____	8. ch ____	12. ch ____	16. y ____

F-28 Tone change for the 3rd tone. Read aloud the following words or phrases:

Part I: 3rd + 3rd → 2nd + 3rd

1.	jǔzhǐ	manner	举止	6.	nǎohǎi	mind	脑海
2.	fǎmǎ	weight used on a balance	砝码	7.	měihǎo	fine	美好
3.	liǎojiě	understand	了解	8.	suǒyǒu	all	所有
4.	shǒubiǎo	watch	手表	9.	chǎnpǐn	product	产品
5.	shuǐguǒ	fruit	水果	10.	wǎnzhuǎn	tactful	婉转

Part II: Half 3rd tone

1.	hěn máng	very busy	很忙	7.	Fǎguó	France	法国
2.	wǒ de	my, mine	我的	8.	lǎoshī	teacher	老师
3.	wǒ shì	I am	我是	9.	kǎoshì	test	考试
4.	Qǐng wèn	May I ask . . . ?	请问	10.	Qǐng gēn wǒ shuō.	Please repeat after me.	请跟我说。
5.	Nǎ guó rén?	What nationality?	哪国人	11.	Dǒng le ma?	Do you understand?	懂了吗?
6.	Měiguó	US	美国	12.	Dì jǐ shēng?	Which tone?	第几声?

F-29 Repeat after the instructor. Mark the tones of "yi" (一) and "bu" (不) in accordance with the "yi-bu" tonal rules:

1. _yí_ gè	one	一个
2. _yì_ bǎi	hundred	一百
3. _yì_ qiān	thousand	一千
4. _yí_ wàn	ten thousand	一万
5. _yí_ zhào	trillion	一兆
6. _yì_ yuán	dollar	一元
7. _yí_ kuài	dollar	一块
8. _yì_ jiǎo	ten cents	一角
9. _yì_ máo	ten cents	一毛
10. _yì_ fēn	cent	一分
11. _bù_ xíng	cannot	不行
12. _bù_ néng	not be able	不能
13. _bù_ xiǎng	don't want	不想
14. _bù_ duō	not many	不多
15. _bù_ shǎo	not few	不少
16. _bú_ dà	not big	不大
17. _bù_ xiǎo	not small	不小
18. _bú_ pà	not afraid	不怕
19. _bú_ liào	not expected	不料
20. _bù_ zǎo	not early	不早
21. _yí_ lùpíng'ān	have a safe trip	一路平安
22. _yì_ gǔzuòqì	get something done in one vigorous effort	一鼓作气
23. _yì_ hūbǎiyìng	be ready to go into action in their hundreds	一呼百应
24. _yì_ míngjīngrén	amaze the world with a single brilliant feat	一鸣惊人
25. _yì_ fānfēngshùn	have a good innings	一帆风顺
26. _bù_ gōngzìpò	collapse of itself	不攻自破
27. _bú_ jìnzétuì	not to advance is to go back	不进则退
28. _bù_ tóngfánxiǎng	out of the common run	不同凡响
29. _bù_ xiāngshàngxià	be equally matched	不相上下
30. _bú_ dòngshēngsè	stay calm and collected	不动声色

F-30 Fun with Pinyin

Read the following ràokǒulìng (tongue twister):

gǔ: 鼓 drum
hǔ: 虎 tiger
bù: 布 cloth
bǔ: 补 patch

Gǔ hé hǔ	**鼓和虎**	**Drum and Tiger**
Yì zhī xiǎo huāgǔ,	一只小花鼓，	A little colored drum,
Gǔ lǐ huà zhī hǔ.	鼓里画只虎。	On the drum a tiger is drawn.
Hǔ pá gǔ pò bù lái bǔ,	虎爬鼓破布来补，	Tiger climbs, drum breaks, a cloth patch is applied,
Bùzhī shì bù bǔ gǔ?	不知是布补鼓？	Is the drum being patched?
Háishì bù bǔ hǔ?	还是布补虎？	Or the tiger being patched?

In-class Practice VI

Comprehensive Pinyin Review

F-31 Read aloud the following Pinyin:

1.	yǔ	yǒu	5.	jūn	zhēn	9.	wō	ōu
2.	xià	xiào	6.	xiōng	jiōng	10.	lián	liáng
3.	niè	lèi	7.	jié	zéi	11.	lǚ	liǔ
4.	zuō	cuō	8.	dàng	dèng	12.	lǜ	nǚ

F-32 Read and compare the following words or phrases:

1.	míngshēng	reputation	名声	4.	shǔsè	light of early dawn	曙色
	míngshèng	scenic spot	名胜		sùshè	dormitory	宿舍
2.	tiáojiě	mediate	调解	5.	chājù	disparity	差距
	tiáojié	adjust	调节		chájù	tea set	茶具
3.	shíqī	period	时期	6.	zhīshi	knowledge	知识
	shíqì	stoneware	石器		zhìshǐ	result in	致使

F-33 In each pair, circle the one your instructor pronounces:

1.	lǚ	nǚ	4.	lián	liáng	7.	xià	xiào
2.	bīn	bīng	5.	xiōng	jiōng	8.	jié	zéi
3.	dàng	dèng	6.	lǚ	liǔ	9.	jūn	zhēn

F-34 Listen to the instructor pronounce the following classroom expressions, and then write them out in Pinyin:

1. 大家好。______________________________

2. 上课。______________________________

3. 中文怎么说？______________________________

4. 没有问题。______________________________

5. 第四声 ______________________________

6. 请打开书。______________________________

F-35 Fun with Pinyin

Read the following ràokǒulìng (tongue twister):

xī:	锡	tin
qī:	漆	paint
xījiàng:	锡匠	tinsmith
qījiàng:	漆匠	lacquerer

Xījiàng hé qījiàng	**锡匠和漆匠**
Xījiàng mài xī, qījiàng mài qī, Xījiàng shuō qījiàng tōu le tāde xī, Qījiàng shuō xījiàng tōu le tāde qī, Bùzhī shì xījiàng tōu le qījiàng de qī, Háishì qījiàng tōu le xījiàng de xī.	锡匠卖锡，漆匠卖漆， 锡匠说漆匠偷了他的锡， 漆匠说锡匠偷了他的漆， 不知是锡匠偷了漆匠的漆， 还是漆匠偷了锡匠的锡。

Tinsmith and Lacquerer

Tinsmith sells tins; lacquerer sells paint,
The tinsmith charges the lacquerer with stealing his tins,
The lacquerer charges the tinsmith with stealing his paints,
Who knows whether the tinsmith has stolen the lacquerer's paints,
Or the lacquerer has stolen the tinsmith's tins.

汉字入门 THE CHINESE WRITING SYSTEM

Chinese characters can be thought of as square-shaped "signs" which fit into blocks that are independent of each other. Generally speaking, a character may consist of one, two, or three parts, each standing for an independent semantic unit. In general, the arrangement of these semantic units in Chinese characters falls into the following patterns:

1. One-semantic-unit characters:

 e.g., 女，山

2. Two-semantic-unit characters:

 e.g., 你，奶

 e.g., 盲，雷

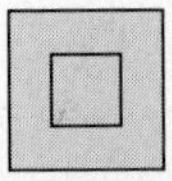 e.g., 回，国

 e.g., 起，这

 e.g., 闻，周

 e.g., 句，气

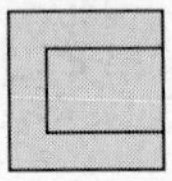 e.g., 巨，匠

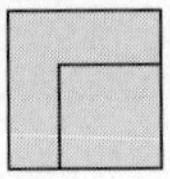 e.g., 床，层

 e.g., 凶

3. Three-semantic-unit characters:

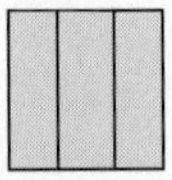 e.g., 谢

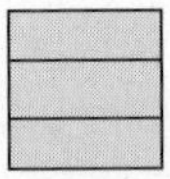 e.g., 意

 e.g., 想

 e.g., 筷

 e.g., 语

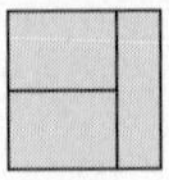 e.g., 部

Radicals

Radicals are pictographs which represent objects in the real world. Some of them can stand alone as independent, one-semantic-unit characters. Examples include 人 (person), 口 (mouth), and 雨 (rain). Radicals may also be combined with other components to form a new character for which the radical serves as a clue to its meaning. Examples include 吹 (to blow) and 妹 (younger sister). Some radicals cannot be used as independent characters but only serve as a part of another character. Their function is to provide a semantic clue to the character, such as 宀 in 家 (home), 艹 in 菜 (vegetable), and 辶 in 逛 (to stroll). According to most dictionaries, there are 214 commonly used radicals in Chinese. Look at the following archaic examples of radicals:

1. 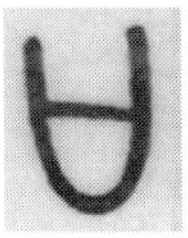
2. 
3. 
4. 
5. 
6. 
7. 
8. 
9. 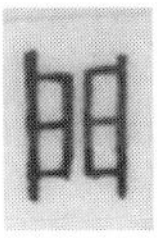
10. 
11. 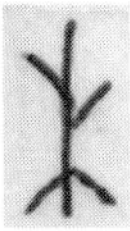
12. 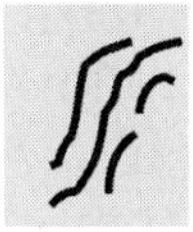

Below are their modern forms. Can you use the archaic forms as clues to figure out the meaning of the modern forms?

人	口	山	水	日	月
rén	kǒu	shān	shuǐ	rì	yuè
( )	( )	( )	( )	( )	( )
土	木	雨	火	女	门
tǔ	mù	yǔ	huǒ	nǚ	mén
( )	( )	( )	( )	( )	( )

Each of these characters, when combined with other components to form a new character, provides a clue to the meaning of that character. For example, 吃 [chī] (to eat) is formed by the radical 口 (mouth) and a phonetic clue 乞 [qǐ]. Characters with the radical 口 generally have meanings related to the mouth, such as 喝 [hē] (to drink), 唱 [chàng] (to sing) and 吸 [xī] (to suck). Here are some more examples:

心	耳	目	手	鱼	马
xīn	ěr	mù	shǒu	yú	mǎ
(heart)	(ear)	(eye)	(hand)	(fish)	(horse)
车	门	刀	足	金	玉
chē	mén	dāo	zú	jīn	yù
(vehicle)	(door)	(knife)	(foot)	(metal)	(jade)

练习一 Practice (1)

Circle the radicals in the following characters:

姐	鳄	晴	悲	驾	轮	劈	枝	聪	期
jiě	è	qíng	bēi	jià	lún	pī	zhī	cōng	qī
sister	crocodile	sunny	grief	to drive	wheel	cleave	branch	clever	period

Some of these characters also take a slightly different form when used as radicals. They often have a specific name commonly used by Chinese when referring to them as radicals. The following are those most frequently used:

人	rén – person	⟶	亻	*dān lìrén* – single standing person e.g., 你 (nǐ – you)	他 (tā – he)
手	shǒu – hand	⟶	扌	*tíshǒu* – lift hand e.g., 打 (dǎ – to strike)	拉 (lā – to pull)
水	shuǐ – water	⟶	氵	*sān diǎn shuǐ* – three dot water e.g., 江 (jiāng – river)	海 (hǎi – sea)
	bīng – ice	⟶	冫	*liǎng diǎn shuǐ* – two dot water e.g., 冷 (lěng – cold)	冰 (bīng – ice)
心	xīn – heart	⟶	忄	*shùxīn* – vertical heart e.g., 忙 (máng – busy)	情 (qíng – feelings)
火	huǒ – fire	⟶	灬	*sì diǎn huǒ* – four dot fire e.g., 煮 (zhǔ – to boil)	蒸 (zhēng – to steam)
刀	dāo – knife	⟶	刂	*lìdāo* – standing knife e.g., 到 (dào – to arrive)	利 (lì – sharp)
邑	yì – town	⟶	阝	*yòu ěr dāo* – right ear knife e.g., 都 (dōu – all)	那 (nà – that)
阜	fǔ – dam	⟶	阝	*zuǒ ěr dāo* – left ear knife e.g., 陡 (dǒu – steep)	陆 (lù – land)
犬	quǎn – dog	⟶	犭	*fǎn quǎn* – reversed dog e.g., 狗 (gǒu – dog)	狐 (chú – fox)

练习二 Practice (2)

F-36 Circle the radicals in the following characters:

冻	伯	怪	摔	信	踢	拔	煎	海	割
dòng	bó	guài	shuāi	xìn	tī	bá	jiān	hǎi	gē
freeze	uncle	strange	tumble	believe	kick	pull	fry	sea	cut

F-37 Match the following radicals with their original characters:

( )	( )	( )	( )	( )	( )
火	水	心	刀	手	人
a. 扌	b. 刂	c. 灬	d. 亻	e. 氵	f. 忄

There are some radicals which are actually only part of the original characters, such as:

丝	sī – silk	⟶	糸(纟)	*jiǎosī (mì)* – tangled silk e.g., 纸 (zhǐ – paper) 绸 (chóu – silk)
草	cǎo – grass	⟶	艹	*cǎo zì tóu* – top of grass character e.g., 花 (huā – flowers) 菜 (cài – vegetable)

The following characters show very little change when used as radicals. For example,

金	jīn – gold	⟶	钅	e.g., 钟 (zhōng – clock)	钱 (qián – money)
食	shí – food/eat	⟶	饣	e.g., 饭 (fàn – rice)	饿 (è – hungry)
衣	yī – clothes	⟶	衤	e.g., 裙 (qún – skirt)	裤 (kù – pants)
示	shì – display/reveal	⟶	礻	e.g., 礼 (lǐ – ritual)	视 (shì – to view)
玉	yù – jade	⟶	王	e.g., 珍 (zhēn – treasure)	珠 (zhū – pearl)
竹	zhú – bamboo	⟶	⺮	e.g., 篮 (lán – basket)	笔 (bǐ – pen)
火	huǒ – fire	⟶	火	e.g., 炸 (zhà – to fry)	爆 (bào – to explode)
足	zú – foot	⟶	足	e.g., 跑 (pǎo – to run)	跳 (tiào – to jump)

A few radicals do not have corresponding characters and can only be used as a component of a character to provide the semantic clue to the character:

宀	mián	*bǎo gài tóu*, precious cover head, which is used to imply "roof" e.g., 家 (jiā – home) 室 (shì – room)
辶	chuò	*zǒuzhī*, walking zhi, used to imply walking or running e.g., 道 (dào – path/way) 逃 (táo – to run/escape)

练习三 Practice (3)

Circle the radicals in the following characters:

缎	逛	珍	笛	钉	衫	饱	烧	神	寓
duàn	guàng	zhēn	dí	dīng	shān	bǎo	shāo	shén	yù
satin	stroll	treasure	flute	nail	jacket	full	burn	god	apartment

Strokes

The basic elements of Chinese characters are strokes. In order to know how to write Chinese characters, one must know how to write each stroke. Knowledge of strokes will not only lay the foundation for character writing, but is essential for looking up a word in a Chinese dictionary.

There are a total of 31 different kinds of strokes used in Chinese writing. Among these are eight basic strokes that are most commonly used. These eight strokes are illustrated as follows:

1. 横 héng (Horizontal stroke)		2. 竖 shù (Vertical stroke)		3. 撇 piě (Left-slanted stroke)		4. 捺 nà (Right-slanted stroke)	
一	王	丨	中	丿	大	㇏	文
5. 点 diǎn (Dot)		**6. 提 tí (Up-lift stroke)**		**7. 钩 gōu (Hook)**		**8. 折 zhé (Bend stroke)**	
丶	游	㇀	泳	亅	小	㇆	姐

In writing Chinese characters, the correct stroke order should be followed so that the characters look "right" to native Chinese. The following principles should be observed in the order of strokes:

Top first, then bottom:

e.g., 交 ⟶ 亠 六 交

Left first, then right:

e.g., 很 ⟶ 彳 很

Horizontal first, then vertical:

e.g., 十 ⟶ 一 十

Left-slanted first, then right-slanted:

e.g., 父 ⟶ 八 少 父

Center first, then both sides:

e.g., 小 ⟶ 亅 小 小

Outside first, then inside:

e.g., 同 ⟶ 冂 同

Enter first, and then close the door:

e.g., 国 ⟶ 冂 国 国

练习四 Practice (4)

F-38 For each of the following characters, write out the first stroke:

交 ______ 月 ______ 水 ______ 去 ______ 中 ______

不 ______ 他 ______ 洪 ______ 吃 ______ 代 ______

F-39 Write the following characters progressively, following the correct stroke order:

再 ____________________

但 ____________________

因 ____________________

京 ____________________

看 ____________________

In writing Chinese characters, the following principles guide the directions of the strokes:

a. Start the horizontal strokes from the left and move to the right.
b. Start the vertical strokes from the top and move downwards.
c. Left-slanted strokes start from the upper right and go towards the lower left.
d. Right-slanted strokes move from top left to bottom right.

Here are some examples:

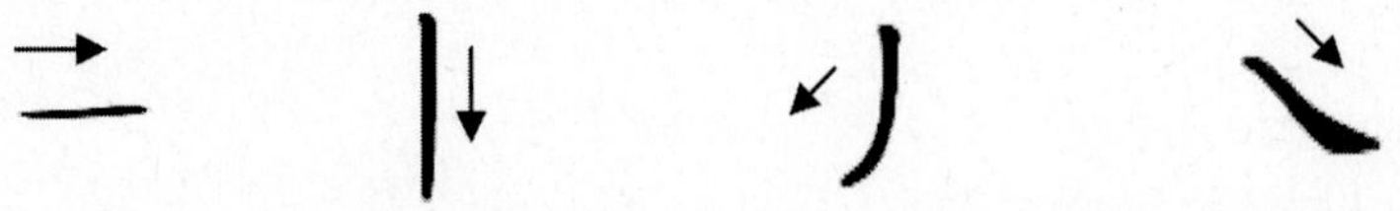

The shape of Chinese character strokes follows strict rules. A tiny change in the shape may change the meaning of the whole character. For example, 贝 [bèi] means "shell" and 见 [jiàn] means "to see." The top parts of the two characters are the same, but the bottom parts are different. Though the difference is not very conspicuous, it needs to be taken seriously. Otherwise, misunderstanding may result.

Writing Chinese characters may be difficult but it is also great fun. Character writing can be an art as well. If you put some effort into it, practice, and learn the cultural implications of characters, you may find writing Chinese an enjoyable and rewarding experience.

道可道，非常道。
Dào kě dào, fēi cháng dào.

The path that can be articulated is not the eternal path.

老子：道德经
Laozi: Dao De Jing

课堂用语 CLASSROOM EXPRESSIONS

课堂用语
Kè táng yòng yǔ

Chinese characters	Pinyin	Meaning
1. 同学们好。	Tóngxuémen hǎo.	Hello, students.
2. 你们好。	Nǐmen hǎo.	Hello, everyone.
3. 大家好。	Dàjiā hǎo.	Hello, everybody.
4. 老师好。	Lǎoshī hǎo.	Hello, teacher.
5. 你好。	Nǐ hǎo.	Hello.
6. 上课。	Shàng kè.	Class begins.
7. 下课。	Xià kè.	Class is dismissed.
8. 请跟我说。	Qǐng gēn wǒ shuō.	Please repeat after me.
9. 对(了)。	Duì (le).	Correct.
10. 不对。	Bú duì.	Incorrect.
11. 很好。	Hěn hǎo.	Very good.
12. 谢谢。	Xièxie.	Thank you.
13. 不客气。	Bú kèqi.	You are welcome.
14. 再见。	Zài jiàn.	Goodbye.
15. 请你再说一遍。	Qǐng nǐ zài shuō yíbiàn.	Please say it again.
16. 中文怎么说?	Zhōngwén zěnme shuō?	How do you say ____ in Chinese?
17. 英文怎么说?	Yīngwén zěnme shuō?	How do you say ____ in English?
18. 请打开书。	Qǐng dǎkāi shū.	Please open your book.
19. 请看第__页。	Qǐng kàn dì __ yè.	Please take a look at page __.
20. 请看第__题。	Qǐng kàn dì __ tí.	Please take a look at question __.
21. 请念课文。	Qǐng niàn kèwén.	Please read the text.
22. 请跟我念。	Qǐng gēn wǒ niàn.	Please read after me.
23. 请你念。	Qǐng nǐ niàn.	You read, please.
24. 请你写。	Qǐng nǐ xiě.	You write, please.
25. 懂了吗?	Dǒng le ma?	Do you understand?
26. 懂了。	Dǒng le.	Understand.
27. 不懂。	Bù dǒng.	Don't understand.
28. 有问题吗?	Yǒu wèntí ma?	Any questions?
29. 我有问题。	Wǒ yǒu wèntí.	I have questions.
30. 没有问题。	Méi yǒu wèntí.	No questions.

Chinese characters	Pinyin	Meaning
31. 练习练习	Liànxi liànxi.	Practice a bit.
32. 表演	biǎoyǎn	Perform
33. 作业	zuòyè	Homework
34. 生词	shēngcí	Vocabulary
35. 考试	kǎoshì	Test
36. 生词考试	shēngcí kǎoshì	Character quiz
37. 第一声	dì yī shēng	The first tone
38. 第二声	dì èr shēng	The second tone
39. 第三声	dì sān shēng	The third tone
40. 第四声	dì sì shēng	The fourth tone
41. 轻声	qīng shēng	Neutral tone
42. 第几声?	Dì jǐ shēng?	Which tone?

43.

一	二	三	四	五	六	七	八	九	十
yī	èr	sān	sì	wǔ	liù	qī	bā	jiǔ	shí
one	two	three	four	five	six	seven	eight	nine	ten

课堂用语练习 CLASSROOM EXPRESSIONS AND EXERCISES

Form groups of two to three students and practice the following situations:

Items 1–14

F-40 The teacher enters the classroom, greets the students, and starts the class. Try to use the following phrases: tóng xué men hǎo, nǐ hǎo, shàng kè, qǐng gēn wǒ shuō, duì (le), hěn hǎo, zài jiàn.

F-41 Students introduce themselves in turn to the class (greeting, their names, where they are from . . . etc.)

Example: Nǐmen hǎo. Wǒ shì ____. Wǒ cóng ____ lái. . . . Hǎo. Xièxie. Zàijiàn.
Hello, everyone, I am ___. I am from _____. . . . OK, thank you. Bye-bye.

Items 15–27

F-42 On campus you run into one of your Chinese classmates. Greet and introduce yourselves to each other in Chinese. (Include greeting, names, where you come from, very good, bye . . . etc.)

Items 28–42

F-43 In the library, you run into one of your Chinese classmates. Greet and introduce yourselves in Chinese, and then practice Pinyin and the four tones. (Remember to give your partners some feedback!)

F-44 Before class, you are waiting outside the classroom with your Chinese classmates. You would like to take the chance to get to know them better (and you might want to review yesterday's lessons).

F-45 On campus, you run into your Chinese teacher. Greet your teacher, and then ask some questions about Pinyin and tones, and how to say something in English or Chinese.

F-46 You have some Chinese friends and would like to ask them some questions. (For example, ask how to say the following words in Chinese or English: textbooks, Chinese, friends — some examples can be from Classroom Expressions items.)

F-47 You are the Chinese teacher teaching Pinyin practice, Lesson 1, Lesson 2, and Classroom Expressions.

词类简称 ABBREVIATIONS OF PARTS OF SPEECH

Adj.	=	adjective	形容词	[xíngróngcí]	e.g.,	好 [hǎo] (good) 美 [měi] (beautiful)
Adv.	=	adverb	副词	[fùcí]	e.g.,	很 [hěn] (very) 也 [yě] (also)
Aux.	=	auxiliary verb	助动词	[zhùdòngcí]		
Conj.	=	conjunction	连词	[liáncí]	e.g.,	可是 [kěshì] (but)
Int.	=	interjection	叹词	[tàncí]	e.g.,	啊 [a] (Ah?)
M.W.	=	measure word (or classifier)	量词	[liàngcí]	e.g.,	一本 [běn] 书 (a book)
N.	=	noun	名词	[míngcí]	e.g.,	老师 [lǎoshī] (teacher) 书 [shū] (book)
Num.	=	numeral	数词	[shùcí]	e.g.,	二 [èr] (two) 十 [shí] (ten)
Part.	=	particle	助词	[zhùcí]	e.g.,	吗 [ma] (turn a sentence into a question)
Prep.	=	preposition	介词	[jiècí]	e.g.,	在 [zài] (in; at) 从 [cóng] (from)
Pron.	=	pronoun	代词	[dàicí]	e.g.,	你 [nǐ] (you) 他 [tā] (he)
V.	=	verb	动词	[dòngcí]	e.g.,	学 [xué] (study) 说 [shuō] (speak) 跑 [pǎo] (run)
V.O.	=	verb + object	动宾	[dòng bīn]	e.g.,	说中文 [shuō Zhōngwén] (speak Chinese)
V.C.	=	verb + complement	动补	[dòng bǔ]	e.g.,	搬过来 [bān guò lái] (move over) 打破 [dǎ pò] (hit-broken)

第十一课
LESSON

11

你要红茶还是绿茶?
Do You Want Black Tea or Green Tea?

教学目标 OBJECTIVES

- Order food at a restaurant
- Present/choose from alternatives
- Ask what someone wants
- Tell someone what you want

A fancy seafood restaurant in Hong Kong.

***饺子** [jiǎozi] (dumplings), a representative Chinese food.*

Traditional food stands are all along the street. Go get a treat!

生词 VOCABULARY

核心词 Core Vocabulary

SIMPLIFIED	TRADITIONAL	PINYIN		
1. 红	紅	hóng	Adj.	red
2. 茶	茶	chá	N.	tea
3. 还是	還是	háishì	Conj.	or
4. 绿	綠	lǜ	Adj.	green
5. 服务员	服務員	fúwùyuán	N.	waiter/waitress
6. 坐	坐	zuò	V.	to sit
7. 小姐	小姐	xiǎojiě	N.	miss
8. 先生	先生	xiānsheng	N.	mister
9. 先	先	xiān	Adv.	first
10. 喝	喝	hē	V.	to drink
11. 杯	杯	bēi	M.W.	cup
12. 冰	冰	bīng	N.	ice
13. 可乐	可樂	kělè	N.	cola
14. 瓶	瓶	píng	M.W.	bottle
15. 啤酒	啤酒	píjiǔ	N.	beer
16. 面	面	miàn	N.	noodle
17. 饺子	餃子	jiǎozi	N.	dumpling (crescent shaped)
18. 盘	盤	pán	M.W.	plate
19. 炒	炒	chǎo	V.	to stir fry
20. 十	十	shí	Num.	ten
21. 碗	碗	wǎn	M.W.	bowl
22. 汤	湯	tāng	N.	soup
23. 双	雙	shuāng	M.W.	pair
24. 筷子	筷子	kuàizi	N.	chopstick

专名 Proper Nouns

SIMPLIFIED	TRADITIONAL	PINYIN		
1. 张正然	張正然	Zhāng Zhèngrán	N.	(name) Zhengran Zhang
2. 孙信美	孫信美	Sūn Xìnměi	N.	(name) Xinmei Sun
3. 杨欢	楊歡	Yáng Huān	N.	(name) Huan Yang

补充词 Supplementary Vocabulary

SIMPLIFIED	TRADITIONAL	PINYIN		
1. 饭馆	飯館	fànguǎn	N.	restaurant
2. 餐厅	餐廳	cāntīng	N.	restaurant
3. 餐馆	餐館	cānguǎn	N.	restaurant
4. 饭店	飯店	fàndiàn	N.	restaurant, hotel
5. 菜单	菜單	càidān	N.	menu
6. 白饭	白飯	báifàn	N.	steamed rice
7. 饮料	飲料	yǐnliào	N.	drink
8. 果汁	果汁	guǒzhī	N.	juice
9. 橙汁	橙汁	chéngzhī	N.	orange juice
10. 柳橙汁 (柳丁汁)	柳橙汁 (柳丁汁)	liǔchéngzhī (liǔdīngzhī)	N.	tangerine juice
11. 咖啡	咖啡	kāfēi	N.	coffee
12. 点菜	點菜	diǎncài	V.O.	to order food
13. 小费	小費	xiǎofèi	N.	tip
14. 买单	買單	mǎidān	V.O.	to pay the bill
15. 结账 (结帐)	結賬 (結帳)	jiézhàng	V.O.	to settle the account
16. 酸	酸	suān	Adj.	sour
17. 甜	甜	tián	Adj.	sweet

SIMPLIFIED	TRADITIONAL	PINYIN		
18. 苦	苦	kǔ	Adj.	bitter
19. 辣	辣	là	Adj.	spicy
20. 咸	鹹	xián	Adj.	salty
21. 清淡	清淡	qīngdàn	Adj.	plain
22. 烫	燙	tàng	Adj.	burning hot
23. 凉	涼	liáng	Adj.	cool

常见食品 [Chángjiàn shípǐn] Common Foods

SIMPLIFIED	TRADITIONAL	PINYIN		
1. 馄饨	餛飩	húntun	N.	wonton
2. 春卷	春捲	chūnjuǎn	N.	spring roll
3. 鱼	魚	yú	N.	fish
4. 虾	蝦	xiā	N.	shrimp
5. 海鲜	海鮮	hǎixiān	N.	seafood
6. 青菜	青菜	qīngcài	N.	vegetable
7. 猪肉	豬肉	zhūròu	N.	pork
8. 牛肉	牛肉	niúròu	N.	beef
9. 鸡肉	雞肉	jīròu	N.	chicken
10. 豆腐	豆腐	dòufu	N.	bean curd
11. 甜点	甜點	tiándiǎn	N.	dessert
12. 饼干	餅乾	bǐnggān	N.	cracker
13. 蛋糕	蛋糕	dàngāo	N.	cake
14. 沙拉	沙拉	shālā	N.	salad
15. 面包	麵包	miànbāo	N.	bread

常见水果 [Chángjiàn shuǐguǒ] Common Fruits

	SIMPLIFIED	TRADITIONAL	PINYIN		
1.	苹果	蘋果	píngguǒ	N.	apple
2.	香蕉	香蕉	xiāngjiāo	N.	banana
3.	桃子	桃子	táozi	N.	peach
4.	梨子	梨子	lízi	N.	pear
5.	西瓜	西瓜	xīguā	N.	watermelon
6.	草莓	草莓	cǎoméi	N.	strawberry
7.	葡萄	葡萄	pútao	N.	grape

语文知识 LANGUAGE LINK

The Sentence Patterns provide models that will help you with the Language in Use section. In both sections, pay attention to the grammar points, vocabulary, and expressions.

句型 Sentence Patterns

A: 你要红茶还是绿茶？
Nǐ yào hóngchá háishì lǜchá?

B: 我要红茶。
Wǒ yào hóngchá.

A: 你想点什么？
Nǐ xiǎng diǎn shénme?

B: 我们点一杯可乐、一瓶啤酒、
Wǒmen diǎn yìbēi kělè, yìpíng píjiǔ,
一盘炒饭、三碗汤和
yìpán chǎofàn, sānwǎn tāng hé
二十个饺子。
èrshíge jiǎozi.

课文 Language in Use: 你要红茶还是绿茶? Nǐ yào hóngchá háishì lǜchá?

服务员： 请问，几位?
Qǐngwèn, jǐ wèi?

张正然： 三位。
Sān wèi.

服务员： 好，请跟我来。请坐。
Hǎo, qǐng gēn wǒ lái. Qǐngzuò.

张正然、孙信美、杨欢： 谢谢!
Xièxie!

服务员： 小姐，先生，请问，你们想先喝点儿什么?
Xiǎojiě, xiānsheng, qǐngwèn, nǐmen xiǎng xiān hē diǎr shénme?

孙信美： 我喜欢喝茶。
Wǒ xǐhuān hē chá.

服务员： 你要红茶还是绿茶?
Nǐ yào hóngchá háishì lǜchá?

孙信美： 我要一杯冰红茶。
Wǒ yào yìbēi bīng hóngchá.

杨欢： 我要一杯可乐。
Wǒ yào yìbēi kělè.

张正然： 我要一瓶啤酒。
Wǒ yào yìpíng píjiǔ.

服务员： 好，一杯冰红茶、一杯可乐、一瓶啤酒。请等一下。
Hǎo, yìbēi bīng hóngchá, yìbēi kělè, yìpíng píjiǔ. Qǐng děng yíxià.

张正然： 对了，你们喜欢吃饭还是吃面?
Duì le, nǐmen xǐhuān chīfàn háishì chīmiàn?

孙信美： 我都喜欢。
Wǒ dōu xǐhuān.

杨欢： 我想吃饺子。
Wǒ xiǎng chī jiǎozi.

服务员： 这是您的冰红茶、可乐、还有啤酒。你们要点菜吗？
Zhè shì nín de bīng hóngchá, kělè, háiyǒu píjiǔ. Nǐmen yào diǎncài ma?

张正然： 好，我们点一盘炒饭、一盘炒面和二十个饺子吧。
Hǎo, wǒmen diǎn yìpán chǎofàn, yìpán chǎomiàn hé èrshí ge jiǎozi ba.

孙信美： 我们还要三碗汤。对了，我们也要三双筷子，谢谢！
Wǒmen háiyào sānwǎn tāng. Duìle, wǒmen yě yào sānshuāng kuàizi, xièxie!

注释 LANGUAGE NOTES

服务员

In Mainland China, this term is used for anyone who provides service, mainly waiters and waitresses. In Taiwan, people use 服务生 instead of 服务员.

位

As was explained previously, 位 is another measure word for people. It is usually used to be courteous to guests or to show respect. In a restaurant, the waiter/waitress usually politely asks "几位?" and the customers reply with a phrase, such as "三位" (three of us) or "五位" (five of us). In this situation, the word "位" is only a response to the question and has nothing to do with courtesy or politeness.

点

点 is used to order (dishes, wine, music pieces, etc.)
Similar to 点, 要 can also be used to order food.

饺子

Instead of 饺子, 水饺 is more commonly used in Taiwan.

语法 GRAMMAR

还是

还是 is a conjunction corresponding to "or" in English. It is used to connect two alternatives in an alternative question (a question of the form "A or B"?). These two alternatives can be noun phrases, verb phrases, adjective phrases, etc., for example,

你要红茶还是绿茶?	Would you like black tea or green tea?
你想打电话还是写信?	Do you want to make a phone call or write a letter?
你今天上午上课还是下午上课?	Do you have class in the morning or in the afternoon?
谁是中国人，你还是他?	Who is Chinese, you or he?

量词 (Measure Words/Classifiers) (3)

Words identifying containers can also be used as measure words. Here are some examples,

Measure word	Example		
杯	一**杯**冰红茶	yì*bēi* bīnghóngchá	a *glass* of iced tea
瓶	两**瓶**啤酒	liǎng*píng* píjiǔ	two *bottles* of beer
盘	三**盘**炒饭	sān*pán* chǎofàn	three *plates* of fried rice
碗	四**碗**酸辣汤	sì*wǎn* suānlàtāng	four *bowls* of hot and sour soup

Also,

Measure word	Example		
壶	一**壶**咖啡	yì*hú* kāfēi	a *pot* of coffee
盒	两**盒**巧克力	liǎng*hé* qiǎokèlì	two *boxes* of chocolate
桶	三**桶**水	sān*tǒng* shuǐ	three *buckets* of water
罐	四**罐**可乐	sì*guàn* kělè	four *cans* of Coke
箱	五**箱**书	wǔ*xiāng* shū	five *cases* of books
袋	六**袋**花生	liù*dài* huāshēng	six *bags* of peanuts

补充课文 SUPPLEMENTARY PRACTICE

This selection will help you test your comprehension of the grammar and vocabulary you have learned in this lesson. Be prepared to answer questions about the meaning of the passage.

今天我们下课以后都饿了，我们就约了几个朋友一起去中国饭馆吃饭。服务员小姐看到我们很亲切地说“欢迎光临”，然后问我们想喝点儿什么饮料。我要了一杯冰红茶，杨欢要了一杯可乐，正然喜欢喝啤酒，他要了一瓶啤酒。

服务员小姐还问我们想吃面还是想吃饭，我们看了看菜单，有很多好吃的东西，最后我们点了一盘炒饭，一盘炒面，二十个饺子和三碗汤。我们不太习惯用叉子，比较喜欢用筷子，我们就跟服务员小姐要了三双筷子。我们一面吃饭一面聊天，大家吃得又饱又高兴。

Notes: 饿 [è]: hungry
了 [le]: an aspect particle indicating completion of an action
约 [yuē]: to make an appointment, invite
看到 [kàndào]: to see; to catch sight of
亲切 [qīnqiè]: cordial; warm
欢迎光临 [huānyíng guānglín]: welcome
然后 [ránhòu]: then
饮料 [yǐnliào]: beverage
还 [hái]: also
菜单 [càidān]: menu
好吃 [hǎochī]: yummy; delicious
最后 [zuìhòu]: finally
习惯 [xíguàn]: to get used to
叉子 [chāzi]: fork
一面 ... 一 面 ... [yímiàn . . . yímiàn . . .]: adverb indicating two simultaneous actions
聊天 [liáotiān]: chat
又 ... 又 ... [yòu]: both . . . and
得 [de]: 得 is used in the “degree of complement” sentence to tell how an action is performed
饱 [bǎo]: to be full
高兴 [gāoxìng]: happy

练习 ACTIVITIES

I. Pinyin Exercises

11-1 Listen to the instructor pronounce the Pinyin below. Mark "√" after the Pinyin if correct, or write in the correct Pinyin:

1. fānguǎn ________	2. lùchá ________	3. píjǔ ________
4. kuāzi ________	5. kěliè ________	6. xiānsheng ________
7. kēchá ________	8. fúwùyuán ________	9. jīwéi ________
10. jiǎozǐ ________	11. bīnhóngchā ________	12. chǎofàn ________

11-2 Listen to the instructor and fill in each blank with the correct Pinyin:

1. qǐng _____	2. _____ shì	3. _____ chá	4. _____ cài
5. liǎng _____ chá	6. sān _____ fàn	7. xiǎo _____	8. yǐn _____
9. yì _____ kuàizi	10. sìwǎn _____	11. kā _____	12. bái _____
13. chǎo _____	14. _____ yào	15. cài _____	16. _____ cài

11-3 Read the following Chinese poem, paying special attention to the tones and rhythm:

Mǐn Nóng
(Lǐ Shēn)

Chú hé rì dāng wǔ,
Hàn dī hé xià tǔ.
Shéi zhī pán zhōng cān,
Lìlì jiē xīnkǔ.

悯农
(李绅)

除禾日当午,
汗滴禾下土。
谁知盘中餐,
粒粒皆辛苦。

Gratefulness to Peasants
(Li, Shen)

Hoeing the crops under the hot sun,
Sweat drips onto the soil beneath the crops.
Who realizes the rice in the bowl
Is every grain produced from hard labor?

II. Character Exercises

11-4 Read the following words, phrases, and sentences:

茶	想
红茶	想吃饭
冰红茶	想吃炒饭
一杯冰红茶	他想吃一盘炒饭
喝一杯冰红茶	他想吃一盘虾炒饭
她要喝一杯冰红茶	他想吃一盘还是两盘虾炒饭

Note: 虾 [xiā]: shrimp

Now try to use the following characters to make words, phrases, and then sentences:

1. 馆	2. 服	3. 坐	4. 喝	5. 红	6. 绿
7. 可	8. 瓶	9. 酒	10. 面	11. 汤	12. 筷

11-5 Insert the proper measure word into the phrases below:

1. 三 小 说	2. 两 车	3. 那 啤 酒
4. 这 炒 饭	5. 多 少 饺 子	6. 三 狗
7. 两 绿 茶	8. 一 老 师	9. 一 工 程 课
10. 一 啤 酒	11. 四 馄 饨 汤	12. 几 筷 子

III. Grammar Exercises

11-6 Substitution exercises:

1. 你想<u>喝茶</u>还是<u>喝咖啡</u>？
   我想<u>喝茶</u>。

喝红茶	喝绿茶
喝可乐	喝啤酒
吃炒饭	吃炒面
看小说	看电视
做功课	上网
学工程	学电脑

2. 请问，你想<u>喝</u>什么？
   我要<u>一杯可乐</u>。

吃	二十个饺子
点	一盘炒面
喝	一瓶啤酒
喝	一杯冰红茶
喝	一杯绿茶

11-7 Fill in the blanks with the words below. Some words may be used more than once.

跟 想 要 还是

1. 你喜欢吃饭 ________ 吃面?
2. 请 ____ 我来。
3. 你 ____ 喝什么?
4. 我 ____ 二十个饺子。
5. 李文中常 ____ 丁明说中文。
6. 吃晚饭以后,你 ____ 上网 ________ 看电视?

11-8 Combine the words or phrases in parentheses with the sentences and the word "还是" to make alternative questions:

For example, 今天下午他有课。 (法语 工程)
→ 今天下午他有法语课还是工程课?

1. 他喜欢学习。 (在图书馆 在宿舍)
2. 杨欢要去图书馆。 (六点半 七点)
3. 李先生是老师。 (日文 中文)
4. 她要一杯茶。 (红 绿)

IV. Communicative Activities

11-9 Situational dialogues:

Situation 1:
Your classmates are visiting you in your apartment. Please act as a good host.

Hints:

1. Topics to cover:
   - Greetings.
   - Ask what your friends would like to eat and drink.
   - Chat about your hobbies, your apartment, your studying schedule, etc.
2. Words and expressions to use:

   喜欢... ...还是...
   想吃/喝... ...吧

Situation 2:

You and several international students are eating together in a Korean restaurant.

Hints:

1. Topics to cover:
   - Greetings.
   - Discuss what kinds of food and drink you like and place an order.
   - Get to know some new friends.
   - Ask about foods in other countries.

2. Words and expressions to use:

   喜欢...　　...还是...　　想吃/喝...
   您贵姓？　　哪国人？　　学什么？
   有没有...？　　是不是...？

Situation 3:

Discuss with your friend what to do after class.

Hints:

1. Topics to cover:
   - Meet the friend on campus and greet each other.
   - Chat for a while about each other's courses this semester and ask about your mutual friends.
   - Discuss what you want to do after class: practice Chinese, visit friends, go to a restaurant, etc.

2. Words and expressions to use:

   你好吗？　忙吗？　是...还是...？
   ...难吗？　喜欢　看朋友

文化知识 Culture Link

文化点滴 CULTURE NOTES

中国菜系介绍 [Zhōngguó càixì jièshào] Chinese Food (1)

Chinese food is among the best-known cuisines in the world. It is abundant in variety, delicious in taste, and pleasing to the eye. Chinese food is also considered to be healthy.

Chinese people have studied the art of cooking for over 3,000 years. It would not be surprising today if you were served at a restaurant in China with 一鸡三味 [yìjī sānwèi] (one chicken with three different flavors), 一鸭四吃 [yìyā sìchī] (one Peking roast duck in four or five courses) or 一鱼二烧 [yìyú èrshāo] (one fish served in two cooking styles). Chinese cooking places emphasis on 色 [sè], 香 [xiāng], and 味 [wèi] (color, flavor, and taste). From simple family meals to the most elaborate banquets (usually over 18 courses), every mouthful manages to combine nutrition, aesthetics, and history.

There are eight styles of Chinese cuisine. They are 鲁菜 [Lǔcài] (Shandong style), 川菜 [Chuāncài] (Sichuan style), 淮阳菜 [Huáiyángcài] (Yangzhou style), 粤菜 [Yuècài] (Cantonese style), 闽菜 [Mǐncài] (Fujian style), 浙菜 [Zhècài] (Zhejiang style), 皖菜 [Wǎncài] (Anhui style), and 湘菜 [Xiāngcài] (Hunan style). Both the 川菜 and 湘菜 are hot and spicy, whereas 淮阳菜 and 浙菜 are a sweet and

A common Chinese breakfast, 粥 [zhōu] (porridge), 酱菜 [jiàngcài] (pickles) and 蛋 [dàn] (eggs).

A banquet feast with fancy decorations.

At Chinese traditional markets 菜市场 [càishìchǎng] you can find processed meat, chicken, pickles, fish balls, baked goods, desserts, vegetables, and seafood.

light in flavor with fresh, tender ingredients. The characteristics of 粤菜 are very special and unique ingredients, consisting mostly of fresh seafood with an emphasis on the "original flavor." 点心 [diǎnxīn] (dim sum), a Cantonese-style brunch with dozens of varieties of light appetizers, is very popular among Chinese both at home and abroad.

Chinese food commonly uses a lot of ingredients with purported healing properties, including ginger, green onion, garlic, cinnamon, yam, eggs, vinegar, mung beans, and rice wine. All ingredients are categorized into groups of three different nature — hot, cold, and neutral. The combination of ingredients is based on Daoist yin-yang theory to strive for balance. Chinese people are interested in 食疗 [shíliáo] (medical treatment with food). They have known for centuries that sea cucumbers strengthen bones and protect against aging. Bitter melon clears the blood. Carp is good for the gallbladder and spleen, as well as for pregnant women and their fetuses. Pig's feet and chicken broth help blood circulation. With these ideas in mind, Chinese people often use herbal medicine together with certain ingredients in their stir-fry dishes and soups to help meet the body's needs.

Food is an extremely important part of people's lives in China. In the Qing Dynasty, there were approximately 2,000 people working to provide food for the emperor and his family. Dining partners have always been a symbol of one's social status. Today, food still plays a great role in the social life of Chinese people. "Business is done at the dining table" is a common saying in China.

Dining in China is often associated with hospitality as well. Chinese usually treat their guests to abundant food of great variety.

Questions:

1. What kind of food do you like best? What do you think are the major differences between Chinese food and Western food?
2. Do you often go to Chinese restaurants? Describe one of your favorite Chinese dishes.

Chinese Food (2)

Western-brand foods are also popular in China, Taiwan, and Hong Kong:

麦当劳		[Màidāngláo]	McDonald's
肯德基	炸鸡	[Kěndéjī zhájī]	Kentucky Fried Chicken
必胜客	匹萨	[Bìshèngkè pǐsà]	Pizza Hut
星巴克	咖啡	[Xīngbākè kāfēi]	Starbucks Coffee

趣味中文 FUN WITH CHINESE

饭后百步走，活到九十九。
Take a walk after each meal and you will live to be 99 years old.

fàn	hòu	bǎi	bù	zǒu	huó	dào	jiǔshíjiǔ
饭	后	百	步	走	活	到	九十九
meal	after	hundred	step	walk	live	to	ninety-nine

Questions:

1. Do you know any similar sayings in a language other than Chinese?
2. Can you give an example?

行动吧！ LET'S GO!

小吃 Chinese Snacks

1. While traveling in China, 小中 saw the following interesting shop signs. Read the signs and answer the following questions.

Useful words and expressions:

小吃 [xiǎochī]: snacks
左边 (左邊) [zuǒbiān]: left side
右边 (右邊) [yòubiān]: right side
馅 (餡) [xiàn]: food filling
熊 [xióng]: bear
之父 [zhīfù]: father of
快餐 [kuàicān]: fast food
店名 [diànmíng]: name of a shop

Question:

左边的店名叫什么，卖什么？右边的店呢？

2. 小中 also visited Taiwan. During his stay there his Chinese friends took him out to eat at the following places. They ate several dishes at each place.

Useful words and expressions:

发财(發財) [fācái]: get rich
排骨 [páigǔ]: ribs or pork chop
香菇 [xiānggū]: mushroom
炸酱面(炸醬麵) [zhájiàng miàn]: noodles with spicy bean sauce
锅贴(鍋貼) [guōtiē]: fried dumpling
鱼丸(魚丸) [yúwán]: fish ball

十二月十八日星期一　　十二月二十二日星期日

Questions:

1. 左边的店名叫什么？
2. 他们十二月十八日星期一吃什么？十二月二十二日星期日呢？
3. 你想点些什么？

第十二课
LESSON

12

我可以借你的车吗？
May I Borrow Your Car?

教学目标 OBJECTIVES

- Make a request
- Express wishes, obligations, capabilities, possibilities, or permissions

Meeting friends at the Guangzhou airport in China.

Have a good trip back to the U.S. **浦东** *[Pǔdōng] International Airport in Shanghai.*

Taxis are plentiful and are a convenient way to get around the city.

生词 VOCABULARY

核心词 Core Vocabulary

SIMPLIFIED	TRADITIONAL	PINYIN		
1. 可以	可以	kěyǐ	Aux.	can, may
2. 借	借	jiè	V.	to borrow
3. 明天	明天	míngtiān	N.	tomorrow
4. 用	用	yòng	V.	to use
5. 得	得	děi	Aux.	must; have to
6. 机场	機場	jīchǎng	N.	airport
7. 接	接	jiē	V.	to pick up
8. 妹妹	妹妹	mèimei	N.	younger sister
9. 玩	玩	wán	V.	to play, have fun
10. 飞机	飛機	fēijī	N.	airplane
11. 到	到	dào	V.	to arrive
12. 手排挡 (手排)	手排擋 (手排)	shǒupáidǎng (shǒupái)	N.	manual transmission
13. 开	開	kāi	V.	to drive
14. 应该	應該	yīnggāi	Aux.	should
15. 问题	問題	wèntí	N.	problem; question
16. 白	白	bái	Adj.	white
17. 色	色	sè	N.	color
18. 停	停	tíng	V.	to park
19. 停车场	停車場	tíngchēchǎng	N.	parking lot
20. 这次	這次	zhècì	Pron.	this time
21. 练习	練習	liànxí	V.	to practice

SIMPLIFIED	TRADITIONAL	PINYIN		
22. 这样	這樣	zhèyàng	Pron.	thus, in this way
23. 就	就	jiù	Adv.	(connects two clauses, the first being the premise of the second)
24. 能	能	néng	Aux.	can, may, be able to
25. 进步	進步	jìnbù	V.	to improve

专名 Proper Nouns

SIMPLIFIED	TRADITIONAL	PINYIN		
1. 于影	于影	Yú Yǐng	N.	(name) Ying Yu
2. 王本乐	王本樂	Wáng Běnlè	N.	(name) Benle Wang
3. 上海	上海	Shànghǎi	N.	Shanghai
4. 洛杉矶	洛杉磯	Luòshānjī	N.	Los Angeles

补充词 Supplementary Vocabulary

SIMPLIFIED	TRADITIONAL	PINYIN		
1. 自动排挡 (自排)	自動排擋 (自排)	zìdòngpáidǎng (zìpái)	Adj.	automatic transmission

语文知识 LANGUAGE LINK

The Sentence Patterns provide models that will help you with the Language in Use section. In both sections, pay attention to the grammar points, vocabulary, and expressions.

句型 Sentence Patterns

A: 我可以借你的车吗？
Wǒ kěyǐ jiè nǐde chē ma?

B: 可以。
Kěyǐ.

A: 你要去接谁?
Nǐ yào qù jiē shéi?

B: 我要去接我妹妹。
Wǒ yào qù jiē wǒ mèimei.

A: 你会不会开车?
Nǐ huìbuhuì kāi chē?

B: 我不会开车。
Wǒ bú huì kāi chē.

课文 Language in Use: 我可以借你的车吗? Wǒ kěyǐ jiè nǐde chē ma?

于影: 本乐, 明天下午你用不用车?
Běnlè, míngtiān xiàwǔ nǐ yòngbuyòng chē?

王本乐: 我不用。你有什么事儿吗?
Wǒ bú yòng. Nǐ yǒu shénme shèr ma?

于影: 我得去机场接人, 可以借你的车吗?
Wǒ děi qù jīchǎng jiē rén, kěyǐ jiè nǐde chē ma?

王本乐: 可以。你要去接谁?
Kěyǐ. Nǐ yào qù jiē shéi?

于影: 我妹妹和她男朋友。他们从上海坐飞机去
Wǒ mèimei hé tā nán péngyou. Tāmen cóng Shànghǎi zuò fēijī qù

洛杉矶玩儿, 明天会到我这儿来。
Luòshānjī wár, míngtiān huì dào wǒ zhèr lái.

王本乐: 我的车是手排挡的, 你会不会开?
Wǒ de chē shì shǒupáidǎng de, nǐ huìbuhuì kāi?

于影: 应该没问题。我爸爸的车也是手排挡的, 我常开他的车。
Yīnggāi méi wèntí. Wǒ bàba de chē yěshì shǒupáidǎng de, wǒ cháng kāi tāde chē.

王本乐： 我的车是白色的，车号是
Wǒ de chē shì báisè de, chēhào shì

BD5730，停在五号停车场。
BD wǔ qī sān líng, tíng zài wǔ hào tíngchē chǎng.

于影： 知道了。谢谢！
Zhīdào le. Xièxie!

王本乐： 不谢。你妹妹他们会说英文吗？
Búxiè. Nǐ mèimei tāmen huì shuō Yīngwén ma?

于影： 会一点儿，这次他们想多学习一点儿英文。
Huì yìdiǎr, zhècì tāmen xiǎng duō xuéxí yìdiǎr Yīngwén.

王本乐： 太好了，我得跟他们多练习一点儿中文。
Tàihǎo le, wǒ děi gēn tāmen duō liànxí yìdiǎr Zhōngwén.

这样，我的中文就能进步了。
Zhèyàng, wǒde Zhōngwén jiù néng jìnbù le.

注释 LANGUAGE NOTES

坐

坐 means "sit." When its object is a means of transportation, 坐 means "to take." For example, 坐飞机 means "to take an airplane."

手排挡 (手排)

手排挡 literally means "hand handle gear." It refers to a manual transmission. In Taiwan, 手排 is commonly used.

这样

这样 is a phrase meaning "in this way."

就

就 here is used as a conjunction meaning "then."

语法 GRAMMAR

Optative Verbs (能愿动词): 要，想，应该，得，能，可以，会

Optative Verbs are placed before the main verb to express one's wish, desire, obligation, capability, possibility, or permission. Following are the commonly used optative verbs.

Optative verbs	Meaning	Examples	Negation
要 [yào]	1. want, will, to be going to	我要去机场。	不想 (irregular negation)
	2. have to, should	你要多练习中文。	不用 (irregular negation)
想 [xiǎng]	want, intend, would like to	他们想多说英文。 我想吃饺子。	不想
应该 [yīnggāi]	should, ought to, to be supposed to	你应该在宿舍学习。 你应该多休息。	不应该
得 [děi]	have to, to be required to	我得去机场接人。	不用 (irregular negation)
能 [néng]	1. have the ability to	我能开手排挡的车。	不会 (irregular negation)
	2. can (depending on circumstances)	他明天能来上课。	不能
	3. permission — may	我能借他的车。	不能
可以 [kěyǐ]	1. permission — may	我可以借他的车。	不能 (irregular negation) 不可以
	2. can (depending on circumstances)	他明天可以来。	不能 (irregular negation)
会 [huì]	1. know how to, have the ability to	你会开车。	不会
	2. be likely to	他明天会来。	不会

从 ... 去(到) ...

从 ... 去(到)... (from . . . to . . .) is a common pattern which is used to describe the movement of something from one place (or time) to another. Note that when describing an event, Chinese word order begins with the starting point, then proceeds to the means, to the arriving point, and then to the action. This reflects the temporal sequence of the event. For example,

Place:	从 Place 1	坐 N	去 (到) Place 2	
他们	从上海	坐飞机	去 (到)洛杉矶	玩。
Subj.	Place 1	Means	Place 2	VP

They, from Shanghai, took an airplane, arrived in Los Angeles, and had fun.

Time: 这学期是从一月到五月。
This semester is from January to May.

多 VP (学习，练习)

多 can be placed before a verb to indicate doing more of the verb. For example,

你要多学习。	You need to study more.
你应该多练习汉字 [hànzì]。	You should practice characters more.
请多吃一点儿。	Please eat a little bit more.
我要多睡一点儿。	I want to sleep a little more.

补充课文 SUPPLEMENTARY PRACTICE

This selection will help you test your comprehension of the grammar and vocabulary you have learned in this lesson. Be prepared to answer questions about the meaning of the passage.

我妹妹和她男朋友要来美国度假，他们要先从上海坐飞机去洛杉矶玩儿，然后再到我这儿来。我得去机场接他们，可是我没有车，我就跟本乐借车。本乐的车是手排挡的，他问我会不会开。我告诉他我虽然比较喜欢开自排的车，但是我以前也常开手排的车，所以应该没问题。

妹妹他们这次来，除了想好好地玩儿以外，他们也想多了解美国文化，多学一点儿英文。本乐说他也可以趁这个机会跟他们多练习一点儿中文，这样，他的中文就能进步了。我觉得这是一个好主意。

Notes: 度假 [dùjià]: to spend one's vacation
虽然...但是... [suīrán . . . dànshì . . .]: though . . . , . . . but
了解 [liǎojiě]: to understand
趁 [chèn]: to take advantage of
觉得 [juéde]: to think
告诉 [gàosù]: to tell
以前 [yǐqián]: before
除了...以外... [chúle . . . yǐwài . . .]: besides
文化 [wénhuà]: culture
机会 [jīhuì]: opportunity
主意 [zhǔyi]: idea

练习 ACTIVITIES

I. Pinyin Exercises

12-1 Listen to the instructor, then write the correct Pinyin for the following characters:

1. 机场 ________	2. 可以 ________	3. 这次 ________
4. 手排挡 ________	5. 飞机 ________	6. 白色 ________
7. 问题 ________	8. 停车场 ________	9. 进步 ________
10. 应该 ________	11. 练习 ________	12. 这样 ________

12-2 Listen to the instructor, then fill in each blank with the correct Pinyin:

1. ____ 练习 ____ ____ 进步	2. 我 ____ 去 ____ 人
3. ____ 纽约到 ____ ____	4. 还不 ____ ____ 车
5. 想 ____ ____ 色的车	6. 我 ____ 上 ____ 车

12-3 Read the following Chinese poem, paying special attention to the tones and rhythm:

Lè Yóuyuán (Lǐ Shāngyǐn)	乐游原 (李商隐)	Wandering about the Pleasant Plateau (Li, Shangyin)
Xiàng wǎn yì bú shì,	向晚意不适，	Feeling slightly sad near dusk,
Qū chē dēng gǔyuán.	驱车登古原。	I drive up to the ancient plateau.
Xīyáng wúxiàn hǎo,	夕阳无限好，	The sunset is endlessly beautiful,
Zhǐshì jìn huánghūn.	只是近黄昏。	But dusk is drawing near.

II. Character Exercises

12-4 Read the following words and phrases:

到	车
到机场	开车
从学校到机场	练习开车
从学校到机场接人	应该练习开车
能从学校到机场接人	应该多练习开车
你能从学校到机场去接人吗	你们都应该多练习开车

Now try to use the following characters to make words, phrases, and then sentences:

1. 借	2. 用	3. 玩	4. 飞	5. 接	6. 色
7. 停	8. 会	9. 排	10. 次	11. 得	12. 进

12-5 Match the following simplified characters with their equivalent traditional forms:

应	机	习	进	飞	场	开	样
(1)	(2)	(3)	(4)	(5)	(6)	(7)	(8)
習	場	機	開	應	進	樣	飛

III. Grammar Exercises

12-6 Substitution exercises:

1. 你会不会开车？
   我会开车。

写小说
用电脑
说法文
写电子邮件
开飞机

2. 你现在能打电话吗？
   我现在能打电话。

喝啤酒
看电视
上网
看中国文学书
跟我一起喝咖啡

3. 王老师要从洛杉矶到纽约看朋友。

公寓	图书馆	看书
英国	日本	学习
家	学校	打球
六点	八点	跟朋友吃饭

12-7 Match the Chinese sentences with their English translations. Pay attention to the optative verbs.

1. 我今天得开车去学校。 D
2. 我今天要开车去学校。 B
3. 我今天应该开车去学校。 A
4. 我今天能开车去学校。 E
5. 我今天会开车去学校。 C

A. I should drive to school today.
B. I will drive to school today.
C. I am likely to drive to school today.
D. I have to drive to school today.
E. I am able to drive to school today.

1.	他不可以打手机。	A.	He doesn't want to use the cell phone.
2.	他不会打手机。	B.	He shouldn't use the cell phone.
3.	他不用打手机。	C.	He is not allowed to use the cell phone.
4.	他不想打手机。	D.	He doesn't know how to use the cell phone.
5.	他不应该打手机。	E.	He doesn't need to use the cell phone.

12-8 Complete the sentences with the following optative words or their negative forms (e.g. 不用), "要、想、应该、得、能、可以、会":

1. 我今天不 ______ 上课。我 ______ 不 ______ 跟你一起去打球?
2. 你 ______ 多休息。
3. 坐飞机不 ______ 打手机。
4. A: 七月你 ______ 去上海玩儿吗?

   B: 我不 ______ 去。我从六月到九月都 ______ 在洛杉矶学习。
5. 我很 ______ 看电影。可是我明天早上六点就 ______ 开车去机场接朋友，今天晚上不 ______ 太晚睡觉。
6. 今天下午我 ______ 借你的数学书用一下，______ 吗?
7. A: 你 ______ 不 ______ 说德语?

   B: ______ 说一点儿。
8. 不 ______ 开夜车。这样你 ______ 很累。

Note: 开夜车 [kāiyèchē]: to burn the midnight oil

IV. Communicative Activities

12-9 Situational dialogues:

Situation 1:

You are going to travel to China next month. Your friend has a guide book on Chinese. Please borrow this book from your friend.

Hints:

1. Topics to cover:
   - Greetings.
   - Tell your friend you want to borrow the guide book on China.
   - Talk about the good scenic spots and delicious food in China.
   - Discuss and determine a possible travel route.

2. Words and expressions to use:

很好玩儿/很美　　从 ... 坐 ... 到/去...
多吃点儿　　要/得/应该/可以去...
喜欢...

Situation 2:

Your friend is borrowing your car to pick up a TV he/she bought from the store. Describe your car to your friend.

Hints:

1. Topics to cover:
   - Greetings.
   - Chat about the TV and the car.
   - Discuss your route.
2. Words and expressions to use:

有事儿吗？　　要/想 ...　　拿[ná] pick up stuff, (items)
会不会　　红/绿/白色的
没问题　　知道了　　应该/能/可以 ...　　从 ... 到 ...

Situation 3:

You are considering taking a Chinese course next semester. You are in the professor's office to ask whether the course will suit you.

Hints:

1. Topics to cover:
   - Greetings.
   - Chat for a while about the courses you are taking this semester.
   - Discuss your course schedule for the next semester and your current knowledge of Chinese.
   - Find out whether you should take the course.
2. Words and expressions to use:

忙吗？　　会说/看/写一点儿 ... 应该 ...　　多练习...
... 点钟要/得上 ... 课　　能/可以

文化知识 Culture Link

文化点滴 CULTURE NOTES

中国的汽车工业 [Zhōngguó de qìchē gōngyè] China's Auto Industry

China on Wheels

China's domestic auto industry celebrated its 50th anniversary in 2003. In 1953 a truck named 解放 [Jiěfàng] (Liberation) and a limousine named 红旗 [Hóngqí] (Red Flag) were first produced at China's First Auto Manufacturer in 长春 [Chángchūn] (Changchun), 吉林省 [Jílín Shěng] (Jilin Province). China's first sedan, branded as 上海 [Shànghǎi] (Shanghai), was also produced that year at Shanghai Auto Manufacturer.

Since the late 1980s many world-renowned auto manufacturers have established facilities in China to take advantage of the largest potential auto market in the world. Now China has Volkswagen and Audi in Changchun; Ford, Chrysler, Suzuki, and Hyundai in 北京 [Běijīng] (Beijing); Toyota in 天津 [Tiānjīn] (Tianjin); Honda and Volvo in 广州 [Guǎngzhōu] (Guangzhou); and Volkswagen and GMC in Shanghai. The auto market in China is now filled with almost all Chinese-made and joint venture-manufactured cars and has only a small number of imported cars. By 2007, 27% of China's auto market will be open to imported cars, as required by the WTO. In October 2003 the first 2,500 BMW sedans from a joint venture at 沈阳[Shěnyáng] (the city of Shenyang) became available to the Chinese auto market. According to an agreement signed in September 2003, China will supply the domestic market with joint-venture Mercedes Benz sedans in 2005.

The auto market for individual Chinese started in the early 1990s when only the wealthy could afford to buy used cars from some foreign embassies and consulates in Beijing. In October 1998 the Central Bank of China started to issue auto loans to individuals for the purchase of cars. The automobile loan business expanded very rapidly. The total loan amount grew from 400 million Yuan RMB (approximately US$50 million) in 1998 to 140 billion Yuan RMB (approximately US$17.5 billion) by 2002. The number of family cars increased eight times in the ten years from 1993 to 2003, and now there are over 7.7 million family cars in China. However, that number accounts for only 10% of all cars in China as compared to a substantially higher average percentage of family cars in other parts of the world. Millions of Chinese are carrying "pocket licenses," forming a gigantic pool of potential customers for the automobile market in China.

As roads in China are not yet ready to support a large number of cars, China has restricted the purchase of private cars for the time being. As a result, a vehicle license plate today may cost as much as US$15,000 at an auction. Also, an annual parking permit in major cities like Shanghai or Beijing costs from 1,000 to 6,000 Yuan RMB (US$125 to $750). That is one reason why you hear people say that you might be able to afford to buy a new car in China, but not to use it. In China, after the purchase of a car, there are also many other additional costs for maintenance, road and bridge tolls, vehicle taxes, insurance, gas, parking, and annual inspection.

Cars also serve as a symbol of one's social status in China.

Auto detailing shops are available for car owners.

A privately owned car on the streets of Guangdong Province 粤 [Yuè]. Do you know how much the license plate costs?

Early morning in Shanghai, privately owned cars on the street.

Small, utilitarian minivans are a popular choice for businesses and families in Taiwan.

This mini truck is owned by a scooter business in Taiwan. It is used for delivering equipment and scooters.

Questions:

1. Some people say that with a large population of 1.3 billion, it is not appropriate for China to encourage its people to purchase their own cars. Do you agree with them? Why or why not?
2. How would you comment on the mentality among some Chinese that owning a car is a sign of high social status? Do you agree? Why or why not?

趣味中文 FUN WITH CHINESE

有借有还，再借不难。

If one borrows something and then returns it, it will make borrowing easier the next time.

yǒu	jiè	yǒu	huán	zài	jiè	bù	nán
有	借	有	还	再	借	不	难
have	borrow	have	return	again	borrow	not	difficult

Question:

How would you comment on this Chinese saying? Do you know any similar sayings in another culture?

行动吧！ LET'S GO!

停车标志和汽车出售
Parking Sign and Car for Sale

正明 is interested in the signs below. Take a look at them, and then answer the questions.

Useful words and expressions:

车位(車位) [chēwèi]: parking space
每 [měi]: every
收费(收費) [shōufèi]: to collect a fee
电洽(電洽) [diànqià]: to contact via phone
觉得(覺得) [juéde]: to think
已 [yǐ]: already
满(滿) [mǎn]: full
小时(小時) [xiǎoshí]: hour
售 [shòu]: for sale
找 [zhǎo]: to look for
贵(貴) [guì]: expensive

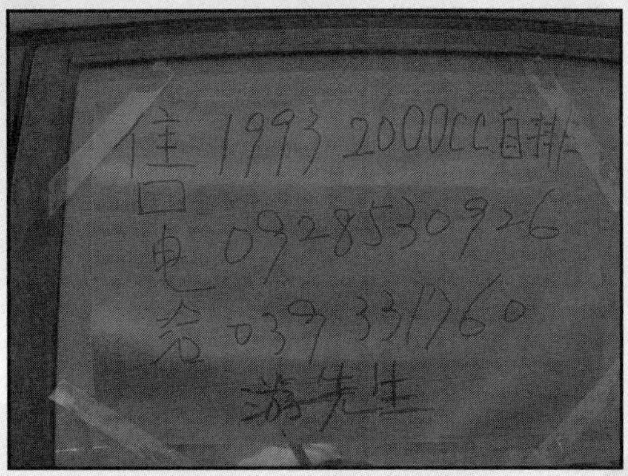

This ad is from the window of the car on the left.

Questions:

1. 正明在找什么？
2. 这个停车场怎么收费？你觉得贵不贵？
3. 是谁要卖车？这辆车是自排的吗？
4. 手机的号码是多少？

复习 Review

LESSON 11 AND LESSON 12

Conversation

Form pairs. Ask your partner the following questions. Then report the information you collect in class.

1. 你喜欢吃饭还是吃面?
2. 你喜欢在图书馆还是在宿舍看书?
3. 你喜欢给朋友打电话还是写电子邮件?
4. 你会开车吗?
5. 你会开自排挡的车还是手排挡的车?
6. 毕业以后你想去中国工作吗?
7. 我们从这里到洛杉矶应该开车还是坐飞机?

Situational Dialogues

You go to a Chinese restaurant. Chat with the waitress/waiter, then order drinks and dishes.

Useful expressions: 还 是; measure words: 杯 瓶 盘 碗 双; 点 (to order), 多 + VP . . . (一点儿); optative verbs: 可以, 要, 想, 应该, 能, 会, 得; time sequence: 从 place 坐 N 到 place

Simplified and Traditional Characters

Read each character aloud. Write its simplified form. Then make a phrase and a sentence using the character.

For example, 學 → 学 → 学生 → 我是学生。

L11: 務 ( ) 樂 ( ) 麵 ( ) 盤 ( ) 湯 ( ) 雙 ( )
L12: 場 ( ) 飛 ( ) 應 ( ) 會 ( ) 習 ( ) 進 ( )

第十三课
LESSON

13

我想买一件衬衫
I Want to Buy a Shirt

教学目标 OBJECTIVES

- Go shopping
- Talk about clothing, colors, and prices
- Provide opinions

Shopping malls, street malls, department stores, and traditional markets are common in Mainland China and Taiwan. They are usually crowded.

生词 VOCABULARY

核心词 Core Vocabulary

SIMPLIFIED	TRADITIONAL	PINYIN		
1. 买	買	mǎi	V.	to buy
2. 件	件	jiàn	M.W.	(measure word for clothes)
3. 衬衫	襯衫	chènshān	N.	shirt
4. 店员	店員	diànyuán	N.	salesman, saleswoman
5. 条	條	tiáo	M.W.	(measure word for skirts/pants)
6. 裙子	裙子	qúnzi	N.	skirt
7. 或者	或者	huòzhě	Conj.	or, either . . . or . . .
8. 裤子	褲子	kùzi	N.	pants
9. 黄	黃	huáng	Adj.	yellow
10. 不错	不錯	búcuò		not bad, pretty good
11. 比较	比較	bǐjiào	Adv.	relatively
12. 穿	穿	chuān	V.	to wear
13. 黑	黑	hēi	Adj.	black
14. 试试	試試	shìshi	V.	to try
15. 帮	幫	bāng	V.	to help
16. 好看	好看	hǎokàn	Adj.	good-looking
17. 让	讓	ràng	V.	to let, allow
18. 觉得	覺得	juéde	V.	to think, feel
19. 钱	錢	qián	N.	money
20. 块	塊	kuài	N.	dollar
21. 张	張	zhāng	M.W.	(measure word for piece of paper)
22. 电影	電影	diànyǐng	N.	movie
23. 票	票	piào	N.	ticket

专名 Proper Nouns

SIMPLIFIED	TRADITIONAL	PINYIN		
1. 毛爱红	毛愛紅	Máo Àihóng	N.	(name) Aihong Mao
2. 方子英	方子英	Fāng Zǐyīng	N.	(name) Ziying Fang

补充词 Supplementary Vocabulary

SIMPLIFIED	TRADITIONAL	PINYIN		
1. 贵	貴	guì	Adj.	expensive
2. 便宜	便宜	piányi	Adj.	inexpensive
3. 卖	賣	mài	V.	to sell
4. 号	號	hào	N.	size
5. 几号	幾號	jǐ hào		what size
6. 特大	特大	tè dà	Adj.	extra large
7. 大	大	dà	Adj.	large
8. 中	中	zhōng	Adj.	medium
9. 小	小	xiǎo	Adj.	small
10. 特小	特小	tè xiǎo	Adj.	extra small

货币 [Huòbì] Currency

SIMPLIFIED	TRADITIONAL	PINYIN		
1. 人民币	人民幣	Rénmínbì	N.	currency of the People's Republic of China
2. 新台币	新台幣	Xīntáibì	N.	currency of Taiwan (New Taiwan dollars)
3. 港币	港幣	Gǎngbì	N.	currency of Hong Kong
4. 美金	美金	Měijīn	N.	U.S. dollar
5. 欧元	歐元	Ōuyuán	N.	euro

钱币表达方法 [Qiánbì biǎodá fāngfǎ] Ways to Express Money in Chinese

Written form:

SIMPLIFIED	TRADITIONAL	PINYIN		
1. 元	元	yuán	N.	dollar
2. 角	角	jiǎo	N.	(10角 = 1元)
3. 分	分	fēn	N.	(100分 = 10角 = 1元)

Spoken form:

SIMPLIFIED	TRADITIONAL	PINYIN		
4. 块	塊	kuài	N.	dollar
5. 毛	毛	máo	N.	(10毛 = 1块)
6. 分	分	fēn	N.	(100分 = 10毛 = 1块)

常见衣服 [Chángjiàn yīfu] Common Items of Clothing

Measure Word: 件

SIMPLIFIED	TRADITIONAL	PINYIN		
1. 上衣	上衣	shàngyī	N.	upper-clothing
2. 大衣	大衣	dàyī	N.	overcoat
3. 外套	外套	wàitào	N.	coat
4. 背心	背心	bèixīn	N.	vest
5. 西装	西裝	xīzhuāng	N.	suit
6. 夹克衫 (夹克)	夾克衫 (夾克)	jiákèshān (jiákè)	N.	jacket
7. 毛衣	毛衣	máoyī	N.	sweater
8. T-恤衫 (T-恤)	T-恤衫 (T-恤)	tīxùshān (tīxù)	N.	T-shirt
9. 内衣	內衣	nèiyī	N.	underwear

Measure Word (Classifier): 条(條)

SIMPLIFIED	TRADITIONAL	PINYIN		
10. 长裤	長褲	chángkù	N.	long pants
11. 短裤	短褲	duǎnkù	N.	shorts
12. 牛仔裤	牛仔褲	niúzǎikù	N.	jeans
13. 内裤	內褲	nèikù	N.	underpants
14. 裙子	裙子	qúnzi	N.	skirt
15. 迷你裙	迷你裙	míníqún	N.	miniskirt

Measure Word (Classifier): 双(雙)

SIMPLIFIED	TRADITIONAL	PINYIN		
16. 鞋子	鞋子	xiézi	N.	shoes
17. 皮鞋	皮鞋	píxié	N.	leather shoes
18. 球鞋	球鞋	qiúxié	N.	sneakers
19. 拖鞋	拖鞋	tuōxié	N.	slippers
20. 凉鞋	涼鞋	liángxié	N.	sandals
21. 靴子	靴子	xuēzi	N.	boots
22. 袜子	襪子	wàzi	N.	socks

常见饰品 [Chángjiàn shìpǐn] Common Accessories

SIMPLIFIED	TRADITIONAL	PINYIN		
1. 手表	手錶	shǒubiǎo	N.	watch
2. 耳环	耳環	ěrhuán	N.	earrings
3. 手镯	手鐲	shǒuzhuó	N.	bracelet
4. 戒指	戒指	jièzhi	N.	ring
5. 项链	項鏈	xiàngliàn	N.	necklace
6. 眼镜	眼鏡	yǎnjìng	N.	glasses

SIMPLIFIED	TRADITIONAL	PINYIN		
7. 帽子	帽子	màozi	N.	hat
8. 手套	手套	shǒutào	N.	gloves
9. 手绢	手絹	shǒujuàn	N.	handkerchief
10. 领带	領帶	lǐngdài	N.	necktie
11. 围巾	圍巾	wéijīn	N.	scarf

常见穿衣动作 [Chángjiàn chuānyī dòngzuò] Common Actions for Clothes

SIMPLIFIED	TRADITIONAL	PINYIN		
1. 穿	穿	chuān	V.	to wear, put on (regular clothes)
2. 穿上	穿上	chuānshàng	V.C.	to put on (regular clothes)
3. 戴	戴	dài	V.	to wear, put on (accessories)
4. 戴上	戴上	dàishàng	V.C.	to put on (accessories)
5. 脱	脫	tuō	V.	to take off (regular clothes)
6. 脱下	脫下	tuōxià	V.C.	to take off (regular clothes)
7. 摘	摘	zhāi	V.	to take off (accessories)
8. 摘下	摘下	zhāixià	V.C.	to take off (accessories)

常见颜色 [Chángjiàn yánsè] Common Colors

SIMPLIFIED	TRADITIONAL	PINYIN		
1. 红色	紅色	hóngsè	Adj.	red
2. 白色	白色	báisè	Adj.	white
3. 黑色	黑色	hēisè	Adj.	black
4. 黄色	黃色	huángsè	Adj.	yellow
5. 绿色	綠色	lǜsè	Adj.	green
6. 蓝色	藍色	lánsè	Adj.	blue

SIMPLIFIED	TRADITIONAL	PINYIN		
7. 紫色	紫色	zǐsè	Adj.	purple
8. 粉红色	粉紅色	fěnhóngsè	Adj.	pink
9. 橙色 (橘色)	橙色 (橘色)	chéngsè (júsè)	Adj.	orange
10. 灰色	灰色	huīsè	Adj.	gray
11. 棕色 (咖啡色)	棕色 (咖啡色)	zōngsè (kāfēisè)	Adj.	brown
12. 金黄色	金黃色	jīnhuángsè	Adj.	gold
13. 银灰色	銀灰色	yínhuīsè	Adj.	silver
14. 深色	深色	shēnsè	Adj.	dark
15. 深蓝色	深藍色	shēnlánsè	Adj.	dark blue
16. 浅色	淺色	qiǎnsè	Adj.	light
17. 浅绿色	淺綠色	qiǎnlǜsè	Adj.	light green
18. 彩色	彩色	cǎisè	Adj.	multicolored

语文知识 LANGUAGE LINK

The Sentence Patterns provide models that will help you with the Language in Use section. In both sections, pay attention to the grammar points, vocabulary, and expressions.

句型 Sentence Patterns

A: 你想买什么?
Nǐ xiǎng mǎi shénme?

B: 我想买一件衬衫。
Wǒ xiǎng mǎi yíjiàn chènshān.

A: 你帮我看看，我穿裙子
Nǐ bāng wǒ kànkan, wǒ chuān qúnzi

好看还是穿裤子好看?
hǎokàn háishì chuān kùzi hǎokàn?

B: 我觉得你穿裙子好看。
Wǒ juéde nǐ chuān qúnzi hǎokàn.

A: 这条裙子多少钱?
Zhètiáo qúnzi duōshǎo qián?

B: 十五块。
Shíwǔ kuài.

课文 Language in Use: 我想买一件衬衫 Wǒ xiǎng mǎi yíjiàn chènshān

店员：两位小姐想买什么?
Liǎngwèi xiǎojiě xiǎng mǎi shénme?

毛爱红：我想买一件衬衫。
Wǒ xiǎng mǎi yíjiàn chènshān.

方子英：我想买一条裙子或者裤子。
Wǒ xiǎng mǎi yìtiáo qúnzi huòzhě kùzi.

店员：这件黄衬衫怎么样?
Zhèjiàn huáng chènshān zěnmeyàng?

毛爱红：还不错。可是我比较喜欢穿黑色的，有没有黑色的?
Hái búcuò. Kěshì wǒ bǐjiào xǐhuān chuān hēisède, yǒuméiyǒu hēisède?

店员：有，在这儿，你试试!
Yǒu, zài zhèr, nǐ shìshi!

方子英：爱红，来，你帮我看看，我穿裙子好看还是
Àihóng, lái, nǐ bāng wǒ kànkan, wǒ chuān qúnzi hǎokàn háishì

穿裤子好看?
chuān kùzi hǎokàn?

毛爱红： 你穿穿，让我看看。我觉得你穿这条裙子好看。
Nǐ chuānchuan, ràng wǒ kànkan. Wǒ juéde nǐ chuān zhètiáo qúnzi hǎokàn.

方子英： 请问，这条裙子多少钱？
Qǐngwèn, zhètiáo qúnzi duōshǎo qián?

店员： 十五块。
Shíwǔ kuài.

方子英： 好，我买了。
Hǎo, wǒ mǎile.

毛爱红： 我要买这件黑衬衫。
Wǒ yào mǎi zhèjiàn hēi chènshān.

店员： 对了，小姐，这张电影票是你的吗？
Duì le, xiǎojiě, zhèzhāng diànyǐngpiào shì nǐde ma?

方子英： 是的，这张电影票是我的。谢谢！我们等一下
Shìde, zhèzhāng diànyǐngpiào shì wǒde. Xièxie! Wǒmen děngyíxià

要去看电影。
yào qù kàn diànyǐng.

注释 LANGUAGE NOTES

不错

不错 literally means "not wrong." It means "good" in Chinese.

好看

好看 means "good-looking." 好 is often used together with a verb to form a new adjective to mean "good to + V." or "easy to + V." For example,

好吃	delicious (good to eat)
好听 [tīng]	beautiful sounding (good to hear)
好玩	funny, interesting (good to play)
好喝	delicious to drink (good to drink)

Also,

好写	easy to write
好说	easy to say
好懂 [dǒng]	easy to understand
好念 [niàn]	easy to read

觉(得)

When 觉 is pronounced as [jué] it means "to feel" or "to think." When 觉 is pronounced as [jiào] in 睡觉 it means "to sleep."

得 (Pronunciation in 得 "must" and 觉得)

When 得 is pronounced as [děi] it means "must" or "have to." When 得 is pronounced as [de] in 觉得 it means "to think" or "to feel."

多少钱

How much (money) is it?

语法 GRAMMAR

Conjunction 或者

或者 is another conjunction meaning "or", similar to 还是. However, while 还是 is only used in alternative questions, 或者 can be used in statements. Here are some examples:

A: 你想买衬衫还是T-恤衫?	Would you like to buy a shirt or a T-shirt?
B: 我想买一条裙子或者裤子。	I want to buy a skirt or a pair of pants.
A: 你喜欢黑色的还是蓝色的?	Do you like black or blue?
B: 我喜欢红色或者白色的。	I like red or white.

量词 (Measure Words/Classifiers) (4): 件，条，张

In previous lessons we have studied the following measure words:

Measure word	Usage	Example
本	For book-like things	一本书 一本词典 [cídiǎn] (dictionary) 一本杂志 [zázhì] (magazine)
辆	For vehicles	一辆汽车 [qìchē] (car) 一辆自行车 [zìxíngchē] (bicycle)
只	For animals	一只狗 一只猫
门	For courses	五门课
个	For people and things in general	两个人
位	A courteous measure word used for guests	三位客人 [kèrén] (guest)
张	For sheet-like things	四张票 [piào] (ticket) 五张桌子 [zhuōzi] (table)

In this lesson, 双 is introduced as a special measure word for certain things in pairs, for example,

Measure word	Usage	Example
双	For pairs of certain things	一双筷子
		一双眼睛 [yǎnjīng] (eyes)
		两双鞋 [xié] (shoes)
		三双袜子 [wàzi] (socks)

Note: Not all things in pairs take 双 as the measure words. Here are some other examples:

Measure word	Usage	Example
副 [fù]: pair	For pairs of certain things (usually for accessories)	一副手套 [shǒutào] (gloves)
对 [duì]: pair		一对耳环 [ěrhuán] (earrings)

This lesson also introduces two measure words used for clothing, 件 and 条.

件 is generally used for upper body clothing, but sometimes it can also be used for clothing in general. For example,

Measure word	Usage	Example
件	For clothing in general	一件衬衫
		一件大衣 [dàyī] (overcoat)
		一件运动衫 [yùndòngshān] (sports shirt)
		一件T-恤衫 [tīxùshān] (T-shirt)
		一件夹克衫 [jiákèshān] (jacket)
		一件滑雪衫 [huáxuěshān] (winter coat)

条 is a measure word used for long-shaped clothing, such as 裤子 and 裙子. For example,

Measure word	Usage	Example
条	For long-shaped items	一条裤子
		一条长裤 [chángkù] (long pants)
		一条牛仔裤 [niúzǎikù] (jeans)
		一条裙子

Duplication of Verbs

Many verbs can be duplicated in spoken Chinese to indicate a quick action — "to do a little bit of something" or to do something in a relaxed way. Here are some examples:

试试	to have a try	看看	to have a look
穿穿	to try on	听听 [tīngting]	to listen for a little while
写写	to write a little	说说	to say a little
想想	to think a little	走走	to take a walk

If the verb is disyllabic, the duplication is as follows:

介绍介绍	to give a little introduction	学习学习	to study a little

Basically, verbs expressing active actions or behaviors can be duplicated. Those that indicate status or existence cannot be duplicated. Sometimes, a duplicated verb expression may have "一" in between, such as,

看一看 试一试 想一想 穿一穿

Notes:
a. Only monosyllabic verbs can take 一 in between when duplicated.
b. The duplicated syllable is always pronounced in the neutral tone.

Such verbs may also be followed by 一下(儿). This has the same effect as duplication.

看看	=	看一看	=	看一下(儿)
想想	=	想一想	=	想一下(儿)
介绍介绍	=	(NA)	=	介绍一下(儿)
学习学习	=	(NA)	=	学习一下(儿)

补充课文 SUPPLEMENTARY PRACTICE

This selection will help you test your comprehension of the grammar and vocabulary you have learned in this lesson. Be prepared to answer questions about the meaning of the passage.

上个周末，我和子英一起去购物中心逛街，买东西。我想买一件衬衫，子英想买一条裙子或者裤子。我们到了一家服饰店，我先挑了一件黄色和一件黑色的衬衫。我试穿了一下，照照镜子，觉得黑色的比较适合我，所以我就买了那件黑衬衫。

子英也拿了一条裙子和一条裤子，然后就到试衣间穿穿，她要我帮她看看，我看了以后，觉得她穿裙子比较好看，最后她决定买那条裙子，店员小姐说那条裙子十五块钱。我们买了衣服以后，就去看电影了。

Notes:
周末 [zhōumò]: weekend
逛街 [guàngjiē]: to go shopping
到 [dào]: to arrive
服饰店 [fúshìdiàn]: clothing shop
试穿 [shìchuān]: to try on
镜子 [jìngzi]: mirror
试衣间 [shìyījiān]: dressing room
决定 [juédìng]: to decide
购物中心 [gòuwù zhōngxīn]: shopping center
东西 [dōngxi]: thing; stuff
家 [jiā]: measure word for shops
挑 [tiāo]: to choose; to pick
照 [zhào]: to reflect; to mirror
适合 [shìhé]: to suit
最后 [zuìhòu]: finally, at last

练习 ACTIVITIES

I. Pinyin Exercises

13-1 Listen to the instructor and write down the sentences in Pinyin:

1. ______________________________
2. ______________________________
3. ______________________________
4. ______________________________
5. ______________________________

13-2 Matching game: Work in groups of three. Prepare three stacks of cards. One stack should have pictures of T-shirts, jackets, shirts, sports shirts, pants, skirts, jeans, shoes, socks, and caps. The second stack should have the words for these items in Pinyin, and the third stack has a price written on each card. One person plays the role of a customer and makes requests for what he/she wants to buy. Another plays the role of the store assistant and picks out the card with the picture that matches the request and gives the price, then the third picks out the cards with the Pinyin and the price. After finishing one round, change roles and continue with the same game.

Useful words and expressions:

件，条，双，顶 [dǐng] (measure word/classifier for hats)

衬衫，裤子，T-恤衫，运动衫，裙子，袜子 [wàzi] (socks)，
帽子 [màozi] (hat, cab)，运动鞋，夹克衫，牛仔裤

13-3 Read the following Chinese poem, paying special attention to the tones and rhythm:

Jué Jù **(Dù Fǔ)**	**绝句** **(杜甫)**
Liǎngge huánglí míng cuìliǔ, Yìháng báilù shàng qīngtiān. Chuāng hán Xīlǐng qiānqiū xuě, Mén bó Dōngwú wànlǐ chuán.	两个黄鹂鸣翠柳， 一行白鹭上青天。 窗含西岭千秋雪， 门泊东吴万里船。

A Quatrain
(Du, Fu)

Two golden orioles are singing on the green willow trees,
White egrets are flying in a line in the blue sky.
Looking out of my window I see the snow-capped Western Mountains,
At my door are parked eastward-going ships that have traveled thousands of miles.

II. Character Exercises

13-4 Read the following words, phrases, and sentences:

衬衫	好看
一件衬衫	裙子好看
一件白衬衫	红裙子好看
一件白色的衬衫	这条红裙子好看
买一件白色的衬衫	穿这条红裙子好看
想买一件白色的衬衫	你穿这条红裙子好看
我想买一件白色的衬衫	我觉得你穿这条红裙子好看
我想买一件白色的或者黑色的衬衫	我觉得你穿这条红裙子比较好看

Now try to use the following characters to make words, phrases, and then sentences:

1. 店　2. 帮　3. 裤　4. 黄　5. 错　6. 票
7. 黑　8. 试　9. 让　10. 钱　11. 块　12. 张

13-5 Identify the radical of each of the following characters and write out the meaning of the radical in English. Then give as many examples of characters with the same radical as you can.

For example,

吗 [口] mouth 呢 吃 喝 和

1. 衫 [ ] ______ ________________
2. 买 [ ] ______ ________________
3. 黄 [ ] ______ ________________
4. 黑 [ ] ______ ________________
5. 钱 [ ] ______ ________________
6. 件 [ ] ______ ________________
7. 试 [ ] ______ ________________
8. 觉 [ ] ______ ________________
9. 块 [ ] ______ ________________
10. 票 [ ] ______ ________________

III. Grammar Exercises

13-6 Substitution exercises:

1. 你想买什么？
   我想买一件衬衫。

件	运动衫
件	T恤衫
件	毛衣
条	长裤
条	裙子
双	鞋子

2. 你想做什么？
   我想买一件衬衫或者一件大衣。

看	中国电影	美国电影
吃	春卷	饺子
穿	皮鞋	运动鞋
开	美国车	韩国车
去	中国饭馆	日本饭馆

3. 你觉得这碗汤怎么样？
   我觉得这碗汤很好喝。

盘	炒饭	好吃
个	汉字	好写
个	句子	好说
部	电影	好玩
条	裙子	好看

Notes: 汉字 [hànzì]: characters
句子 [jùzi]: sentence
部 [bù]: measure word for 电影

4. 这件运动衫不贵
   多少钱？
   二十五块八毛九分。

大衣	很便宜	五十六块
皮鞋	很贵	四十三块九毛五分
袜子	很好	两块二毛六分

13-7 Insert an appropriate measure word in each of the following:

1. 两 ______ 书　　2. 五 ______ 车票　　3. 三 ______ 衬衫

4. 一 ______ 皮鞋　　5. 四 ______ 裙子　　6. 六 ______ 牛仔裤

13-8 Complete the following sentences with duplication of the verb phrases given:

1. 这件衬衫我穿太大了，你 ________ 吧。(to have a try)
2. 这是谁的车？我来 ________ 车号。(to have a look)
3. 这是我的室友。来，你们 ____________ 。(to get to know each other)
4. 这首歌很好听，你也 ____________ 。(to listen to it)
5. 你知道这本书吗？我来给你 ______________ 。
   (to give you a little introduction)

Notes: 首 [shǒu]: measure word for song
歌 [gē]: song
听 [tīng]: to listen

13-9 Answer the following questions, using the word 或者 in your answer:

1. 先生，您想买什么？
   ____
2. 子英，你喜欢黑色的衬衫吗？
   ____
3. 爱红，你说我穿什么好看？
   ____
4. 于信，你今天晚上做什么？
   ____

IV. Communicative Activities

13-10 猜猜他/她是谁？(Play "Guess the classmate")

Divide the class into groups. Each group secretly decides on a classmate for the other groups to guess. Each member of the group says one or two sentences to describe the person, and then the other groups try to guess who the person is. For example,

他(她)今天穿一件白衬衫，黑裤子……
你们猜猜他/她是谁？

Note: 猜 [cāi]: to guess

13-11 In groups of three, act out the following scenario:

It is your first week in China. You go shopping with your friend Fang Mingming. You see a T-shirt and a pair of blue jeans. You like the style but are not sure of the color. You ask Fang Mingming for suggestions and he gives you a lot of good ones regarding your selection.

Words and expressions to use:

式样 [shìyàng] (style)		合适 [héshì] (suitable, fit)
试试	觉得	怎么样
还是	或者	比较

文化知识 Culture Link

文化点滴 CULTURE NOTES

中国的传统服饰
[Zhōngguó de chuántǒng fúshì]
Chinese Traditional Dress

The most typical representative items of traditional Chinese clothing are the 旗袍 [qípáo] for women, and the 唐装 [tángzhuāng] and traditional vests and suits for both genders. The material is usually silk with either patterned or picturesque embroidery on it. At first glance these clothes all look alike when compared to Western dress. It is this simplicity that people value in traditional Chinese clothing. Without using much cloth, the clothing accents the shape of the body to create an elegant and neat look.

This beautiful and delicate Qipao is made of silk and has the lucky colors of silver, red, and gold as well as lucky flowers and the phoenix embroidered on it.

Ladies in qipao and tangzhuang.

A gentleman in tangzhuang.

Chinese traditional dress is frequently worn to celebrate cultural festivals.

Around the 17th century, noble Manchurian men and women wore long, loose, tube-shaped robes. Each generation made subtle changes until the 1930s when it truly became the 旗袍 we associate with Chinese culture today. The choice of having sleeves or no sleeves, as well as certain differences in the collars and lengths of the dresses, all show the progression. The 1930s was a period of strong Western influence, and it was at this time that the 旗袍 became internationally popular.

An additional type of common clothing is the Chinese traditional suit. This is less formal and is unisex in shape. The only distinction between male and female suits is color. Men usually wear dark colors, while women prefer pastels. This outfit consists of loose pants and a shirt all made out of the same type of cloth. For children, an embroidered vest would sometimes accompany this suit.

Today, Western-style clothing is much more common in China. Chinese traditional dress is usually worn during cultural festivals. Parents also often dress their young children in traditional outfits. 旗袍 and 唐装 are also often seen in Chinese TV programs and movies that depict the 30s. Another example would be traditional wedding banquets, where the 旗袍 and 唐装 are popular among the newlyweds as well as the guests. In Chinese culture, red symbolizes good luck, so red outfits are very common.

Questions:

1. Besides red, what other lucky colors do you think Chinese people like to wear on happy occasions?
2. Have you ever seen any unique clothes worn by Chinese minorities? If so, describe them to your classmates.
3. Have you seen any movies where people wear traditional Chinese clothes?

趣味中文 FUN WITH CHINESE

情人眼里出西施。
Any woman becomes a beauty in the eyes of her lover.
Love makes one blind to all imperfections.

qíngrén	yǎn	lǐ	chū	Xīshī
情人	眼	里	出	西施
lover	eye	inside	come out	Xishi

西施 [Xīshī] is the name of a famous beauty in Chinese history. She lived in the 越国 [Yuèguó] Yue state in the 春秋 [Chūnqiū] Spring and Autumn period (722 to 484 B.C.).

Questions:

1. Do you know of any other famous beauties in Chinese history?
2. Can you think of any stories that are examples of 情人眼里出西施?
3. How do you feel about the imperfections of your boyfriend or girlfriend?

行动吧！ LET'S GO!

购物：钱币，收据和发票
Shopping: Bill, Receipt, and Invoice

1. Below are samples of currency in 人民币, 新台币 and 港币:

Useful words and expressions:

正面 [zhèngmiàn]: front side
样本(樣本) [yàngběn]: sample
反面 [fǎnmiàn]: reverse

(正面样本) (反面样本)

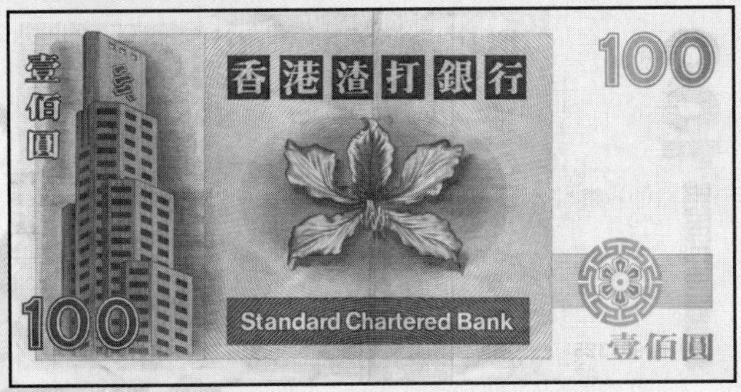

Questions:

1. What are the names of the central banks in China and Taiwan?
2. Do you notice any similarities or differences in these samples?

2. 在台湾，这是美英去超市买菜付钱以后收银员给她的一张统一发票：

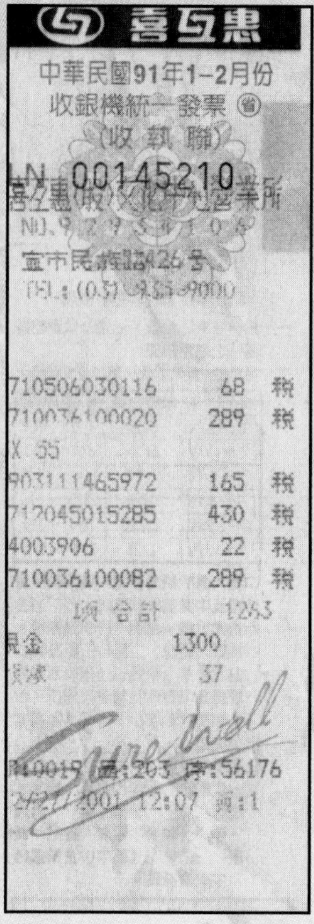

Useful words and expressions:

- 统一发票(統一發票) [tǒngyī fāpiào]: name of the receipts commonly used in Taiwan
- 合计(合計) [héji]: total
- 超市 [chāoshì]: supermarket
- 收银员(收銀員) [shōuyínyuán]: cashier
- 收银机(收銀機) [shōuyínjī]: cashier machine
- 便利商店 [biànlì shāngdiàn]: convenience store
- 收执联(收執聯) [shōuzhílián]: to receive and keep a sheet receipt
- 税(稅) [shuì]: tax

Questions:

1. 这个超市叫什么？
2. 美英一共 [yígòng] (in total) 花了多少钱？

第十四课
LESSON

14

我今年二十岁
I Am 20 This Year

教学目标 OBJECTIVES

- Say the days of the week
- Extend/accept an invitation
- Talk about people's birthdays

Eating cake at home, going out to eat at a steak house, and singing songs at KTV are all fun ways to celebrate birthdays.

生词 VOCABULARY

核心词 Core Vocabulary

SIMPLIFIED	TRADITIONAL	PINYIN		
1. 岁	歲	suì	N.	age, years
2. 有空	有空	yǒukòng	V.O.	to have free time
3. 星期	星期	xīngqī	N.	week
4. 过	過	guò	V.	to spend (life, time); to celebrate (e.g. birthday)
5. 生日	生日	shēngrì	N.	birthday
6. 为	為	wèi	Prep.	(indicates the object of one's act of service)
7. 舞会	舞會	wǔhuì	N.	dance party
8. 参加	參加	cānjiā	V.	to participate; to join
9. 一定	一定	yídìng	Aux.	certainly; surely
10. 做	做	zuò	V.	to make; to do
11. 蛋糕	蛋糕	dàngāo	N.	cake
12. 送	送	sòng	V.	to give as a present
13. 棒	棒	bàng	Adj.	wonderful
14. 不客气。	不客氣。	búkèqi		You are welcome.
15. 多大	多大	duōdà		how old
16. 地图	地圖	dìtú	N.	map

补充词 Supplementary Vocabulary

SIMPLIFIED	TRADITIONAL	PINYIN		
1. 日历	日曆	rìlì	N.	calendar
2. 月历	月曆	yuèlì	N.	monthly calendar
3. 庆生	慶生	qìngshēng	V.O.	to celebrate a birthday
4. 礼物	禮物	lǐwù	N.	gift
5. 蜡烛	蠟燭	làzhú	N.	candle
6. 祝你生日快乐。	祝你生日快樂。	Zhù nǐ shēngrì kuàilè.		Happy birthday to you.

三 月

星期一	星期二	星期三	星期四	星期五	星期六	星期日
		1	2	3	4	5
6	7	8	9	10	11	12
13	14	15	16	17	18	19
20	21	22	23	24	25	26
27	28	29	30	31		

语文知识 LANGUAGE LINK

The Sentence Patterns provide models that will help you with the Language in Use section. In both sections, pay attention to the grammar points, vocabulary, and expressions.

句型 Sentence Patterns

A: 今天是星期几?
Jīntiān shì xīngqī jǐ?

B: 今天是星期六。
Jīntiān shì xīngqī liù.

A: 你今年多大?
Nǐ jīnnián duō dà?

B: 我今年二十岁。
Wǒ jīnnián èrshí suì.

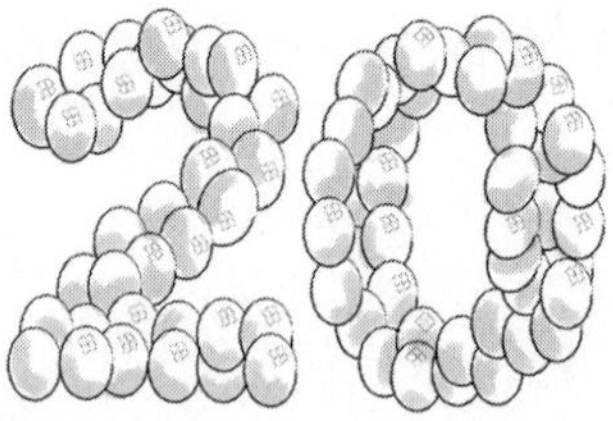

A: 你的生日是几月几号?
Nǐ de shēngrì shì jǐ yuè jǐ hào?

B: 我的生日是十月三号。
Wǒ de shēngrì shì shí yuè sān hào.

课文 Language in Use: 我今年二十岁 Wǒ jīnnián èrshí suì

方子英: 爱红，二月十八日你有没有空?
Àihóng, èr yuè shíbā rì nǐ yǒuméiyǒu kòng?

毛爱红: 二月十八日那天是星期几?
Èr yuè shíbā rì nàtiān shì xīngqī jǐ?

方子英: 星期六。
Xīngqī liù.

毛爱红: 我有空。有什么事儿吗?
Wǒ yǒu kòng. Yǒu shénme shèr ma?

方子英: 那天我过生日，我男朋友要为我
Nàtiān wǒ guò shēngrì, wǒ nánpéngyou yào wèi wǒ

开一个生日舞会，我想请你参加。
kāi yíge shēngrì wǔhuì, wǒ xiǎng qǐng nǐ cānjiā.

毛爱红: 谢谢你，我一定去。还有谁会去?
Xièxie nǐ, wǒ yídìng qù. Hái yǒu shéi huì qù?

方子英: 我们想请我们的同学和朋友都参加。
Wǒmen xiǎng qǐng wǒmen de tóngxué hé péngyou dōu cānjiā.

毛爱红: 我会做蛋糕。我送你一个生日蛋糕，怎么样?
Wǒ huì zuò dàngāo. Wǒ sòng nǐ yíge shēngrì dàngāo, zěngmeyàng?

方子英: 太棒了! 谢谢你!
Tàibàngle! Xièxie nǐ!

毛爱红： 不客气。你今年多大？
Búkèqi. Nǐ jīnnián duō dà?

方子英： 我今年二十岁。你呢？你的生日是几月几号？
Wǒ jīnnián èrshí suì. Nǐ ne? Nǐ de shēngrì shì jǐ yuè jǐ hào?

毛爱红： 我的生日是十月三号，我今年二十二岁。你的舞会在哪儿开？
Wǒ de shēngrì shì shí yuè sān hào, wǒ jīnnián èrshíèr suì. Nǐ de wǔhuì zài nǎr kāi?

方子英： 在我男朋友的家，这是他的地址。你知道怎么去吗？
Zài wǒ nánpéngyou de jiā, zhè shì tāde dìzhǐ. Nǐ zhīdào zěnme qù ma?

毛爱红： 没问题！我有地图。星期六下午五点见。
Méi wèntí! Wǒ yǒu dìtú. Xīngqīliù xiàwǔ wǔdiǎn jiàn.

方子英： 再见。
Zàijiàn.

注释 LANGUAGE NOTES

开舞会(晚会/派对)

开 here means "to hold (a party)," 开舞会 means "to hold a dance party." For parties, the following terms are commonly used: 晚会 [wǎnhuì] and 派对 [pàiduì].

太棒了

太棒了 is a phrase meaning "Great!," "Terrific!" "棒" here is an adjective meaning "good," "great." It is similar to "太好了！"

不客气

不客气 is a phrase meaning "You are welcome." It is similar to 不谢.

多大

多大 means "How old?" It is generally used to ask the age of adults and children over ten years old. For young children under ten years old, 几岁 ("How old?") is commonly used. For older people, it is appropriate to use "您多大年纪[niánjì] (age)?"

地址(住址)

For "address," both 地址 and 住址 are commonly used. When writing an address, Chinese word order progresses from the larger unit to the smaller unit. For example,

中国北京市中山路12号 No. 12, Zhongshan Road, Beijing, China

语法 GRAMMAR

Days of the Week

The ways to express the days of the week in Chinese are illustrated below:

Monday	Tuesday	Wednesday	Thursday	Friday	Saturday	Sunday
星期一	星期二	星期三	星期四	星期五	星期六	星期日 星期天
周一	周二	周三	周四	周五	周末 [zhōumò] weekend	

- 礼拜 [lǐbài] is also commonly used for indicating the days of the week.

For example, 礼拜一, 礼拜五, and 礼拜天.

- 星期几 and 礼拜几 mean "Which day of the week?"

For Chinese, a week starts on Monday instead of Sunday.

Expressing Dates, Year, Month, and Days of the Week

前天 the day before yesterday	昨天 yesterday	今天 today	明天 tomorrow	后天 the day after tomorrow
前年 the year before last year	去年 last year	今年 this year	明年 next year	后年 the year after next year
上上个星期 the week before last week	上个星期 last week	这个星期 this week	下个星期 next week	下下个星期 the week after next week
上上个月 the month before last month	上个月 last month	这个月 this month	下个月 next month	下下个月 the month after next month

Preposition 为

为 is a preposition meaning "for." Together with its object it forms a prepositional phrase (P.P.), which occurs before a verb phrase (V.P.). For example,

他	为我 P.P.	开一个晚会。 V.P.	He is having a party for me.

补充课文 SUPPLEMENTARY PRACTICE

This selection will help you test your comprehension of the grammar and vocabulary you have learned in this lesson. Be prepared to answer questions about the meaning of the passage.

二月十八日　　　　星期六　　　　天气：晴

今天我真高兴，我过了一个很难忘的二十岁生日。我男朋友在他家为我举办了一个庆生会，他还邀请了很多朋友来参加，我收到了很多礼物，爱红还为我做了一个生日蛋糕，太棒了！

每个人都祝我生日快乐，为我唱生日快乐歌，我许了一个愿，吹了蜡烛，然后切蛋糕给大家吃。

我们一起唱卡拉 OK，听流行音乐，跳舞，聊天……很好玩！

啊！我的二十岁生日，真特别！

Notes: 天气 [tiānqì]: weather
晴 [qíng]: sunny
难忘 [nánwàng]: unforgettable
举办 [jǔbàn]: to hold
庆生会 [qìngshēnghuì]: birthday party
邀请 [yāoqǐng]: to invite
收到 [shōudào]: to receive
生日快乐歌 [shēngrì kuàilè gē]: happy birthday song
许愿 [xǔyuàn]: to make a wish
吹 [chuī]: to blow
蜡烛 [làzhú]: candle
切 [qiē]: to cut; to slice
卡拉OK [kǎlā ōukēi]: karaoke
流行音乐 [liúxíng yīnyuè]: popular music
特别 [tèbié]: special

练习 ACTIVITIES

I. Pinyin Exercises

14-1 Listen to the phrases and write them down in Pinyin:

1. ____________ 2. ____________ 3. ____________ 4. ____________
5. ____________ 6. ____________ 7. ____________ 8. ____________

14-2 Listen to the instructor and fill in each blank with the correct Pinyin:

Àimíng: Zhège ___________ shì wǒde __________ . Wǒ yào kāi yígè _________ . Nǐ néng lái ma?

Xiǎoyīng: Tài hǎo le! Wǒ _________ qù. Nǐ jīnnián _________ ?

Àimíng: Wǒ èrshíyī ______ . Nǐde shēngrì shì _______________ ?

Xiǎoyīng: Wǒde shēngrì shì _______________ . Wǒ jīnnián ___________ suì.

14-3 Read the following Chinese poem, paying special attention to the tones and rhythm:

Xiāng Sī **(Wáng Wéi)** Hóngdòu shēng nánguó, Chūn lái fā jǐ zhī. Yuàn jūn duō cǎi xié, Cǐ wù zuì xiāngsī.	**相思** **(王维)** 红豆生南国， 春来发几枝。 愿君多采撷， 此物最相思。

Remembrance
(Wang, Wei)

The red bean grows in the southern lands,
In spring its slender twigs bloom.
Gather more of them, I hope,
Of loving remembrance they evince.

II. Character Exercises

14-4 Read the following words, phrases, and sentences:

号 几号 几月几号 今天是几月几号	舞会 生日舞会 我的生日舞会 参加我的生日舞会 请参加我的生日舞会 请你参加我的生日舞会 我请你参加我的生日舞会 我想请你参加我的生日舞会
地址 家的地址 我家的地址 这是我家的地址 这是我男朋友家的地址	

Now try to use the following characters to make words, phrases, and then sentences:

1. 岁 2. 空 3. 星 4. 过 5. 为 6. 定
7. 做 8. 蛋 9. 送 10. 棒 11. 客 12. 图

14-5 From the dialogue in Language in Use, find words that have the following radicals:

宀		土		木	
米		月		力	
门		辵(辶)		厶	

14-6 Match the following characters with their English definitions:

地址	to join	送	birthday
舞会	surely	岁	years old
蛋糕	cakes	客气	week
参加	dance party	星期	to give
一定	address	生日	to be polite

III. Grammar Exercises

14-7 Substitution exercises:

1. 你的生日是几月几号星期几?
   我的生日是<u>十二月七号星期六</u>。

四月二十八日	星期一
十一月十三日	星期二
一月二十九日	星期三
十月十六日	星期四
九月三十日	星期五
八月七日	星期天

2. 你要怎么为你的男朋友庆祝生日?
   我要为他<u>开</u><u>一个生日舞会</u>。

买	一件衬衫
做	一个蛋糕
唱	一首生日歌
买	一个新手机
做	两个中国菜

Notes: 庆祝 [qìngzhù]: to celebrate
唱 [chàng]: to sing
首 [shǒu]: measure word for songs
歌 [gē]: song

14-8 Say aloud the following expressions of time in Chinese:

1. Feb. 5, 2003 ______________
2. Sept. 12, 2001 ______________
3. Mar. 8, 1998 ______________
4. Oct. 1, 1949 ______________
5. Jan. 31, 1986 ______________
6. Dec. 25, 2008 ______________
7. Last Wednesday ______________
8. Next Sunday ______________
9. 10:30 yesterday morning ______________________________
10. 2:45 P.M. day after tomorrow ______________________________

14-9 In pairs, ask and answer the following questions:

1. 今天是几月几号星期几?

   ____

2. 你今年多大了?

   ____

3. 你家在哪儿?

   ____

4. 今年是哪一年?

   ____

14-10 This is 子英's to-do list. In pairs, ask and answer questions about what 子英 is going to do:

1. Hold an evening party for her boyfriend ____________________
2. Write an e-mail to her roommate ____________________
3. Make a birthday cake for her younger sister____________________
4. Buy a movie ticket for Dazhong's girlfriend ____________________

IV. Communicative Activities

14-11 Situational dialogue:

Next Saturday is your birthday. You want to hold a birthday party and invite all your friends. You are phoning a friend you met at the beginning of the semester. Act out the phone conversation with the help of the clues below. You do not have to be restricted to the following. Add whatever you want to say.

You:
1. Your birthday is next Saturday, Feb. 26.
2. You will hold a party in the evening and you are going to invite your friends.
3. You want to know whether he/she will be able to come.
4. Make sure your friend knows where you live.

Your friend:
1. Express happy surprise at the invitation.
2. Assure your friend you will come to the party.
3. You want to know what time you should be there.
4. Do not forget to get the address of your friend's home.

文化知识 Culture Link

文化点滴 CULTURE NOTES

十二生肖 [Shí'èr shēngxiào] Chinese Zodiac

十二生肖, or the Chinese Zodiac, refers to the 12 农历年 [nónglì nián] (lunar years) in a cycle of the Chinese lunar calendar, and to the 12 animals to which they correspond, namely the rat, ox, tiger, rabbit, dragon, snake, horse, sheep, monkey, rooster, dog, and boar. Since the lunar calendar does not exactly match the Gregorian calendar, we cannot match the Chinese Zodiac directly with our calendar years. For example, calendar 2004 is referred to as the year of the monkey, but the first month of 2004 was actually still in the lunar year of the sheep.

No one really knows for certain the origin of the 十二生肖 system, or how it has evolved over time. One hypothesis says that the ancient Chinese invented the 10 天干 [tiāngān] (the heavenly stems) and 12 地支 [dìzhī] (the earthly branches) for chronological purposes. Later, to make things easier, people selected the 12 animals to represent the 12 earthly branches. Another story says that the ancestors divided one day and one night duration into 12 equal periods, with the first period from 11:00 P.M. to 1:00 A.M. Each period is named after the animal that is most active at that time. For example, the rat took the first position because it is most active around midnight. Other explanations for the system exist, but it is debatable how accurate and complete they are.

People born in a certain lunar year are believed to share some of the special characteristics of the animal that represents that year in the 十二生肖 system. In fact, instead of directly asking your age, Chinese people will often ask your 生肖, from which they can not only deduce your age, but also ascribe to you the qualities of the animal that represents that year. This is why 生肖 plays a big role in marriage proposals in China — people want to find a partner who is a good 生肖 match. Some very superstitious couples purposely schedule pregnancies so that their children will be born in a certain year in the hope that their children will pick up the characteristics of that year's representative 生肖 animal.

CHINESE ZODIAC

Chinese Zodiac 12 animals	Year of Birth / Features	Chinese Zodiac 12 animals	Year of Birth / Features
	1924, 1936, 1948, 1960, 1972, 1984, 1996, 2008		1918, 1930, 1942, 1954, 1966, 1978, 1990, 2002
	charming, bright, creative, and thrifty		social, competitive, and stubborn
鼠 [shǔ] Rat		**马 [mǎ] Horse**	
	1925, 1937, 1949, 1961, 1973, 1985, 1997, 2009		1919, 1931, 1943, 1955, 1967, 1979, 1991, 2003
	steadfast, dependable, and methodical		artistic, fastidious, and indecisive
牛 [niú] Ox		**羊 [yáng] Sheep**	
	1926, 1938, 1950, 1962, 1974, 1986, 1998, 2010		1920, 1932, 1944, 1956, 1968, 1980, 1992, 2004
	dynamic, warm, sincere, and a leader		witty, popular, good-humored, and versatile
虎 [hǔ] Tiger		**猴 [hóu] Monkey**	
	1927, 1939, 1951, 1963, 1975, 1987, 1999, 2011		1921, 1933, 1945, 1957, 1969, 1981, 1993, 2005
	humble, artistic, and clear-sighted		aggressive, alert, and a perfectionist
兔 [tù] Rabbit		**鸡 [jī] Rooster**	
	1916, 1928, 1940, 1952, 1964, 1976, 1988, 2000		1922, 1934, 1946, 1958, 1970, 1982, 1994, 2006
	flamboyant, lucky, and imaginative		honest, conservative, sympathetic, and loyal
龙 [lóng] Dragon		**狗 [gǒu] Dog**	
	1917, 1929, 1941, 1953, 1965, 1977, 1989, 2001		1923, 1935, 1947, 1959, 1971, 1983, 1995, 2007
	discreet, refined, and intelligent		caring, industrious, and home-loving
蛇 [shé] Snake		**猪 [zhū] Boar**	

Questions:

1. 你是属什么的？ What's your sign?
2. 你的生肖个性怎么样？ What kind of personality is your sign supposed to have?
3. 准不准？ Is that an accurate description of your personality?

Notes: 属 [shǔ]: to belong to
个性 [gèxìng]: personality
准 [zhǔn]: accurate

趣味中文 FUN WITH CHINESE

女大十八变。
A girl changes quickly in physical appearance from childhood to adulthood.

nǚ	dà	shíbā	biàn
女	大	十八	变
girl	big/grow up	eighteen	change

Chinese people usually use 女大十八变 to show their admiration of the changing appearance of a girl, or their surprise at seeing a girl grow up to become a young lady.

Questions:

1. Has your appearance changed much as you have grown? Can your friends or relatives who haven't seen you for a long time still recognize you?
2. Can you apply "女大十八变" to some movie stars you are familiar with?

行动吧！ LET'S GO!

庆祝贺词
Common Phrases for Congratulations and Best Wishes

Read the following congratulatory phrases, which Chinese people use often on various social occasions.

1. 祝你生日快乐 [Zhù nǐ shēngrì kuàilè]: Wishing you a happy birthday.
2. 福如东海，寿比南山 [fú rú dōnghǎi, shòu bǐ nánshān]: happiness as immense as the Eastern Sea; life span as lofty as the Southern Mountain (commonly heard in relation to the birthday of someone aged 60 or older).
3. 永浴爱河 [yǒng yù àihé]: bathe in the river of love forever (used for newlyweds).
4. 步步高升 [bùbù gāoshēng]: to get promotions step by step.
5. 金榜题名 [jīnbǎng tímíng]: to emerge successful from a competitive examination.
6. 学业进步 [xuéyè jìnbù]: to make progress in one's studies.
7. 恭贺新禧 [gōnghè xīnxǐ]: best wishes for a happy new year.
8. 事事如意 [shìshì rúyì]: everything will go well and smoothly.
9. 祝你好运 [zhù nǐ hǎo yùn]: wishing you good luck.
10. 吉祥如意 [jíxiáng rúyì]: hope things go well and smoothly.

复习 Review

LESSON 13 AND LESSON 14

Conversation

Form pairs to chat about clothes and movies. Your conversation should include the following topics. Then report the information you collect to the class.

1. 你比较喜欢穿T-恤衫还是衬衫?
2. 你常穿什么色的裤子?
3. 上次 (last time) 你自己 [zìjǐ] (oneself) 买新衣服是什么时候? (几月几号星期几?)
4. 你帮我看看, 你觉得我今天穿这样 (this way) 好看吗?
5. 你喜欢看电影吗? 你常在哪儿看电影?
6. 现在一张电影票要多少钱? 你觉得贵不贵?
7. 你今年多大? 你是属 [shǔ] (to belong to) [zodiac sign]) 什么的?
8. 你的生日是几月几号? 去年 (last year) 你是怎么 (how) 过你的生日的?

Situational Dialogues

Today is your birthday. Please invite your friend to your birthday dance party (生日舞会) tonight at your dorm, if your friend has time (有没有空). Please also make sure that your friend knows how to get to your address (地址) by offering a map (地图).
Ask for suggestions from your friend about what you should wear tonight for the party (穿什么好看).

Useful grammar points and expressions:

L13: 觉得 measure words (classifiers): 件, 条, 张 或者/还是 看看, 穿穿, 试试
L14: 开...; 多大; 太棒了; 不客气; 年, 月, 日, 星期 为 Subject + V.P.

Simplified and Traditional Characters

Read each character aloud. Write its simplified form. Then tell a story (at least five sentences) using the following characters.

For example, 學 → 学 → 学生 → 我是一个学生, 我学.......

L13: 買 ( ) 幫 ( ) 條 ( ) 褲 ( ) 讓 ( ) 錢 ( )
L14: 歲 ( ) 為 ( ) 過 ( ) 參 ( ) 氣 ( ) 圖 ( )

第十五课
LESSON

15

图书馆在宿舍前边
The Library Is in Front of the Dorm

教学目标 OBJECTIVES

- Show people around
- Ask where something is located
- Explain where something is located

A fancy Japanese-style, four-story house in Taiwan. We will learn to use 在, 有, 是 to describe the layout.

This sign 听雨轩 [tīng yǔ xuān] (Listen to Rain Pavilion) is on the wall of a Chinese restaurant. Can you guess where it leads? (Answer: bathroom)

生词 VOCABULARY

核心词 Core Vocabulary

SIMPLIFIED	TRADITIONAL	PINYIN		
1. 前边	前邊	qiánbiān	N.	in front of
2. 参观	參觀	cānguān	V.	to visit
3. 欢迎	歡迎	huānyíng	V.	to welcome
4. 里边	裡邊	lǐbiān	N.	inside
5. 厨房	廚房	chúfáng	N.	kitchen
6. 公用	公用	gōngyòng	Adj.	for public use, communal
7. 旁边	旁邊	pángbiān	N.	beside, nearby
8. 客厅	客廳	kètīng	N.	living room
9. 走	走	zǒu	V.	to walk
10. 对面	對面	duìmiàn	N.	opposite
11. 餐厅	餐廳	cāntīng	N.	dining room
12. 洗澡间	洗澡間	xǐzǎojiān	N.	bathroom; restroom
13. 卧室	臥室	wòshì	N.	bedroom
14. 中间	中間	zhōngjiān	N.	middle
15. 桌子	桌子	zhuōzi	N.	table
16. 上边	上邊	shàngbiān	N.	on top of; above; over
17. 后边	後邊	hòubiān	N.	behind, at the back
18. 公园	公園	gōngyuán	N.	park
19. 真	真	zhēn	Adv.	really

专名 Proper Nouns

SIMPLIFIED	TRADITIONAL	PINYIN		
1. 田进	田進	Tián Jìn	N.	(name) Jin Tian
2. 梁园生	梁園生	Liáng Yuánshēng	N.	(name) Yuansheng Liang
3. 包志中	包志中	Bāo Zhìzhōng	N.	(name) Zhizhong Bao

补充词 Supplementary Vocabulary

SIMPLIFIED	TRADITIONAL	PINYIN		
1. 左边	左邊	zuǒbiān	N.	on the left
2. 右边	右邊	yòubiān	N.	on the right
3. 门	門	mén	N.	door
4. 书桌	書桌	shūzhuō	N.	desk
5. 窗户	窗戶	chuānghu	N.	window
6. 椅子	椅子	yǐzi	N.	chair
7. 衣橱	衣櫥	yīchú	N.	wardrobe
8. 床	床	chuáng	N.	bed
9. 教室	教室	jiàoshì	N.	classroom
10. 杂志	雜誌	zázhì	N.	magazine
11. 乱	亂	luàn	Adj.	messy
12. 整齐	整齊	zhěngqí	Adj.	tidy
13. 干净	乾淨	gānjìng	Adj.	clean
14. 脏	髒	zāng	Adj.	dirty
15. 整理	整理	zhěnglǐ	V.	to arrange, put in order

语文知识 LANGUAGE LINK

The Sentence Pattern provides models that will help you with the Language in Use section. In both sections, pay attention to the grammar points, vocabulary, and expressions.

句型 Sentence Patterns

A: 宿舍里边有没有厨房?
Sùshè lǐbiān yǒuméiyǒu chúfáng?

B: 有厨房，是公用的。
Yǒu chúfáng, shì gōngyòng de.

A: 客厅的对面是什么?
Kètīng de duìmiàn shì shénme?

B: 客厅的对面是餐厅。
Kètīng de duìmiàn shì cāntīng.

A: 图书馆在哪儿?
Túshūguǎn zài nǎr?

B: 图书馆在宿舍前边。
Túshūguǎn zài sùshè qiánbiān.

课文 Language in Use: 图书馆在宿舍前边 Túshūguǎn zài sùshè qiánbiān

(<u>Situation:</u> 今天是宿舍参观日，在学生宿舍)
(Jīntiān shì sùshè cānguān rì, zài xuésheng sùshè)

田进: 你们好！欢迎你们来看我的宿舍。请跟我来。
Nǐmen hǎo! Huānyíng nǐmen lái kàn wǒde sùshè. Qǐng gēn wǒ lái.

梁园生: 田进，你的宿舍里边有没有厨房?
Tiánjìn, nǐde sùshè lǐbiān yǒuméiyǒu chúfáng?

田进： 有厨房，是公用的。
Yǒu chúfáng, shì gōngyòng de.

包志中： 你的房间在哪儿？
Nǐde fángjiān zài nǎr?

田进： 我的房间在旁边，从这儿走。来，请进。这是客厅，
Wǒde fángjiān zài pángbiān, cóng zhèr zǒu. Lái, qǐng jìn. Zhèshì kètīng,

客厅的对面是一个餐厅。
kètīng de duìmiàn shì yíge cāntīng.

梁园生： 洗澡间呢？
Xǐzǎojiān ne?

田进： 洗澡间在客厅和卧室的中间。你看，这是我的卧室。
Xǐzǎojiān zài kètīng hé wòshì de zhōngjiān. Nǐ kàn, zhèshì wǒde wòshì.

包志中： 桌子上边的中文书都是你的吗？
Zhuōzi shàngbiān de Zhōngwén shū dōushì nǐde ma?

田进： 有的是我的，有的是我朋友的。
Yǒude shì wǒ de, yǒude shì wǒ péngyou de.

包志中： 你常在宿舍学习吗？
Nǐ cháng zài sùshè xuéxí ma?

田进： 不，我不常在宿舍学习，我常去图书馆学习。
Bù, wǒ bù cháng zài sùshè xuéxí, wǒ cháng qù túshūguǎn xuéxí.

梁园生： 图书馆在哪儿？
Túshūguǎn zài nǎr?

田进： 图书馆在宿舍前边。图书馆的
Túshūguǎn zài sùshè qiánbiān. Túshūguǎn de

后边还有一个公园。
hòubiān háiyǒu yíge gōngyuán.

我常去那儿打球。
Wǒ cháng qù nàr dǎqiú.

梁园生，包志中： 你们的宿舍真不错。
Nǐmen de sùshè zhēn búcuò.

注释 LANGUAGE NOTES

洗澡间(洗手间，厕所)

洗澡 means "to take a bath." 间 means "room." 洗澡间 is "bathroom."
洗手间 [xǐshǒujiān], which literally means "wash hands room," and 厕所 [cèsuǒ] are also common terms for the restroom or bathroom.

有的

有的 means "some (of the) N." Thus 有的(书) means "some books."

语法 GRAMMAR

Position Words

A position word is used to specify a relative location. The following are examples of position words:

Position words	English	Position words	English
前边/前面	front	后边/后面	back
上边/上面	top	下边/下面	under, beneath
里边/里面	inside	外边/外面	outside
左 [zuǒ] (left) 边	left	右 [yòu] (right) 边	right
旁边	beside		
中间	middle		
对面	opposite		

- The suffix 边 literally means "side." It is usually interchangeable with 面.
- However, in 左边, 右边, and 旁边 the 边 cannot be replaced with 面.
- 面 literally means "face." 对面 means "opposite, face to face."

- In Chinese, the word order for specifying a location is different from that of English. For example,

图书馆	在宿舍的 The reference point (landmark)	前边。 location	The library is in front of the dorm.

State the reference point (宿舍) first, then specify the location (前边)

- 的 can be either present or not. Therefore we can use both 宿舍前边 or 宿舍的前边
- 里边 means "inside." It is never used with a place word that is a geographical name, building, or organization. For example,

他在北京学中文。	He studies Chinese in Beijing.
他在银行 [yínháng] 工作。	He works in a bank.

Sentences Expressing Location and Existence with 在, 有, and 是

在, 有, and 是 are commonly used to indicate location and existence. Some of their sentence patterns are shown below:

Pattern	Example	English
N. (definite) + 在 + Place	图书馆在宿舍(的)前边。	The library is in front of the dorm. (focus on location)
Place + 有 + N. (indefinite)	宿舍(的)前边有一个图书馆。	There is a library in front of the dorm. (focus on existence)
Place + 是 + N. (definite or indefinite)	宿舍(的)前边是图书馆。	In front of the dorm is the library. (focus on identification)

Notes: Example of definite noun: the library.
Example of indefinite noun: a library.

Example	English	Situation
这儿有厕所吗?	Is there a bathroom here?	(e.g., when traveling and asking someone whether there is a bathroom)
厕所在哪儿?	Where is the bathroom?	(e.g., at a friend's house, asking for the location of the bathroom)
这儿是厕所吗?	Is this the bathroom?	(e.g., to identify whether this is or isn't a bathroom)

补充课文 SUPPLEMENTARY PRACTICE

This selection will help you test your comprehension of the grammar and vocabulary you have learned in this lesson. Be prepared to answer questions about the meaning of the passage.

今天下午我和包志中去看田进。田进住在学校的宿舍里，他常常说他的宿舍很不错，所以我们今天去看看，他非常高兴。

田进的卧室不太大，可是很明亮。他的客厅很大。卧室和客厅的中间有一个洗澡间。厨房在卧室的旁边，客厅的对面是餐厅。厨房和餐厅都是公用的，虽然不大，可是很干净。

田进的书桌上有很多书，有的是他的，有的是他朋友的。他不常在宿舍看书，他喜欢去图书馆学习。图书馆离他的宿舍很近，就在宿舍的前边，那儿也很安静。图书馆的后边还有一个很大的公园，每天有很多人在那儿锻炼，打太极拳。田进有时候也喜欢去那儿打球。

田进非常喜欢他的宿舍，我和包志中也都觉得田进的宿舍真的很不错。

Notes: 明亮 [míngliàng]: bright
虽然……可是…… [suīrán . . . . . . kěshì . . . . . .]: although . . . (but) . . .
干净 [gānjìng]: clean
锻炼 [duànliàn]: to exercise
安静 [ānjìng]: quiet
打 [dǎ]: to play
太极拳 [tàijíquán]: tai chi

练习 ACTIVITIES

I. Pinyin Exercises

15-1 Listen to the instructor and circle the correct Pinyin:

1. a. gòngyòng chǔfàng
   b. gǒngyōng chùfáng
   c. gōngyòng chúfáng

2. a. kètīng/cāntīng
   b. kétīng/càntīng
   c. kètíng/cántìng

3. a. túshūguán
   b. túshūguǎn
   c. tūshúguàn

4. a. hǒubiàn
   b. hòubiān
   c. hōubián

5. a. cánguàn
   b. cànguàn
   c. cānguān

6. a. dìzhǐ
   b. dīzhǐ
   c. dǐzhì

15-2 Listen to the dialogue from Language in Use, and then use Pinyin to answer the following questions:

1. Tián Jìn de sùshè yǒuméiyǒu chúfáng?

 ____

2. Tián Jìn de fángjiān zài chúfáng de nǎbiān?

 ____

3. Kètīng hé wòshì de zhōngjiān shì shénme?

 ____

4. Tián Jìn chángcháng zài nǎr xuéxí?

 ____

5. Gōngyuán zài nǎr? Tián Jìn cháng qù nàr zuò shénme?

 ____

15-3 Read the following Chinese poem, paying special attention to the tones and rhythm:

Wàng Lúshān Pùbù **(Lǐ Bó/Lǐ Bái)**	**望庐山瀑布** **(李白)**
Rì zhào xiānglú shēng zǐyān,	日照香炉生紫烟，
Yáo kàn pùbù guà qiánchuān.	遥看瀑布挂前川。
Fēi liú zhí xià sānqiān chǐ,	飞流直下三千尺，
Yí shì yínhē luò jiǔ tiān.	疑是银河落九天。

Viewing the Waterfall on Mount Lu
(Li, Bo)

The sunshine on the incense burner produces a purple cloud,
Looking from afar the waterfall is like a huge curtain hanging high.
Its torrent rushes down three thousand feet from above,
I feel as if the Milky Way fell from the sky.

Note: 李白 Lǐ Bái is pronounced as Lǐ Bó in Classical Chinese.

II. Character Exercises

15-4 Read the following words, phrases, and sentences:

宿舍	旁边
我的宿舍	在旁边
参观我的宿舍	在客厅旁边
来参观我的宿舍	卧室在客厅旁边
欢迎来参观我的宿舍	我的卧室在客厅旁边
欢迎你们来参观我的宿舍	我的卧室在客厅和餐厅旁边

Now try to use the following characters to make words, phrases, and then sentences:

1. 前	2. 里	3. 房	4. 公	5. 间	6. 面
7. 洗	8. 卧	9. 桌	10. 后	11. 园	12. 真

15-5 Identify the radicals of the following characters, then give an example, selected from Language in Use, of a character with the same radical:

For example, 吗 ___口___ ___呢___

1. 边 ________ ________ 2. 厨 ________ ________

3. 洗 ________ ________ 4. 园 ________ ________

15-6 Match the simplified characters with their traditional equivalents:

欢 园 边 厅 厨 观 后

觀 歡 後 邊 園 廳 廚

III. Grammar Exercises

15-7 Substitution exercises:

1. 我们的<u>房间</u>在<u>客厅</u>的<u>右边</u>。

图书馆	公园	前边
厨房	客厅	后边
洗澡间	卧室	旁边
书房	餐厅	左边
字典	书桌	上边
车库	客厅	下边

Notes: 书房 [shūfáng]: study room
书桌 [shūzhuō]: desk
左边 [zuǒbiān]: left
字典 [zìdiǎn]: dictionary
车库 [chēkù]: garage

2. 宿舍的后边有一个公园。

书桌	上边	一本字典
卧室	后边	一个洗澡间
客厅	旁边	一个厨房
椅子	下边	一个球
床	旁边	一个衣橱
炒饭	前边	一双筷子

Note: 衣橱 [yīchú]: closet

3. 卧室的旁边是洗澡间。

中国饭馆	后边	公园
停车场	左边	宿舍
机场	前边	商店
宿舍和图书馆	中间	停车场
书房和客厅	中间	厕所

Note: 厕所 [cèsuǒ]: bathroom, restroom

15-8 Fill in the blanks with 有，在，or 是：

1. 卧室 ______ 客厅的右边。
2. 卧室的前边 ______ 书房。
3. 客厅 ______ 卧室和厨房的中间。
4. 饭厅的后边 ______ 厨房。
5. 洗澡间 ______ 洗衣房的后边，卧室的右边。

Notes: 洗衣房 [xǐyīfáng]: laundry room
右边 [yòubiān]: right

IV. Communicative Activities

15-9 Situational dialogue:

Your friend has just arrived at your place. He has enrolled to study at your university. Before he came he asked you to help him find an apartment. You have found a very nice one-bedroom apartment for him. Tell him everything you know about this apartment. The following pictures can serve as clues.

Useful expressions:

有 是 在　　前边　旁边　对面

不错　　干净 [gānjìng] (clean)

大 小

文化知识 Culture Link

文化点滴 CULTURE NOTES

风水[Fēngshuǐ] Feng Shui The Chinese Art of Placement

风水 [fēng shuǐ] (winds and waters) in its literal sense refers to the topography of the earth, its mountains, valleys, and waterways whose shape and size, direction, and levels are created by the continuous interactions of these two powerful forces of nature.

The goal of 风水 is to maintain harmony and balance between 阴 [yīn] and 阳 [yáng] in the universe and in nature. According to Chinese culture, all living things are interrelated by the cosmic energy known as 气 [qì]. 气 is the invisible flow of energy that circulates through the earth and sky, bringing the life force with it. The practice of 风水 is concerned with harnessing this vital energy to maximize the positive effects that it bestows. It is believed that, we can influence our fate and fortune, by enhancing and directing the flow of 气.

风水, which originated over 4,000 years ago, is the ancient Chinese art of placement. The farmers in southern China developed certain 风水 principles because of their dependence on the earth and the forces governing it. They learned that living in harmony with nature made life much easier. Building homes on hills protected them from floods and also made it easier for them to defend themselves from attackers. Homes were also built to face the south, so that they would not face the storms of yellow dust that blew down from Mongolia. Besides, facing the south exposed them to the winter sunshine so that they would be bright and warm during the cold months but comparatively cool in summer. In addition to being used by farmers, 风水 also played a vital role in ancient Chinese burials, important because of the tradition of ancestor veneration in Chinese culture. It was thought that ancestors made happy with good 风水 guiding the placement of their tombs would shower the blessings of prosperity, honor, long life, and healthy offspring on the living.

In the family home, good 风水 positioning is believed to facilitate harmonious relationships between husband and wife, foster good health, attract abundance and prosperity, and help to build good reputations.

In Chinese cultures, where family life and honor are important, good 风水 is seen as helping husbands and wives beget many good and loving children, who will bring honor to the family name.

In business, following 风水 rules in the selection and design of the premises is thought to create opportunities for growth, raise one's business profile and standing in the community, attract customers, and increase profits and turnover. It is also believed that adhering to good 风水 practices in business will help ensure loyal employees and smooth working relationships.

It is said that a fish tank will bring good luck. These two homes, one in Hong Kong and one in Taiwan, have fish tanks placed to provide decoration and improve Feng shui.

八卦 [bāguà] (The Eight Trigrams) is used to help measure a location's Feng shui.

This is a classy residential building in Hong Kong. Why is there a hole in the building? It is said that the structure continually collapsed while being built. The builder consulted with a Feng shui master and learned that there was a dragon who lived nearby and the mansion was blocking its way. The builder was told to leave a hole for the dragon to pass through.

To Chinese communities the world over, 风水 has been a common mystical practice for centuries, which blends ancient wisdom with cultural traditions. It is the art of living in harmony with our environment for health, wealth, and happiness. It has also attained popularity in many Western countries where its benefits are now being increasingly recognized.

Questions:

1. Do you believe in 风水? Will you consult a 风水 master when you buy a house?
2. Do you think 风水 is a superstition or a science?

趣味中文 FUN WITH CHINESE

有缘千里来相会，无缘对面不相识。

If it is fated, even those separated by one thousand *li* will meet each other.

If it is not fated, even those who are face to face will not know each other.

yǒu	yuán	qiān	lǐ	lái	xiāng	huì,
有	缘	千	里	来	相	会，
have	fate	thousand	kilometer	come	mutually	meet,

wú	yuán	duìmiàn	bù	xiāng	shí.
无	缘	对面	不	相	识。
no	fate	face to face	no	mutually	know.

The concept of fate or destiny is very important in Chinese culture. This saying shows how Chinese people emphasize the importance of their acquaintances. It is usually used to refer to couples who are meant to be together, or to remind people that friends are very precious.

Questions:

1. Do you know where your classmates come from? Are you all "有缘千里来相会"?
2. Can you think of any movie in which the characters come to meet each other from thousands of miles away?

行动吧！ LET'S GO!

北京观光景点 Scenic Spots in Beijing

东东 just returned from visiting Beijing. He is showing you some of the scenic spots that he has visited. Ask the location of some of the spots, such as 十三陵在北京市的哪一边？北京的南边有什么？北边是故宫吗？

Useful words and expressions:

观光(觀光) [guānguāng]: sightseeing
景点(景點) [jǐngdiǎn]: scenic spots
名胜(名勝) [míngshèng]: a scenic spot
故宫(故宮) [Gùgōng]: the Imperial Palace
颐和园(頤和園) [Yí Hé Yuán]: the Yi He Garden (the Summer Palace)
十三陵(十三陵) [Shísān Líng]: the Thirteen Emperors' Tombs
天坛(天壇) [Tiān Tán]: the Altar of Heaven
东边(東邊) [dōng biān]: east side
东南边(東南邊) [dōngnán biān]: southeast side
东北边(東北邊) [dōngběi biān]: northeast side
南边(南邊) [nán biān]: south side
西边(西邊) [xī biān]: west side
西南边(西南邊) [xīnán biān]: southwest side
西北边(西北邊) [xīběi biān]: northwest side
北边(北邊) [běi biān]: north side

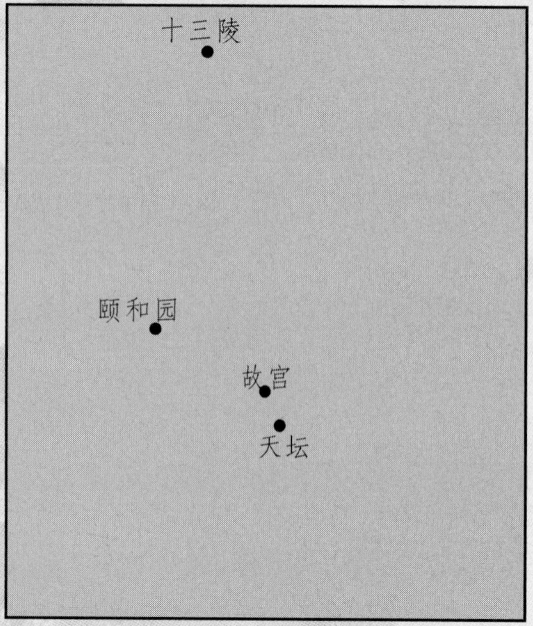

北京观光景点地图

第十六课
LESSON

16

她打篮球打得很好
She Plays Basketball Very Well

教学目标 OBJECTIVES

- Describe how an action is performed
- Talk about hobbies and exercises

to run **跑步** *[pǎobù]*

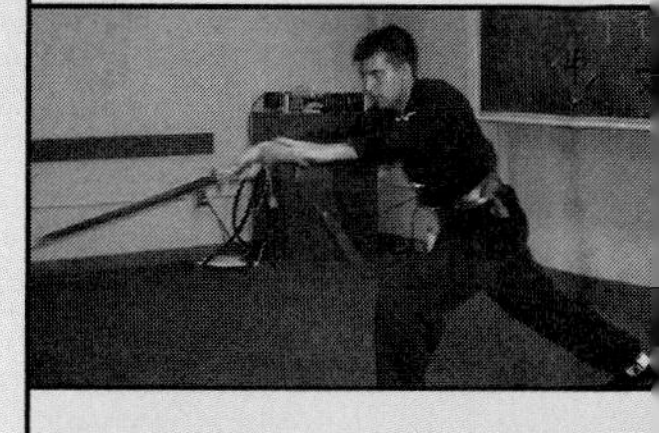

martial arts **功夫** *[gōngfu]*

to play the violin **拉小提琴** *[lā xiǎotíqín]*

Do you have any of these hobbies? How good are you at them?

Warm-up Exercises

1. Instructor leads the students in reading aloud the Chinese term for each activity
2. Instructor asks students about their hobbies. Use 得 to ask how well they do them. For example,

   A: 你的爱好 [àihào] 是什么？ (你喜欢做什么？)
   B: 我喜欢跑步 [pǎobù]。
   A: 你跑步跑得怎么样?
   B: 我跑得很快。

self-defense* 防身术 *[fángshēn shù]

to read* 看书 *[kànshū]

to draw* 画画 *[huàhuà]

to play ball* 打球 *[dǎqiú]

to use a computer* 打电脑 *[dǎ diànnǎo]

to sing* 唱歌 *[chànggē]

to eat* 吃东西 *[chī dōngxi]

to swim* 游泳 *[yóuyǒng]

生词 VOCABULARY

核心词 Core Vocabulary

SIMPLIFIED	TRADITIONAL	PINYIN		
1. 篮球	籃球	lánqiú	N.	basketball
2. 得	得	de	Part.	(used between a verb or an adjective and its complement to indicate result, possibility, or degree)
3. 俩	倆	liǎ		(colloquial) two people
4. 教练	教練	jiàoliàn	N.	coach, trainer
5. 教	教	jiāo	V.	to teach; to coach
6. 游泳	游泳	yóuyǒng	V.O.	to swim
7. 非常	非常	fēicháng	Adv.	very
8. 快	快	kuài	Adj.	fast
9. 体育馆	體育館	tǐyùguǎn	N.	gymnasium
10. 游泳池	游泳池	yóuyǒngchí	N.	swimming pool
11. 健身房	健身房	jiànshēnfáng	N.	gym
12. 锻炼	鍛煉	duànliàn	V.	to exercise
13. 现在	現在	xiànzài	Adv.	now
14. 昨天	昨天	zuótiān	N.	yesterday
15. 球赛	球賽	qiúsài	N.	ball game; match
16. 作业	作業	zuòyè	N.	homework
17. 包	包	bāo	V.	to wrap
18. 慢	慢	màn	Adj.	slow

补充词 Supplementary Vocabulary

SIMPLIFIED	TRADITIONAL	PINYIN		
1. 社团	社團	shètuán	N.	organization
2. 俱乐部	俱樂部	jùlèbù	N.	club
3. 球季	球季	qiújì	N.	season (of a sport)

运动项目 [Yùndòng xiàngmù] Sports Items

(1)  qí zìxíngchē 骑自行车 to ride a bike (V.O.)	(2)  huáchuán 划船 to row a boat (V.O.)	(3) 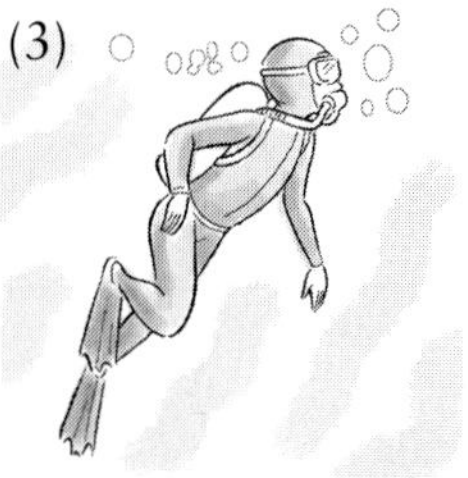 qiánshuǐ 潜水 to dive (V.O.)	(4) 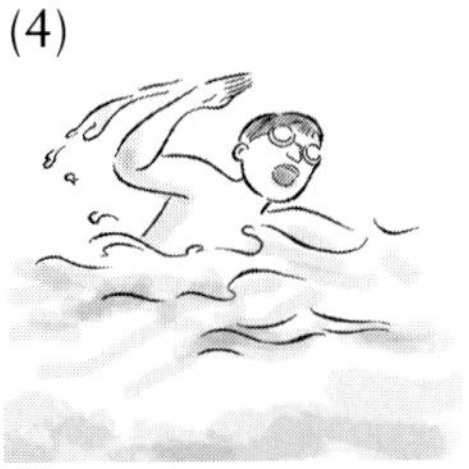 yóuyǒng 游泳 to swim (V.O.)	(5)  diàoyú 钓鱼 to fish (V.O.)
(6)  huáxuě 滑雪 to snow ski (V.O.)	(7)  huábīng 滑冰 to skate (V.O.)	(8)  bīngqiú 冰球 ice hockey	(9)  páshān 爬山 to climb a mountain (V.O.)	(10)  yuǎnzú 远足 hiking
(11) 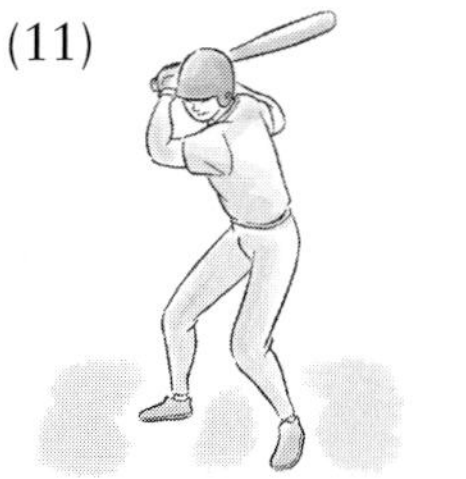 bàngqiú 棒球 baseball	(12)  gǎnlǎnqiú 橄榄球 football	(13)  zúqiú 足球 soccer	(14)  lánqiú 篮球 basketball	(15)  wǎngqiú 网球 tennis
(16)  gāo'ěrfūqiú 高尔夫球 golf	(17)  páiqiú 排球 volleyball	(18)  yǔmáoqiú 羽毛球 badminton	(19)  jǔzhòng 举重 to lift weights (V.O.)	(20)  pǎobù 跑步 to run (V.O.)

语文知识 LANGUAGE LINK

The Sentence Patterns provide models that will help you with the Language in Use section. In both sections, pay attention to the grammar points, vocabulary, and expressions.

句型 Sentence Patterns

A: 你游泳游得怎么样?
Nǐ yóuyǒng yóude zěnmeyàng?

B: 我游泳游得非常快。
Wǒ yóuyǒng yóude fēicháng kuài.

A: 你做饭做得好不好?
Nǐ zuòfàn zuòde hǎobuhǎo?

B: 我做饭做得不太好。
Wǒ zuòfàn zuòde bútàihǎo.

课文 Language in Use: 她打篮球打得很好 Tā dǎ lánqiú dǎde hěnhǎo

张正然:	你们俩要去哪儿? Nǐmenliǎ yàoqù nǎr?
孙信美，杨欢:	我们去打篮球。 Wǒmen qù dǎ lánqiú.
张正然:	你们篮球打得怎么样? Nǐmen lánqiú dǎde zěngmeyàng?
孙信美:	杨欢篮球打得很好。我还不太会打篮球， Yáng Huān lánqiú dǎde hěnhǎo. Wǒ hái bú tài huì dǎ lánqiú, 她是我的教练，她教得很好。 tā shì wǒde jiàoliàn, tā jiāode hěnhǎo.
杨欢:	不行，我还打得不太好。 Bùxíng, wǒ hái dǎde bú tài hǎo.

张正然： 我不常打篮球，我常常和我室友去游泳，
Wǒ bù cháng dǎ lánqiú, wǒ chángcháng hé wǒ shìyǒu qù yóuyǒng,

他游泳游得非常快。
tā yóuyǒng yóude fēicháng kuài.

杨欢： 你们常去哪儿游泳？
Nǐmen cháng qù nǎr yóuyǒng?

张正然： 我们常去体育馆里边的游泳池游泳，
Wǒmen cháng qù tǐyùguǎn lǐbiān de yóuyǒngchí yóuyǒng,

我们也常去健身房锻炼。
wǒmen yě cháng qù jiànshēnfáng duànliàn.

孙信美： 你现在要不要跟我们去打篮球？
Nǐ xiànzài yàobuyào gēn wǒmen qù dǎ lánqiú?

张正然： 现在不行。我昨天看球赛看得太晚了，今天起得很晚，
Xiànzài bùxíng. Wǒ zuótiān kàn qiúsài kànde tàiwǎn le, jīntiān qǐde hěnwǎn,

现在得去做作业。
xiànzài děi qù zuò zuòyè.

杨欢： 昨天我们那儿包饺子、做中国菜。你晚上到我们
Zuótiān wǒmen nàr bāo jiǎozi, zuò Zhōngguó cài. Nǐ wǎnshàng dào wǒmen

那儿吃饺子吧。
nàr chī jiǎozi ba.

张正然： 太好了！我很喜欢吃饺子。
Tàihǎo le! Wǒ hěn xǐhuān chī jiǎozi.

你们包饺子包得快不快？
Nǐmen bāo jiǎozi bāode kuàibukuài?

孙信美： 我们包得很慢。
Wǒmen bāode hěnmàn.

杨欢： 信美很会做饭。她做饭做得很好。
Xìngměi hěn huì zuòfàn. Tā zuòfàn zuòde hěnhǎo.

注释 LANGUAGE NOTES

得 [de, děi]

得 has two pronunciations that have different meanings and functions. 得 [de] is used for degree of complement sentences, whereas [děi] is an optative verb meaning "have to."

俩

俩 means "two people." It is used with pronouns. For example, 我们俩 (us two), 你们俩 (you two), and 他们俩 (they two).

教 [jiào, jiāo]

When 教 is used as a noun, it is pronounced as [jiào], such as 教练, 教授 [jiàoshòu] (professor), or 教育 [jiàoyù] (education). When 教 is used as a verb, it is pronounced as [jiāo].

锻炼

锻炼 means "exercise, work out." In Taiwan, the term 运动 [yùndòng] is more commonly used.

语法 GRAMMAR

Degree of Complement Sentences

A degree of complement sentence is used to assess or tell how an action is performed (such as how fast, how well, how soon, etc.). The word 得 is used. For example,

Single verb	Subject V. 得 Adv. Adj.
你游得怎么样?	How well do you swim?
我游得很快。	I swim very fast.
我游得不快。	I don't swim fast.
你游得快不快?	Do you swim fast or not?

Verb Object (V.O.)	Subject V.O.V. 得 Adv. Adj.
他打篮球打得怎么样?	How well does he play basketball?
他打篮球打得好不好?	Does he play basketball well or not?
他打篮球打得很好。	He plays basketball very well.
他打篮球打得不太好。	He doesn't play basketball very well.

V.: 游，说，学，吃，锻炼，介绍，练习，参观，学习

V.O.: 游泳，上课，教书，做饭，吃饭，开车，打球，上网，睡觉

The object can also be placed at the beginning of a sentence for emphasis. For example,

<u>饺子</u>我包得很慢。
<u>篮球</u>他打得非常好。

补充课文 SUPPLEMENTARY PRACTICE

This selection will help you test your comprehension of the grammar and vocabulary you have learned in this lesson. Be prepared to answer questions about the meaning of the passage.

大家好！我叫孙信美。我和杨欢是好朋友。我们俩都喜欢游泳，常常一起去体育馆里边的游泳池游泳。我不太会游泳，现在正在学。杨欢游泳游得非常好，她也是我的游泳教练。她教我教得很好，所以我学得很快。

张正然是杨欢的男朋友。他不常游泳，可是他特别喜欢打篮球。我们学校有一个很好的健身房，他常常跟他的室友一起去那儿打篮球。他的室友篮球打得非常好，他还是学校篮球队的队长。他们常常一起出去参加比赛。

我们四个人都是体育活动爱好者，常常去健身房锻炼。我们有时候也一起吃饭。杨欢包饺子包得又快又好，我包饺子包得很慢，可是我做中国饭做得特别好吃，他们都喜欢吃我做的饭。

Notes: 特别 [tèbié]: especially, particularly
还 [hái]: used as an adverb, to mean "also," "as well"
队 [duì]: team
队长 [duìzhǎng]: team leader
参加 [cānjiā]: to participate
比赛 [bǐsài]: contest
爱好者 [àihàozhě]: one who loves (a sport, a hobby, etc.)

练习 ACTIVITIES

I. Pinyin Exercises

16-1 Listen to the instructor and select the correct Pinyin:

1. a. dǎ lánqiú
   b. dà lànqiú
   c. dá lānqiú
2. a. bāo jiàozi
   b. bāo jiǎozi
   c. bǎo jiāozi
3. a. kán qiùsài
   b. kān qiùsài
   c. kàn qiúsài

4. a. jiāo yóuyǒng	5. a. tìyùguán	6. a. zuō zuóyè
b. jiáo yōuyòng	b. tǐyúguǎn	b. zuò zuòyè
c. jiào yòuyōng	c. tǐyùguǎn	c. zuò zuǒyè

16-2 Listen to the instructor and complete the sentences in Pinyin:

1. Nǐmen __________ zhème kuài, yào qù nǎr?
2. Yáng Huān ____________________ fēicháng hǎo.
3. Zhāng Zhèngrán yóuyǒng ______________________.
4. Wǒ zuótiān wǎnshàng __________________________.
5. Shéi zuò fàn ____________________?

16-3 Read the following Chinese poem, paying special attention to the tones and rhythm:

Fēngqiáo Yè Bó **(Zhāng Jì)**	**枫桥夜泊** **(张继)**
Yuè luò wū tí shuāng mǎn tiān, Jiāng fēng yúhuǒ duì chóu mián. Gūsū chéngwài Hánshānsì, Yè bàn zhōngshēng dào kèchuán.	月落乌啼霜满天， 江枫渔火对愁眠。 姑苏城外寒山寺， 夜半钟声到客船。

Night Docking at Maple Bridge
(Zhang, Ji)

The moon is setting, the magpie chirping and the sky full of frost,
Accompanied by the Maple River water and fishing candles I sleep with worries on my mind.
Outside Suzhou is the Hanshan Temple,
At midnight the sound of its bell reaches my boat.

II. Character Exercises

16-4 Read the following words, phrases, and sentences:

篮	快
篮球	非常快
打篮球	说得非常快
他打篮球	王老师说得非常快
他打篮球打得很好	王老师说中文说得非常快
他和他室友篮球都打得很好	王老师和方老师中文都说得非常快

Now try to use the following characters to make words, phrases, and then sentences:

1. 俩	2. 教	3. 游	4. 体	5. 池	6. 健
7. 身	8. 锻	9. 赛	10. 业	11. 包	12. 慢

16-5 Find some characters from the lesson that begin with the same stroke as the following characters:

1. 你 ____ ____ ____ ____ ____ ____ ____
2. 要 ____ ____ ____ ____ ____ ____ ____
3. 室 ____ ____ ____ ____ ____ ____ ____

16-6 Circle the radical of each of the following characters. Then provide the meaning of the radical and write at least two other characters that share the same radical.

For example, 快 heart 忙 想

游 ____________ 球 ____________

锻 ____________ 篮 ____________

常 ____________ 赛 ____________

III. Grammar Exercises

16-7 Substitution exercises:

1. 他开车开得怎么样?
   他开车开得很快。

游泳	好
教书	累 [lèi] tired
学电脑	慢
做饭	好
包饺子	快
吃饭	高兴

Notes: 累 [lèi]: tired
高兴 [gāoxìng]: happy

2. 你的生日过得好不好?
   我的生日过得很好。

中国菜	做	好
中文	说	棒
功课	做	好
篮球	打	棒
德国车	买	贵

Note: 贵 [guì]: expensive

16-8 Ask questions with "得" based on the pictures, and then provide an answer:

1. 

游泳 [yóuyǒng]: swimming

Q. ______________________________

A. ______________________________

2. 

篮球 [lánqiú]: basketball

Q. ______________________________

A. ______________________________

3. 

棒球 [bàngqiú]: baseball

Q. ______________________________

A. ______________________________

4. 

排球 [páiqiú]: volleyball

Q. ______________________________

A. ______________________________

5. 

踢 [tī]: to kick 足球 [zúqiú]: soccer

Q. ______________________________

A. ______________________________

16-9 Complete the following sentences with "得" and an expression to indicate the degree of complement (clues are provided):

1. 我妈妈做饭 (fast) ______________________________
2. 杨欢打篮球 (well) ______________________________
3. 你们做作业 (late) ______________________________
4. 我锻炼 (little) ______________________________
5. 谁包饺子 (slow) ______________________________

IV. Communicative Activities

You and your friend are chatting about your extracurricular interests. Create a dialogue. Be sure that the following words and expressions are used (but do not limit your dialogue to these words):

Useful words and expressions:

球赛 (篮球，排球 [páiqiú] (volleyball)，足球 [zúqiú] (soccer)，
棒球 [bàngqiú] (baseball)，乒乓球 [pīngpāngqiú] (table tennis)，
高尔夫球 [gāo'ěrfūqiú] (golf))
健身房　游泳　锻炼　体育馆
社团 (俱乐部) [shètuán (jùlèbù)] (organization, club)

文化知识 Culture Link

文化点滴 CULTURE NOTES

中国体育 [Zhōngguó tǐyù] Chinese Sport

In international sports competitions, such as 奥运会 [Àoyùnhuì] (the Olympics) and 世界锦标赛 [Shìjiè jǐnbiāosài] (World Championships), China is famous for its excellence in many events. Chinese athletes are top ranked in the world in sports such as volleyball, table tennis, basketball, gymnastics, swimming, women's soccer, and diving.

Soccer is one of the most popular sports in China. Currently, China has a professional soccer league. Famous Chinese soccer teams include 上海申花 [Shànghǎi Shēnhuā] (Shanghai Shen Hua) and 大连实德 [Dàlián Shídé] (Dalian Shi De). Whenever there is a major soccer game, Chinese fans either want to go to the stadium or to watch it on television. The games are so popular that the tickets are generally sold out. Fans even buy some tickets that might cost more than an average salesman's monthly salary! The Chinese professional soccer league has attracted talented players from other countries and has adopted foreign soccer

Exercises such as running, swimming, and using the hula hoop are popular in China.

The professional baseball league in Taiwan has many fans.

systems, resulting in that audiences at soccer matches are growing. Soccer analysts predict that China will have a strong soccer team in the near future. Soccer is also very popular in Hong Kong.

In Taiwan, the most popular sports are baseball and basketball. They both have professional leagues. Fans are of all ages and their favorite players become their idols. Through promotions of the American National Basketball Association (NBA) and visits from superstars such as Michael Jordan, basketball has become one of the most popular sports in Taiwan. Having the Chinese player 姚明 [Yáo Míng] in the NBA definitely attracts more Chinese fans and has opened the NBA market in China. With so many popular sports in Chinese societies, Chinese people are excited about and looking forward to the Olympics coming to Beijing in 2008!

Questions:

1. Can you introduce the Chinese sports star that you like the most?
2. What sports activities do you think Chinese people are especially good at?

趣味中文 FUN WITH CHINESE

临时抱佛脚

To embrace Buddha's feet and pray for help in time of emergency (i.e., to do something too late and without preparation).

lín	shí	bào	fó	jiǎo
临	时	抱	佛	脚
encounter	time	embrace	Buddha	feet

Questions:

1. Do you know any similar sayings describing procrastinators in English?
2. Do you often do things at the last minute? If so, do you plan to change this habit?

行动吧！ LET'S GO!

公布告示 Announcements and Notifications

The following are some common announcement and notification signs from which we can learn some survival Chinese.

Useful words and expressions:

公布(公佈) [gōngbù]: announcement
营业(營業) [yíngyè]: business operation
疏散 [shūsàn]: to disperse
安全 [ānquán]: safe
出口 [chūkǒu]: exit
轻声(輕聲) [qīngshēng]: quiet voice
意见箱(意見箱) [yìjiànxiāng]: opinion box
告示 [gàoshi]: notification
随手关门(隨手關門) [suíshǒu guānmén]: close the door after one enters or leaves a room
讲话(講話) [jiǎnghuà]: to speak
慢走 [mànzǒu]: walk slowly
同样的(同樣的) [tóngyàng de]: same, similar
信息 [xìnxī]: information
牌子 [páizi]: sign

Questions:

1. 在图书馆里边，我们可以看到哪些同样的信息？
2. 你在哪儿会看到像这样的牌子？

复习 Review

LESSON 15 TO LESSON 16

Conversation

1. You and your friend are chatting about your dormitory/apartment. Your conversation should include the following topics.

   A: 你的宿舍/公寓 [gōngyù] (apartment) 在哪儿？
   B: 你的宿舍/公寓在你的学校 [xuéxiào] (school) 的旁边吗？
   C: 你的床 [chuáng] (bed) 的旁边是什么？客厅呢？客厅的旁边是厨房吗？
   你的书桌上面常常有什么？
   D: 你住的地方 [dìfang] (place) 附近 [fùjìn] (neighborhood) 都有什么？
   (商店 [shāngdiàn] (store)，饭馆、图书馆、公园、飞机场、停车场…)
   (Use the position words: 旁边、后边、前边、对面、etc. to describe.)

2. You and your friend are chatting about extracurricular activities, hobbies, and exercises. Topics to include are:

   A: 你最 [zuì] (the most) 喜欢的课外活动 [kèwài huódòng] (extracurricular activities) 是什么？
   B: 你常在什么时候、在哪儿做这些活动？
   C: 你常常和谁一起进行 [jìnxíng] (to do) 这些活动？你做得怎么样？你的朋友呢？

Situational Dialogue

Today is orientation day for the freshmen in your department and you have volunteered to show them around the campus. You and the freshmen are in front of the library and you are pointing out all the main campus buildings to them and telling them what their function is. (Use the map on the next page for reference.)

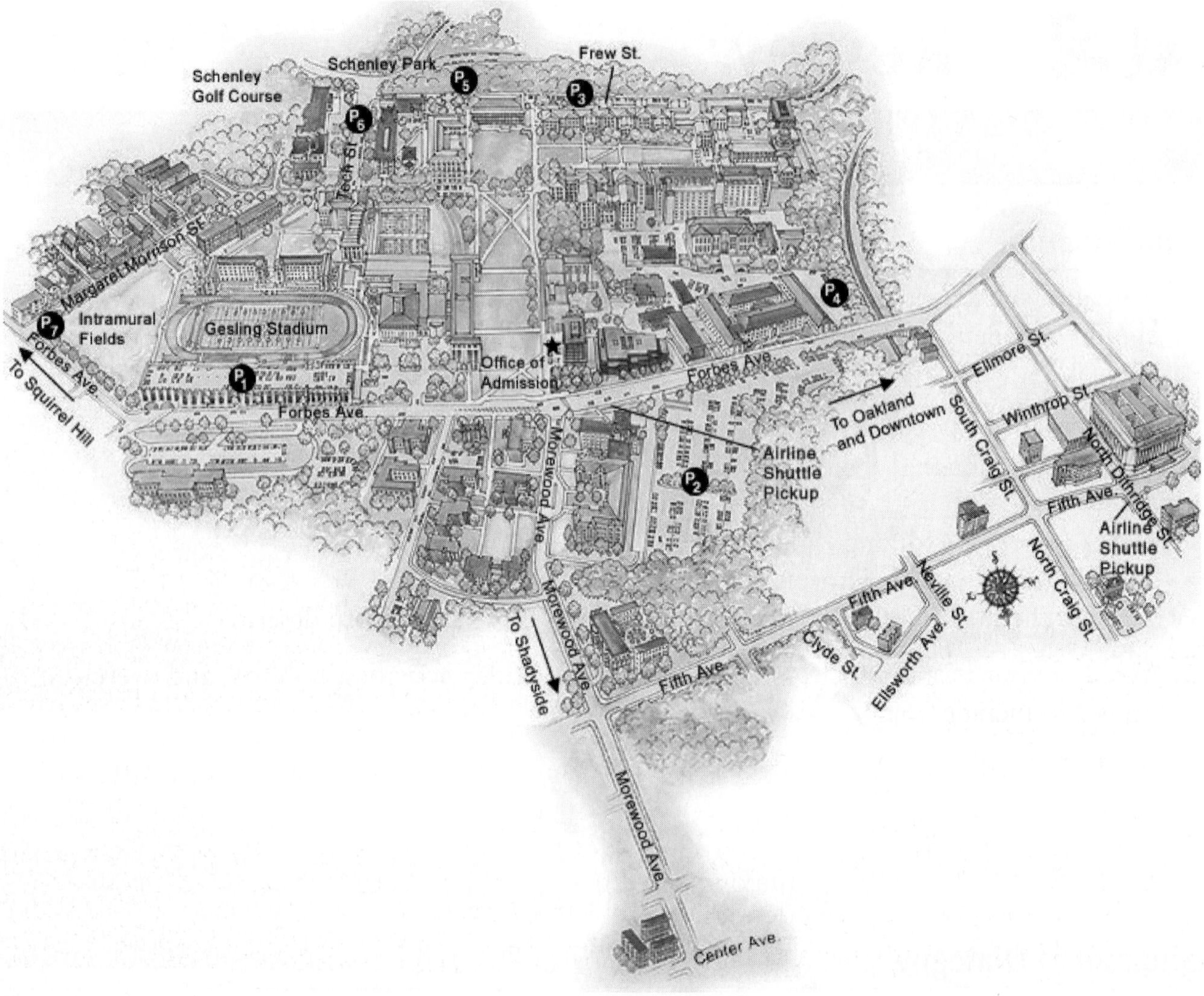

P1: 停车场　　P2: 学生宿舍　　P3: 中文系　　P4: 书店
P5: 图书馆　　P6: 商业系　　P7: 中国饭馆

Notes: 系 [xì]: (department)
商业 [shāngyè]: (business)

Useful grammar points and expressions:

N. + 在 + Place; Place + 有 + N.; Place + 是 + N.; V. + 得 + Complement
Position words: 前边, 后边, 左边, 右边, 上边, 下边, 里边, 外边, 旁边, 中间, 对面

Simplified and Traditional Characters

Read each character aloud. Write its simplified form. Then tell a story (at least five sentences) using the following characters.

For example, 學 → 学 → 学生 → 我是一个学生，我学.......

L15: 邊 (　) 觀 (　) 裡 (　) 廳 (　) 後 (　)
L16: 籃 (　) 練 (　) 體 (　) 賽 (　) 業 (　)

第十七课
LESSON

17

春天就要来了
Spring Is Coming Soon

教学目标 OBJECTIVES

- Talk about the four seasons
- Describe the weather
- Express that something will happen in the near future

There are four seasons in China. However, as China is a large country, a winter day might mean heavy snow in the north but comfortable sunshine in the south.

December in Taiwan.

December in Beijing.

July in Hong Kong.

July in Taiwan: hot and sunny.

生词 VOCABULARY

核心词 Core Vocabulary

SIMPLIFIED	TRADITIONAL	PINYIN		
1. 春天	春天	chūntiān	N.	spring
2. 久	久	jiǔ	Adj.	for a long time
3. 时间	時間	shíjiān	N.	time
4. 过	過	guò	V.	to pass
5. 放	放	fàng	V.	to have, start (a vacation)
6. 春假	春假	chūnjià	N.	spring break
7. 气候	氣候	qìhòu	N.	climate
8. 夏	夏	xià	N.	summer
9. 秋	秋	qiū	N.	autumn
10. 冬	冬	dōng	N.	winter
11. 其中	其中	qízhōng		among (whom, which)
12. 最	最	zuì	Adv.	(indicates the superlative degree)
13. 暖和	暖和	nuǎnhuo	Adj.	warm
14. 短	短	duǎn	Adj.	short
15. 有时候	有時候	yǒushíhou	Adv.	sometimes
16. 热	熱	rè	Adj.	hot
17. 华氏	華氏	huáshì	N.	Fahrenheit
18. 百	百	bǎi	Num.	hundred
19. 度	度	dù	N.	degree
20. 极	極	jí	Adv.	extremely
21. 刮风	刮風	guāfēng	V.O.	(wind) to blow

SIMPLIFIED	TRADITIONAL	PINYIN		
22. 下雨	下雨	xiàyǔ	V.O.	to rain
23. 冷	冷	lěng	Adj.	cold
24. 雪	雪	xuě	N.	snow
25. 见面	見面	jiànmiàn	V.O.	to meet each other

专名 Proper Nouns

SIMPLIFIED	TRADITIONAL	PINYIN		
1. 小玲	小玲	Xiǎo Líng	N.	(name) Xiao Ling

补充词 Supplementary Vocabulary

SIMPLIFIED	TRADITIONAL	PINYIN		
1. 天气	天氣	tiānqì	N.	weather
2. 四季	四季	sìjì	N.	four seasons
3. 放假	放假	fàngjià	V.O.	to have holidays
4. 寒假	寒假	hánjià	N.	winter holiday
5. 暑假	暑假	shǔjià	N.	summer holiday
6. 假期	假期	jiàqī	N.	holiday
7. 摄氏	攝氏	shèshì	N.	centigrade
8. 长	長	cháng	Adj.	long
9. 气温	氣溫	qìwēn	N.	temperature
10. 上升	上升	shàngshēng	V.	to increase
11. 下降	下降	xiàjiàng	V.	to decrease

语文知识 LANGUAGE LINK

The Sentence Patterns provide models that will help you with the Language in Use section. In both sections, pay attention to the grammar points, vocabulary, and expressions.

句型 Sentence Patterns

A: 春天就要来了。
Chūntiān jiùyào lái le.

B: 太好了！我们快要放春假了。
Tài hǎo le! Wǒmen kuàiyào fàng chūnjià le.

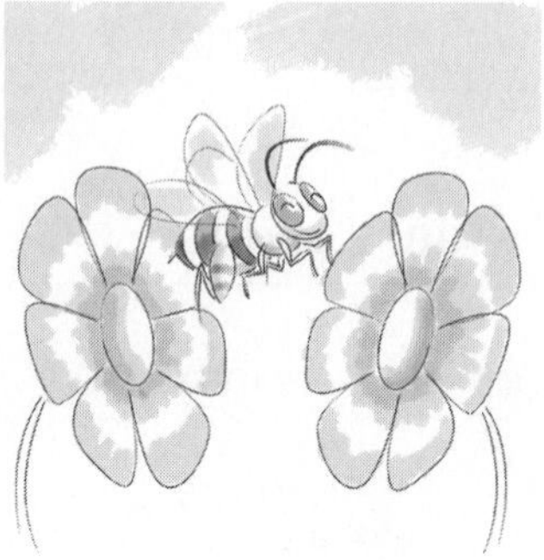

A: 春夏秋冬，其中
Chūn xià qiū dōng, qízhōng

你最喜欢哪一个？
nǐ zuì xǐhuān nǎ yíge?

B: 我最喜欢春天。你呢？
Wǒ zuì xǐhuān chūntiān. Nǐ ne?

A: 这儿的夏天热不热？
Zhèr de xiàtiān rèburè?

B: 这儿的夏天热极了！
Zhèr de xiàtiān rè jí le!

课文 Language in Use: 春天就要来了! Chūntiān jiùyào lái le!

小玲，
Xiǎolíng,

好久不见。
Hǎojiǔ bújiàn.

你现在怎么样？时间过得真快，春天就要来了，我们也
Nǐ xiànzài zěnmeyàng? Shíjiān guòde zhēnkuài, chūntiān jiùyào lái le, wǒmen yě

快要放春假了。
kuàiyào fàng chūnjià le.

我们这儿的气候春夏秋冬都有。其中我最喜欢春天，
Wǒmen zhèr de qìhòu chūn xià qiū dōng dōuyǒu. Qízhōng wǒ zuì xǐhuān chūntiān,

很暖和，可是很短。夏天有时候很热，最热的时候，会到华氏
hěn nuǎnhuo, kěshì hěnduǎn. Xiàtiān yǒushíhou hěn rè, zuì rè de shíhou, huì dào huáshì

一百度，热极了。秋天有时候会刮风、下雨。这儿的冬天非常冷，
yìbǎi dù, rè jí le. Qiūtiān yǒushíhou huì guāfēng, xiàyǔ. Zhèr de dōngtiān fēicháng lěng,

常常下雪。
chángcháng xiàxuě.

放春假的时候我想去你那儿玩玩，我们很快就要见面了！
Fàng chūnjià de shíhou wǒ xiǎng qù nǐ nàr wánwan, wǒmen hěnkuài jiùyào jiànmiàn le!

祝
Zhù

好！
Hǎo!

大中
Dàzhōng

二〇〇四年三月十日
èr líng líng sì nián sān yuè shí rì

注释 LANGUAGE NOTES

好久不见

好久不见, “long time no see,” is a common phrase used by acquaintances to greet each other when they haven’t seen each other for a while.

和

When 和 is pronounced as [hé] ([hàn] in Taiwan), it means “and.” In the phrase 暖和, it is pronounced as [huo].

华氏

华氏 refers to the Fahrenheit system, which is used in the United States. 摄氏 [shèshì] refers to the Celsius system, which is used in Mainland China, Taiwan, Japan, Hong Kong, and most of the rest of the world.

The Verb 刮

The verb 刮 has two traditional forms: 刮 and 颳. In traditional forms, 颳風 [guāfēng] “blowing wind” can also be written as 刮風 [guāfēng]. The difference between the two verbs 刮 and 颳 is that 刮 has more usages than 颳. 颳 is only used in the context of blowing wind. However, 刮 as a verb can have several meanings, including “to blow (wind),” and “to pare, to shave, or to scrape.”

For examples,	刮大风	[guā dàfēng]	“a big wind is blowing”
	刮破	[guāpò]	“to cut or hurt (someone) while shaving”
	刮胡子	[guāhúzi]	“to shave”
	刮掉	[guādiào]	“to scrape off”

语法 GRAMMAR

就/快要…了

Both 就要…了 and 快要…了 are patterns that are used to indicate that a certain action or event is about to happen. For example,

春天就要来了。	Spring is coming soon.
我们快要见面了。	We are going to see each other soon.

最

最 is used for the superlative meaning “the most.” It occurs before a verb or an adjective. For example,

我最喜欢秋天。	I like autumn the most.
他游泳游得最快。	He is the fastest swimmer.
她最好看。	She is the prettiest.

Adj. + 极了

极了 is an intensifier. It occurs after an adjective to indicate a very high degree of the adjective. For example,

热极了!	It is extremely hot!
冷极了!	It is extremely cold!
我忙极了!	I am extremely busy!
晚会好极了!	The party went very well!

补充课文 SUPPLEMENTARY PRACTICE

This selection will help you test your comprehension of the grammar and vocabulary you have learned in this lesson. Be prepared to answer questions about the meaning of the passage.

小玲：喂，大中，是你吗？

大中：小玲啊，是我。好久不见，你现在怎么样？

小玲：还不错。时间过得真快，现在已经是三月了，我们就要放春假了。

大中：是啊，春天就要来了，我们这儿的天气也快要暖和了。

小玲：我们这儿已经很暖和了。今天是华氏六十二度，听说明天要到七十度，树叶也绿了。

大中：真的吗？那太好了！我们这儿今天还是三十五度。这儿冬天太长，也太冷，还常常下雪。不过我们的秋天很美，也很舒服，不太冷，也不太热，可是太短了。

小玲：我们这儿春夏秋冬四季分明，不过冬天不太冷，可是夏天太热了，有时候最高温度会到华氏一百度，热极了。我最喜欢春天，这儿的春天非常漂亮，不常常刮风、也很少下雨。对了，放春假的时候你能来我这儿玩吗？

大中：好啊！我也很想去看看你，我们可以一起出去玩玩。

小玲：太好了！我真高兴，我们很快就要见面了！

Notes: 树叶 [shùyè]: leaves (of tree)
舒服 [shūfu]: comfortable
分明 [fēnmíng]: distinctively different
温度 [wēndù]: temperature
不过 [búguò]: but; nevertheless
四季 [sìjì]: four seasons
最高 [zuìgāo]: highest
漂亮 [piàoliang]: beautiful

练习 ACTIVITIES

I. Pinyin Exercises

17-1 Listen to the instructor. Mark "√" if the Pinyin is correct, or write the correct Pinyin if it is incorrect:

1. cūntiān ________	2. shíjiā ________	3. fàngjià ________
4. qìhòu ________	5. jízhōng ________	6. shíhòu ________
7. huáshì ________	8. xiàoyǔ ________	9. shèxì ________
10. shuòshì ________	11. qízhōng ________	12. sàjiàng ________

17-2 Listen to the instructor and fill in each blank with the correct Pinyin:

1. 很快 _____ 考试了，我忙 _____ 了。
2. 我 _____ 没有回家了，放 _____ 的 _____ 我想回家看看。
3. 北京的 _____ 春夏秋冬都有，_____ 我比较喜欢 _____ 。
4. 香港的 _____ 很 _____，有时候非常 _____，还会 _____、_____ 。
5. _____ 就要来了，_____ 就要 _____ 了。

Notes: 北京 [Běijīng]: Beijing
香港 [Xiānggǎng]: Hong Kong

17-3 Read the following Chinese poem, paying special attention to the tones and rhythm:

Zǎo Fā Báidìchéng **(Lǐ Bó/Lǐ Bái)** Zhāo cí Báidì cǎiyún jiān, Qiānlǐ jiānglíng yírì huán. Liǎng'àn yuánshēng tí bú zhù, Qīngzhōu yǐ guò wàn chóng shān.	**早发白帝城** **(李白)** 朝辞白帝彩云间， 千里江陵一日还。 两岸猿声啼不住， 轻舟已过万重山。
Departing Baidi at Dawn **(Li, Bo/Li, Bai)** At dawn I depart Baidi amid the colorful clouds, After a day I reach Jiangling, a thousand miles away. On the riverbanks monkey calls ring endlessly, My little boat has already passed ten thousand mountains.	

Note: 李白 Lǐ Bái is pronounced as Lǐ Bó in Classical Chinese.

II. Character Exercises

17-4 Read the following words, phrases, and sentences:

就	最
就要	最快
就要到了	游得最快
就要到上海了	游泳游得最快
飞机就要到上海了	教练游泳游得最快
飞机很快就要到上海了	王教练游泳游得最快

Now try to use the following characters to make words, phrases, and then sentences:

1. 春	2. 久	3. 放	4. 气	5. 其	6. 暖
7. 短	8. 热	9. 华	10. 度	11. 风	12. 雨

17-5 Write the following adjectives in Chinese:

1. warm ________	2. hot ________	3. cold ________
4. (time) long ________	5. short ________	6. fast ________
7. slow ________	8. difficult ________	9. many ________
10. few ________	11. big ________	12. small ________

III. Grammar Exercises

17-6 Substitution exercises:

1. 我们什么时候去<u>游泳</u>?
   马上就要去了。

上课
打球
中国饭馆
看电影
参加舞会
买衬衫

Note: 马上 [mǎshàng]: immediately

2. 谁<u>打球打</u>得最<u>好</u>?
   他<u>打球打</u>得最<u>好</u>。

包饺子	慢
开车	快
做蛋糕	好
学习	久
吃饭	少

17-7 Match the second part of the sentence with its first part:

1.	天气热极了，	A.	其中我最喜欢红色的那条。
2.	这儿的裙子都很好看，	B.	有时候她会请我们去她家吃饭。
3.	他们认识的时间很短，	C.	我想坐飞机去中国玩儿。
4.	她的中国菜做得不错，	D.	夏天就要到了。
5.	就要放春假了，	E.	才不到一个月。

17-8 Rewrite the following sentences using the pattern of "就/快要…了":

For Example, 春天来了。→ 春天就要来了。
春天快要来了。

1. 小玲明天和大中见面。

____

2. 我的朋友下个月从加拿大回美国。

____

3. 爸爸等一会儿给我打电话。

____

4. 我们下午去公园玩儿。

____

5. 杨老师下个学期教我们中文。

____

6. 同学们下课以后去游泳。

____

IV. Communicative Activities

17-9 Situational dialogues:

<u>**Situation 1:**</u>
You and your roommate will be picked up by another friend to attend a party together. Your friend's car will arrive soon, but your roommate is still trying on his/her best suit/dress for the party.

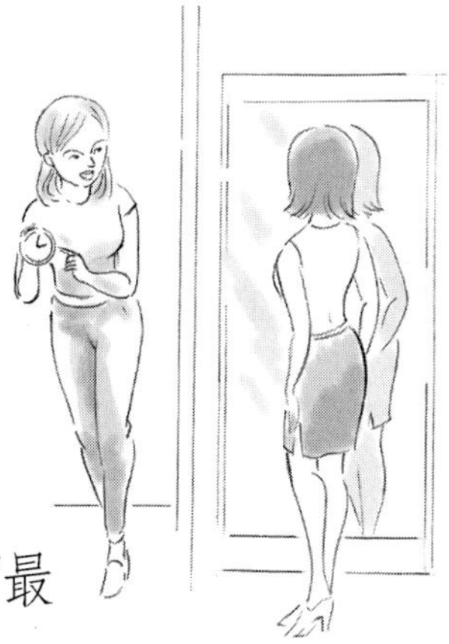

Hints:

1. Topics to cover:
   - Talk about the time of the party and your friend's arrival time.
   - Ask your roommate to be quick.
   - Help him/her select which clothing to wear.

2. Words and expressions to use:

   就/快要…了　　快一点儿
   这件/条还是那件/条好看…　　我觉得　　比较/最

Situation 2:
Your professor is going to teach in China next week. You and your friend are planning to see him/her off at the airport.

Hints:

1. Topics to cover:
   - Chat about your professor's schedule for the trip.
   - Talk about the weather of the city he/she is visiting.
   - Discuss when and how to get to the airport.

2. Words and expressions to use:

   热/冷极了　　坐/开车去　　从…到…
   就/快要…了　　教什么？　　有没有…？

Situation 3:
Your sister's son will turn six next week and will attend school soon. Give your sister some ideas about what to get him as a present.

Hints:

1. Topics to cover:
   - Greeting.
   - Chat about your nephew's birthday.
   - Make some suggestions about what kind of birthday present would be good.

2. Words and expressions to use:

   几岁？　　就/快要…了，是吗？　　应该…
   喜欢　　买自行车/衣服/书/蛋糕　　好极了

文化知识 Culture Link

文化点滴 CULTURE NOTES

中国的主要节庆 [Zhōngguó de zhǔyào jiéqìng] The Three Main Chinese Festivals

The three main Chinese festivals are 春节 [Chūnjié] Chinese New Year, 端午节 [Duānwǔjié] the Dragon Boat Festival, and 中秋节 [Zhōngqiūjié] the Mid-Autumn Festival. They are celebrated according to the Chinese lunar calendar on January 1, May 5, and August 15, respectively.

Chinese New Year preparations begin well before New Year's Day and include such activities as making cakes 年糕 [niángāo], cleaning the house, and planning the reunion dinner. Schools have their winter break during the New Year celebration, and almost all businesses take the week off. A family reunion dinner is held on New Year's Eve, and then the New Year is welcomed by setting off fireworks. Children wear new clothes for the first day of the year and receive 红包 [hóngbāo] (red envelopes) with cash inside for good fortune. The second day of the New Year is a traditional time for married women to visit their parents and family. During the New Year holidays Chinese people also take time to visit temples to pray for good fortune and health, visit friends and relatives, and go sightseeing. The atmosphere of the New Year will last until January 15, which is 元宵节 [Yuánxiāojié] the Lantern Festival. The Lantern Festival is celebrated at night by hanging lanterns and having a lantern parade.

端午节 is also called 龙舟节 [Lóngzhōujié] (the Dragon Boat Festival). It falls on May 5. The story behind this festival is that there was a famous ancient Chinese scholar and official called 屈原 [Qū Yuán] who served the king of 楚 [Chǔ] (Chu). As a loyal minister, he gave clever advice to the king. However, the king didn't listen to his advice and the kingdom was destroyed. Qu Yuan was so upset that he committed suicide by jumping into a river. In order to remember Qu Yuan's patriotism, people made special treats called 粽子 [zòngzi], consisting of rice and other fillings wrapped in bamboo leaves, and threw them into the river, hoping the fish would eat the 粽子 instead of Qu Yuan's body. Chinese people still carry on the tradition by making 粽子 and racing dragon boats.

Next is the Mid-Autumn Festival, sometimes called the Moon Festival. Families usually celebrate this festival by gathering together, eating 月饼 [yuèbǐng] (mooncakes: round-shaped pastries that symbolize perfection and union), and watching the bright moon. There are a few legends behind the Moon Festival. Among them are those of 后羿 [Hòu Yì] and his wife 嫦娥 [Cháng É], 吴刚 [Wú Gāng] chopping the tree, and 玉兔 [Yù Tù] (the Jade Rabbit) making medicine.

The legend of Hou Yi is that once there were ten suns over the earth causing a great drought. 后羿 was a great archer and shot them down one by one until only one remained. 后羿 received an immortality pill from 西王母娘娘 [Xī Wángmǔ Niángniang] (Goddess of the Western Heaven). 嫦娥, without telling 后羿, swallowed the immortality pill. Then she flew to the moon and lived there forever.

吴刚 was a very impatient but ambitious man. He was an apprentice to many immortals. Because he lacked patience, he could not stay with any one apprenticeship, which eventually angered one of the deities. As a result he was sent to the moon. He was required to stay on the moon until he cut down a giant cassia tree. He has spent an eternity trying to chop down this tree, because it regenerated every time it was hit.

The story of the 玉兔 is that one day three deities pretended to be beggars and went down to earth. They bumped into a fox, a monkey, and

Chinese New Year Celebrations.

Chinese New Year Celebrations.

Chinese New Year celebrations.

Dragon boats for the Dragon Boat Festival.

Tasty mooncakes for the Mid-Autumn Festival.

Making dumplings for a celebration!

a rabbit. They asked for food and both the fox and the monkey offered their food to them. The rabbit, however, had no food to give so he jumped into a pot and offered himself to the beggars. The deities, awed by the rabbit's altruism, made the rabbit immortal and let him live on the moon.

It is thought that 嫦娥, 吴刚, and 玉兔 can be seen on the moon when the moon is at its brightest in mid-autumn.

Questions:

1. Do you know of any other traditional Chinese festivals? Do you know the legends behind them? What special foods do people eat? What special presents do people send each other?
2. If you send a festival greeting card to your Chinese friends, what Chinese greetings can you write on the card?

趣味中文 FUN WITH CHINESE

热锅上的蚂蚁
extreme anxiety, restlessness, or fidgeting due to deep worry

rè	guō	shàng	de	mǎyǐ
热	锅	上	的	蚂蚁
hot	pan	on	(particle)	ant

The slang, 热锅上的蚂蚁, literally means an ant on a hot pan. It is used as a metaphor to describe someone who is worried and restless. Of course an ant on a hot pan must be very worried and anxious!

Question:

Is there any similar saying in English that describes a person being worried and anxious?

行动吧！ LET'S GO!

天气预报 Weather Forecast

书文 is visiting 上海 for a week. He is looking for a weather forecast in the newspaper.

Useful words and expressions:

预报(預報) [yùbào]: forecast
气象报告(氣象報告)[qìxiàng bàogào]: weather forecast (term used in Taiwan)
紫外线(紫外線) [zǐwàixiàn]: ultraviolet rays
转(轉) [zhuǎn]: to turn
强 [qiáng]: strong
弱 [ruò]: weak
风力(風力) [fēnglì]: wind power
微风(微風) [wēifēng]: breeze
伞(傘) [sǎn]: umbrella
抹 [mǒ]: to apply to
防晒油(防曬油) [fángshài yóu]: sunscreen
温差 [wēnchā]: temperature difference

上海今日天气

九月十八日	星期一	天气：晴	最高气温：28度	最低气温：26度

一周天气预告

日期	周	天气	最高气温	最低气温	风力	紫外线
九月十九日	周二	阴转晴	22 度	19 度	微风	中弱
九月二十日	周三	晴	26 度	23 度	轻	中强
九月二十一日	周四	多云	23 度	20 度	轻	弱
九月二十二日	周五	晴转阵雨	31 度	25 度	轻	中强
九月二十三日	周六	雨	21 度	18 度	轻	弱
九月二十四日	周日	晴	26 度	23 度	微风	强

Questions:

1. 今天他要穿外套吗？
2. 书文星期五要出外旅行，他应该带伞吗？
3. 星期日要去海边玩，他应该戴帽子，抹防晒油吗？
4. 一天的温差最大的是哪一天？

第十八课
LESSON

18

我们要坐火车去旅行
We Are Going to Take a Train Trip

教学目标 OBJECTIVES

- Describe means of transportation
- Talk about travel plans

Scooters are very practical and popular in Taiwan.

Double-decker bus and boats in Hong Kong.

Bicycles in China.

生词 VOCABULARY

核心词 Core Vocabulary

SIMPLIFIED	TRADITIONAL	PINYIN		
1. 火车	火車	huǒchē	N.	train
2. 旅行	旅行	lǚxíng	V.	to travel
3. 离	離	lí	V.	to be off, away, from
4. 学校	學校	xuéxiào	N.	school
5. 远	遠	yuǎn	Adj.	far
6. 只要	只要	zhǐyào	Adv.	only
7. 分钟	分鐘	fēnzhōng	N.	minute
8. 骑	騎	qí	V.	to ride
9. 自行车	自行車	zìxíngchē	N.	bicycle
10. 公共汽车	公共汽車	gōnggòngqìchē	N.	bus
11. 走路	走路	zǒulù	V.O.	to walk
12. 近	近	jìn	Adj.	near
13. 西部	西部	xībù	N.	west
14. 先	先	xiān	Adv.	first
15. 风景	風景	fēngjǐng	N.	scenery
16. 船	船	chuán	N.	ship
17. 南部	南部	nánbù	N.	south
18. 听说	聽說	tīngshuō	V.	to be told; to hear of; it is said
19. 海边	海邊	hǎibiān	N.	seaside
20. 景色	景色	jǐngsè	N.	scenery; view
21. 一共	一共	yígòng	Adv.	altogether; in all
22. 租	租	zū	V.	to rent, to hire; to lease

专名 Proper Nouns

SIMPLIFIED	TRADITIONAL	PINYIN		
1. 季长风	季長風	Jì Chángfēng	N.	(name) Changfeng Ji
2. 白秋影	白秋影	Bái Qiūyǐng	N.	(name) Qiuying Bai
3. 加拿大	加拿大	Jiānádà	N.	Canada

补充词 Supplementary Vocabulary

SIMPLIFIED	TRADITIONAL	PINYIN		
1. 海滩	海灘	hǎitān	N.	seashore
2. 东	東	dōng	N.	east
3. 北	北	běi	N.	north
4. 旺季	旺季	wàngjì	N.	busy season
5. 淡季	淡季	dànjì	N.	off-season
6. 单车 (脚踏车)	單車 (腳踏車)	dānchē (jiǎotàchē)	N.	bicycle
7. 汽车	汽車	qìchē	N.	car
8. 摩托车 (机车)	摩托車 (機車)	mótuōchē (jīchē)	N.	motorcycle, scooter
9. 出租汽车 (计程车)	出租汽車 (計程車)	chūzūqìchē (jìchéngchē)	N.	taxi
10. 火车	火車	huǒchē	N.	train
11. 公车 (巴士)	公車 (巴士)	gōngchē (bāshì)	N.	bus
12. 面包车 (包型车)	麵包車 (包型車)	miànbāochē (bāoxíngchē)	N.	minibus, van
13. 吉普车	吉普車	jípǔchē	N.	jeep
14. 跑车	跑車	pǎochē	N.	sports car
15. 大货车	大貨車	dàhuòchē	N.	truck

SIMPLIFIED	TRADITIONAL	PINYIN		
16. 四轮驱动 (四轮传动)	四輪驅動 (四輪傳動)	sìlúnqūdòng (sìlúnchuándòng)	N.	four-wheel drive
17. 越野车	越野車	yuèyěchē	N.	off-road vehicle
18. 车站	車站	chēzhàn	N.	stop; station
19. 捷运	捷運	jiéyùn	N.	MRT (Mass Rapid Transportation) in Taiwan
20. 地铁	地鐵	dìtiě	N.	subway
21. 磁浮铁路	磁浮鐵路	cífú tiělù	N.	magnetic railway
22. 天桥	天橋	tiānqiáo	N.	overhead bridge
23. 马路	馬路	mǎlù	N.	road, street
24. 地下道	地下道	dìxiàdào	N.	underground passage
25. 隧道	隧道	suìdào	N.	tunnel
26. 码头	碼頭	mǎtóu	N.	wharf; dock; pier
27. 司机	司機	sījī	N.	driver

语文知识 LANGUAGE LINK

The Sentence Patterns provide models that will help you with the Language in Use section. In both sections, pay attention to the grammar points, vocabulary, and expressions.

句型 Sentence Patterns

A: 你家离学校远不远?
Nǐ jiā lí xuéxiào yuǎnbuyuǎn?

B: 不太远。开车只要五分钟。
Bú tài yuǎn. Kāichē zhǐyào wǔ fēnzhōng.

A: 你每天怎么来学校?
Nǐ měitiān zěnme lái xuéxiào?

B: 我常骑自行车,
Wǒ cháng qí zìxíngchē,

有时候坐公共汽车。
yǒushíhou zuò gōnggòng qìchē.

你呢?
Nǐ ne?

A: 你们怎么去旅行?
Nǐmen zěnme qù lǚxíng?

B: 我们先坐火车,
Wǒmen xiān zuò huǒchē,

然后坐船去加拿大,
ránhòu zuò chuán qù Jiānádà,

再从加拿大坐飞机回来。
zài cóng Jiānádà zuò fēijī huílai.

课文 Language in Use: 我们要坐火车去旅行 Wǒmen yào zuò huǒchē qù lǚxíng

季长风: 秋影, 你住在校外吗? 离学校远不远?
Qiūyǐng, nǐ zhù zài xiàowài ma? Lí xuéxiào yuǎnbuyuǎn?

白秋影: 不太远, 开车只要五分钟。
Bú tài yuǎn, kāichē zhǐyào wǔ fēnzhōng.

季长风: 你每天怎么来学校?
Nǐ měitiān zěnme lái xuéxiào?

白秋影: 我常骑自行车, 下雨下雪的时候就坐公共汽车,
Wǒ cháng qí zìxíngchē, xiàyǔ xiàxuě de shíhou jiù zuò gōnggòng qìchē,

有时候我也走路, 可以锻炼锻炼。你呢?
yǒushíhou wǒyě zǒulù, kěyǐ duànlian duànlian. Nǐ ne?

季长风: 我住在宿舍, 离学校很近, 我每天走路来学校。
Wǒ zhùzài sùshè, lí xuéxiào hěnjìn, wǒ měitiān zǒulù lái xuéxiào.

白秋影: 对了, 这个春假你要做什么?
Duìle, zhège chūnjià nǐ yào zuò shénme?

季长风： 我要跟我的室友一起去西部旅行。
Wǒ yào gēn wǒde shìyǒu yìqǐ qù xībù lǚxíng.

白秋影： 你们怎么去？
Nǐmen zěnme qù?

季长风： 我们想先坐火车去，路上可以看看风景。
Wǒmen xiǎng xiān zuò huǒchē qù, lùshang kěyǐ kànkan fēngjǐng.

然后坐船去加拿大，再从加拿大坐飞机回来。你呢？
Ránhòu zuò chuán qù Jiānádà, zài cóng Jiānádà zuò fēijī huílai. Nǐ ne?

白秋影： 我很想我爸爸、妈妈和妹妹，我要先回家。
Wǒ hěn xiǎng wǒ bàba, māma hé mèimei, wǒ yào xiān huíjiā.

然后再跟朋友开车去玩儿。
Ránhòu zài gēn péngyou kāichē qù wár.

季长风： 你们要去哪儿玩儿？
Nǐmen yào qù nǎr wár?

白秋影： 我们想去南部玩儿。听说那儿的海边景色很美。
Wǒmen xiǎng qù nánbù wár. Tīngshuō nàr de hǎibiān jǐngsè hěn měi.

季长风： 你们有几个人去？
Nǐmen yǒu jǐge rén qù?

白秋影： 我们一共有五个人去，我们想租一辆车。
Wǒmen yígòng yǒu wǔge rén qù, wǒmen xiǎng zū yíliàng chē.

注释 LANGUAGE NOTES

自行车

自行车 means "bicycle." A more colloquial form used mostly in Taiwan is 脚踏车 [jiǎotàchē], and 单车 [dānchē] is also used in Mainland China and Hong Kong. The bicycle is currently the most common means of transportation in China.

公共汽车

公共汽车 means "(public) bus." In Taiwan, it is more commonly called 公车 or 巴士 [bāshì].

路上

路上 is an idiomatic expression commonly used to mean "on the way."

语法 GRAMMAR

离

The verb 离 means "to be away from . . ." It is used in the following pattern:

A + 离 + B + adjective phrase

For example,	宿舍	离	学校	很近。	The dorm is very close to the school.
	中国	离	美国	很远。	China is very far from the U.S.

Note: While English modifiers of distance such as "very close" and "very far" are placed between the names of two places, Chinese modifiers of distance are placed at the end of the sentence, as shown in the examples above.

先……(再)…… 然后……

Both 先 and 再 are adverbs, but 然后 is a conjunction. All three words are used to show sequence. Look at the following examples:

他先去吃饭，再去图书馆，然后回宿舍。
He first went to eat, then to the library and after that he went back to the dorm.

我先去找老师，然后去看你。
I will go to see the professor first, and then to see you.

Note that when you want to indicate sequence, you must use 先 first, and then 然后. If there are more than two actions involved, you need to use 再 as well. The order of the three expressions can be either 先……, 再……, 然后…… or 先……, 然后……再……. For example, for the sentence "Xiaomei will go to Beijing first, then to Hong Kong, and then to Taiwan to visit her Grandma," the Chinese sentence can be either

小美要先去北京，再去香港，然后去台湾看奶奶。

or 小美要先去北京，然后去香港，再去台湾看奶奶。

坐, 骑 and 开

These three verbs are used for different kinds of vehicles:

Verb	Vehicle	Translation
坐 to take, to ride in	汽车	to take (ride in) a car
	长途汽车 [chángtú qìchē]	to take (ride in) a long-distance bus
	出租汽车 [chūzū qìchē] 公共汽车 [gōnggòng qìchē] 火车 飞机	to take (ride in) a taxicab to take (ride in) a (public) bus to take (ride in) a train to take (fly in) an airplane
	轮船 [lúnchuán]	to take a ship
骑 to ride	自行车	to ride a bike
	马 [mǎ]	to ride a horse
开 to drive	车	to drive a car

补充课文 SUPPLEMENTARY PRACTICE

This selection will help you test your comprehension of the grammar and vocabulary you have learned in this lesson. Be prepared to answer questions about the meaning of the passage.

四月十日　　星期六　　晴

今天下午我去看大中。他住在校外的公寓里，他的公寓离学校很近，开车只要五分钟就到了。他常常骑自行车去学校，有时候也走路，他觉得走路可以锻炼身体，下雨下雪的时候他就坐公共汽车。

大中跟他的室友正在上网。因为他们想在放假的时候一起去西部旅行，所以他们想看看网上有没有便宜的火车票和飞机票。他们想先坐飞机到旧金山，在旧金山玩两天，然后坐火车去西雅图，一路上可以欣赏一下外边的风景，在西雅图再玩两天，然后坐船去加拿大，最后再从加拿大坐飞机回来。

我好久没有回家了，我很想家。放假以后我要先回家，看看我的爸爸、妈妈和妹妹。然后我想租一辆车，跟我的朋友一起开车去南部的海边玩儿。听说那儿的风景很美，还可以游泳、晒太阳，所以我想在那儿好好地玩儿几天再回家。

Notes: 晴 [qíng]: sunny
公寓 [gōngyù]: apartment
便宜 [piányì]: inexpensive
旧金山 [Jiùjīnshān]: San Francisco
西雅图 [Xīyǎtú]: Seattle
欣赏 [xīnshǎng]: to enjoy
晒太阳 [shàitàiyáng]: to get a suntan
几: an indefinite pronoun used here to indicate "some"

练习 ACTIVITIES

I. Pinyin Exercises

18-1 Fill in the blanks with the correct Pinyin:

1. Wǒ měitiān ___________ lái xuéxiào.

   a. zhǒulú   b. zǒulù   c. zhòunù

2. ___________ wǒ yào gēn péngyou ___________ qù wár.

   a. Chūnjià/kāichē   b. Cúnjià/kāichē   c. Chǔnjiǎ/kàichē

3. Wǒmen xià ___________ xià ___________ de shíhou zuò ___________ qù xuéxiào.

   a. yù/xuè/gǒnggóng qìchē   b. yú/xuè/gōnggōng qīchē   c. yǔ/xuě/gōnggòng qìchē

4. Dào ___________ qù kěyi kàndào hěnduō ___________.

   a. xībù/fēngjǐng   b. xíbù/féngjíng   c. xìbù/fēngjìng

5. Wǒ tèbié xǐhuān ___________ de ___________.

   a. háibiàn/fèngjǐng   b. hāibiǎn/fēngjíng   c. hǎibiān/fēngjǐng

18-2 Read the following poem, paying special attention to the tones and rhythm:

Tí Xīlínbì (Sū Shì)	题西林壁 (苏轼)
Héng kàn chéng lǐng cè chéng fēng,	横看成岭侧成峰，
Yuǎn jìn gāo dī gè bùtóng.	远近高低各不同。
Bù shí Lúshān zhēn miànmù,	不识庐山真面目，
Zhǐ yuán shēn zài cǐ shān zhōng.	只缘身在此山中。

Inscription on the Xilin Cliff
(Su, Shi)

Looking transversely we see a mountain ridge and sidewise a peak,
The cliff looks very different from all directions.
The true face of Mount Lushan cannot be seen,
Just because you are in the mountains.

II. Character Exercises

18-3 Read the following words and phrases:

火	走
火车	走路
坐火车	走路去学校
从上海坐火车	我每天走路去学校
从上海坐火车去北京	我每天跟我室友走路去学校
我们想从上海坐火车去北京玩儿	我每天跟我室友走路去学校上课

Now try to use the following characters to make words, phrases, and then sentences:

1. 旅	2. 离	3. 远	4. 只	5. 骑	6. 汽
7. 近	8. 西	9. 景	10. 船	11. 听	12. 租

18-4 Write the following phrases in characters:

1. Zhù zài xiào wài ______________	2. Zū yíliàng chē______________
3. Zuò fēijī ______________	4. Qí zìxíngchē ______________
5. Zuò chuán qù wán______________	6. Xībù fēngjǐng ______________
7. Lí xuéxiào hěnjìn ______________	8. Kāichē lǚxíng ______________
9. Hǎibiān jǐngsè ______________	10. Zuò huǒchē ______________

18-5 Group the following characters according to how many components they have:

骑 自 远 离 风 西 海 租 船 景 近
汽 行 旅 先 路 春 部 雪 假 机 开

1. One component

____

2. Two components

____

____

____

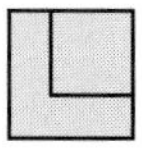
____

3. Three components

____

____

III. Grammar Exercises

18-6 Substitution exercises:

1. 宿舍<u>离</u>学校很近。

a.

我家

远

海边

b.

厨房

近

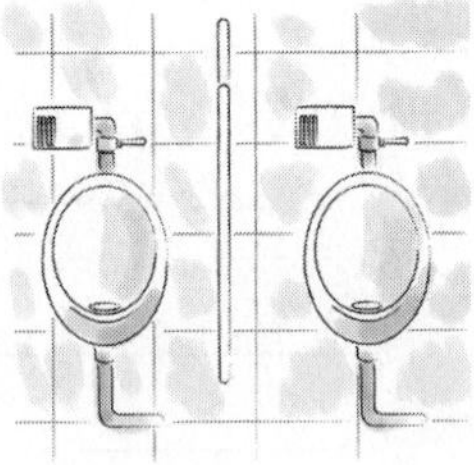

厕所 [cèsuǒ]: bathroom

c.

停车场

近

图书馆

d.

加拿大

远

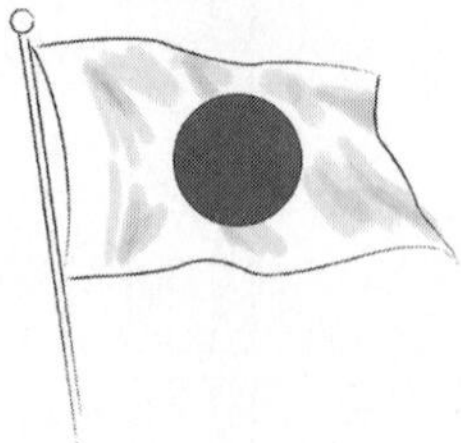

日本

2. 我先去饭馆吃饭，再去喝咖啡 [kāfēi]: coffee，然后回家。

a.  →  → 

健身房 游泳池 洗澡

b.  →  → 

图书馆 书店 宿舍

c.  →  → 

汤 饺子 蛋糕

18-7 Fill in each blank with 坐, 开, 骑, 租:

1. 我每天 ________ 公共汽车来学校。
2. 你 ________ 车 ________ 得快吗？
3. **A：** 他会不会 ________ 自行车？

   B： 会。他 ________ 得很好。
4. ________ 火车比较慢，可是很舒服。
5. 我们应该 ________ 一辆面包车，我的汽车太小了。

IV. Communicative Activities

18-8 In one month your summer vacation will begin. You and your friend are discussing a possible trip to Canada. Your discussion should include (but not be limited to) the following:

1. Time of the trip
2. Route
3. How to travel
4. Vehicles

18-9 You and a few of your friends are planning to travel during the summer. You are now discussing the specifics of your plan. Form groups of two or three and work out a detailed plan for your travel, including where to go, when to go, how to go, and why. While giving your suggestions, try to refer to your or someone else's past travel experiences.

Useful words and expressions:

离……远/近，先……然后……再……，　东/南/西/北部，　只要，
一共，　听说，　觉得，　坐(船/火车/飞机/出租汽车，etc.)，
风景/景色，　海边，　租

文化知识 Culture Link

文化点滴 CULTURE NOTES

中国的交通标志与规则
[Zhōngguó de jiāotōng biāozhì yǔ guīzé]
Traffic in China
Traffic Signs and Rules in China

The traffic rules and regulations in China are basically the same as those in other countries of the world. People in China also drive on the right side of the road, as in the U.S.

However, 交通标志 [jiāotōng biāozhì] (traffic signs) in China are not always the same as those in the U.S. When driving in China, one must pay attention to the following differences.

Stop signs/Traffic lights: Before stop signs or traffic lights, there is frequently very little warning before the stopping point.

Pedestrian signs: A series of lines painted in white (like a zebra) on roads indicates a crossing for pedestrians.

百米牌

Merge signs: Before the merge point on highways, there are signs indicating 200 meters, 100 meters and 50 meters, informing the driver of the distance to the merge point.

Street signs: Street name signs in China contain large characters arranged horizontally and are located at each street corner. Most of the signs are made of enamel with a white background and blue Chinese characters.

Highway signs: The signs for newly built interstate highways in China are all bilingual, in both Chinese and English.

Speed limit signs: In cities or towns in China, there are no speed limit signs, because drivers are not able to drive their vehicles faster than 50 kph (30 mph) due to the narrow streets or high volume of bicycles and pedestrians in the streets. The speed limit on interstate highways is 80–120 kph (50–75 mph).

Traffic timers: In most cities in China, there are traffic timers next to traffic lights to inform drivers and pedestrians how long they have to wait before they should move or stop.

License plates: License plates for vehicles in China all look the same with a white background and blue Chinese characters and numbers. For joint-venture company vehicles, however, the plates use a black background and white characters and numbers. The character before the numbers on the plate indicates the city or province where the vehicle is registered, for example 京 [Jīng] for Beijing, 沪 [Hù] for Shanghai, 粤 [Yuè] for Guangdong.

Traffic in Guangzhou.

Street sign.

Traffic in Beijing.

Traffic in I-lan (city in northeast Taiwan).

Blowing horns is prohibited in some places, and a driver will be penalized for using the horn in prohibited areas, especially near schools, libraries, especially hospitals. Towing fees are expensive in China. If a vehicle breaks down on the highway or parks in a no-parking zone, it usually costs around US$40 to $60 to have it towed to a nearby police station, and another US$50 penalty to collect it.

To obtain a driver's license in China, one must pass a written test and a road test. Almost all the driving schools in China are state-owned and are part of the Public Safety Bureau (the police). To learn to drive costs approximately US$500 at a driving school. You not only learn how to drive, but also how to fix some mechanical problems. The learning and training period usually takes three or four months before permission is given to take the road test.

Questions:

1. Have you ever been to China or any other country? Share your experience or a story about local traffic in these countries with the class.
2. While traveling in the U.S., have you noticed any differences in driving style, traffic rules, or roads among different states or cities?
3. Compare the traffic in your hometown with the city where you are attending school.

趣味中文 FUN WITH CHINESE

读万卷书，行万里路。

Interpretation 1:
Having read ten thousand rolls of books, (is as good as) having traveled ten thousand miles.

Interpretation 2:
To read ten thousand rolls of books is not as good as traveling ten thousand miles — seeing is believing.

Interpretation 3:
One should seek opportunities to read and travel as much as possible.

dú	wàn	juàn	shū,	xíng	wàn	lǐ	lù.
读	万	卷	书，	行	万	里	路。
read	ten thousand	roll	book,	travel	ten thousand	mile	road.

Question:

Do you believe Interpretation 1, 2, or 3? Why?

行动吧！ LET'S GO!

火车和飞机票 Train and Airplane Tickets

While in China 小谢 took a train and then an airplane to Beijing. Below are his train ticket, airport fee receipt, and boarding pass. Read them and then answer the questions.

火车票

B0099632 广 B 售
广州东 —— 深圳 T877次
2003年03月04日 16:27开 03车 62号
全价70.00元 新空调一等软座准高速
日使用一次有效

机场管理费收据

国财1006034 民航机场管理建设费
CAAC AIRPORT MANAGEMENT AND CONSTRUCTION FEE
当地当日一次使用
人民币玖拾圆整
RMB 90 圆
旅客联（报销凭证）
PASSENGER COUPON
02 SD00627725

飞机登机牌

中国南方航空 CHINA SOUTHERN
登机牌 BOARDING PASS
姓名 NAME: XIEDEJUN
到达站 DESTN.: 北京 BEIJING
登机口 GATE: 17
航班号 FLIGHT: CZ3153
舱位 CLASS: U
登机时间 BD TIME: 1130
日期 DATE: 07MAR
座位号 SEAT: 23F
登机闸口于起飞前15分钟关闭 GATES CLOSE 15 MINUTES BEFORE DEPARTURE

Useful words and expressions:

(I) 火车(火車):

广州东(廣州東) [Guǎngzhōu dōng]: refers to the East Train Station in Guangzhou city, a city in Guangdong Province in southern China
深圳 [Shēnzhèn]: a city next to Hong Kong in Guangdong Province
全价(全價) [quán jià]: total price
空调(空調) [kōngtiáo]: air conditioning
一等 [yīděng]: first class
软座(軟座) [ruǎnzuò]: soft seat
硬座 [yìngzuò]: hard seat
准高速(準高速) [zhǔn gāosù]: close to high speed
使用 [shǐyòng]: to use
有效 [yǒuxiào]: to be valid

(II) 机场管理费(機場管理費):

民航 [mínháng]: civil aviation
管理 [guǎnlǐ]: to manage, maintain
建设费(建設費) [jiànshè fèi]: development fee
整 [zhěng]: exact
当地(當地) [dāngdì]: this place
当日(當日) [dāngrì]: on this day

(III) 飞机(飛機):

登机牌(登機牌) [dēngjī pái]: boarding pass
到达站(到達站) [dàodá zhàn]: destination
登机口(登機口) [dēngjīkǒu]: gate
航班号 [hángbān hào]: flight number
舱位 [cāngwèi]: class
登机时间(登機時間) [dēngjī shíjiān]: boarding time
日期 [rìqī]: date
座位 [zuòwèi]: seat
登机闸口(登機閘口) [dēngjī zhákǒu]: boarding gate
关闭(關閉) [guānbì]: to close

Questions:

1. 他先从哪儿坐火车到哪儿去，然后他再坐飞机去北京?
2. 火车有空调吗? 他坐的是什么座 (软坐还是硬座)?
3. 小谢付了多少钱的机场管理费?
4. 当地、当日的口语怎么说?
5. 小谢是什么时候的班机? 他的登机口在哪儿?

复习 Review

LESSON 17 TO LESSON 18

Conversation

Form pairs and chat about the following topics. Then report the information you collect to the class.

1. 你喜欢这里的气候吗？为什么？
2. 春夏秋冬四季 [sìjì] (four seasons) 里面，你比较喜欢哪一个？为什么？
3. 很快就要放暑假了，你有什么计划 [jìhuà] (plan) 呢？
4. 你每天怎么去学校？坐公车还是开车去？骑自行车还是走路去？
5. 你是不是快要毕业了？你学了很多门课，其中你最喜欢哪一门？为什么？

Situational Dialogue

Your friend is travelling to China next week. You are planning to see him/her off at the airport. And since you've been to China before, you are going to relate your experience to him/her. Chat about the schedule for the trip, the weather, the cities you like and dislike, etc.

Useful expressions:

就/快要…了；	从…到…；	我觉得；	比较/最；
…极了；有没有；	坐/开车去；	喜欢；	应该

Simplified and Traditional Characters

Read each character aloud. Write its simplified form. Then tell a story (at least five sentences) using the following characters.

For example, 學 → 学 → 学生 → 我是一个学生，我学……

L17: 熱（ ） 機（ ） 華（ ） 歡（ ） 會（ ）

L18: 離（ ） 遠（ ） 騎（ ） 風（ ） 聽（ ）

第十九课
LESSON

19

我感冒了
I Caught a Cold

教学目标 OBJECTIVES

- Describe the symptoms of an illness
- Describe something that has happened

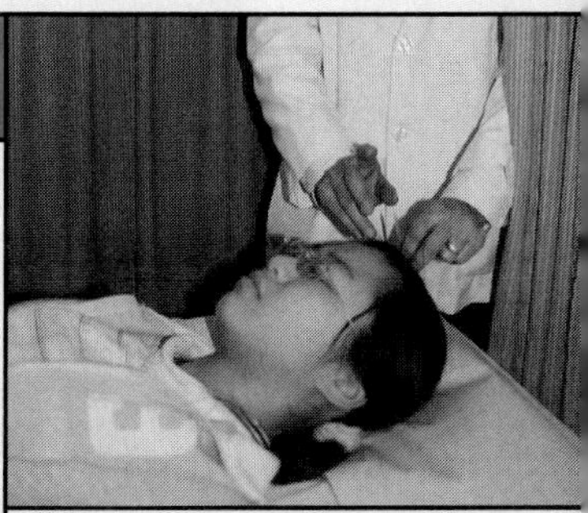

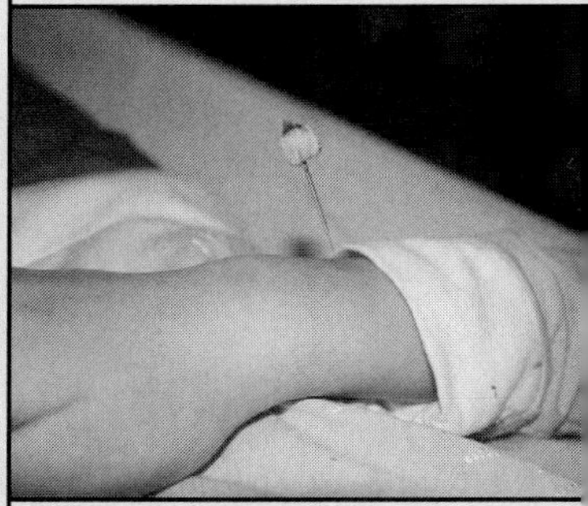

针灸 [zhēnjiǔ] acupuncture is a popular therapy for curing headache, back pain, joint pain, and arthritis. Treatments are commonly administered at a Chinese medicine hospital.

脚底按摩 [jiǎodǐ ànmó] foot massage is believed to be able to detect and cure diseases of the inner organs.

生词 VOCABULARY

核心词 Core Vocabulary

SIMPLIFIED	TRADITIONAL	PINYIN		
1. 感冒	感冒	gǎnmào	N.	cold, flu
2. 饿	餓	è	Adj. V.	hungry to starve
3. 好像	好像	hǎoxiàng	V.	to be like; to seem
4. 舒服	舒服	shūfu	Adj.	comfortable; well
5. 头疼	頭疼	tóuténg	V.	to have a headache
6. 发烧	發燒	fāshāo	V.O.	to have a fever
7. 咳嗽	咳嗽	késòu	V.	to cough
8. 生病	生病	shēngbìng	V.O.	to fall ill
9. 考试	考試	kǎoshì	N.	exam
10. 复习	復習	fùxí	V.	to review
11. 所以	所以	suǒyǐ	Conj.	therefore; consequently
12. 医生	醫生	yīshēng	N.	doctor
13. 吃药	吃藥	chīyào	V.O.	to take medicine
14. 地	地	de	Part.	(attached to an adjective to transform the whole unit into an adverb)
15. 休息	休息	xiūxi	V.	to rest
16. 准备	準備	zhǔnbèi	V.	to prepare
17. 笔记	筆記	bǐjì	N.	notes
18. 感谢	感謝	gǎnxiè	V.	to thank; to be grateful

专名 Proper Nouns

SIMPLIFIED	TRADITIONAL	PINYIN		
1. 欧阳迎	歐陽迎	Ōuyáng Yíng	N.	(name) Ying Ouyang
2. 唐志信	唐志信	Táng Zhìxìn	N.	(name) Zhixin Tang

补充词 Supplementary Vocabulary

SIMPLIFIED	TRADITIONAL	PINYIN		
1. 医务室 (医护室)	醫務室 (醫護室)	yīwùshì (yīhùshì)	N.	clinic
2. 打针	打針	dǎzhēn	V.O.	to give or receive an injection
3. 护士	護士	hùshi	N.	nurse
4. 医院	醫院	yīyuàn	N.	hospital
5. 诊所	診所	zhěnsuǒ	N.	clinic
6. 严重	嚴重	yánzhòng	Adj.	severe
7. 厉害	厲害	lìhài	Adj.	severely; very much
8. 体温	體溫	tǐwēn	N.	body temperature
9. 流感 (流行性感冒)	流感 (流行性感冒)	liúgǎn (liúxíngxìng gǎnmào)	N.	flu
10. 预防针	預防針	yùfángzhēn	N.	immunization shot
11. 流感疫苗	流感疫苗	liúgǎn yìmiáo	N.	flu shot

语文知识 LANGUAGE LINK

The Sentence Patterns provide models that will help you with the Language in Use section. In both sections, pay attention to the grammar points, vocabulary, and expressions.

句型 Sentence Patterns

A: 你吃饭了吗?
Nǐ chīfàn le ma?

B: 还没有呢。我不饿。
Hái méiyǒu ne. Wǒ bú è.

A: 你怎么了? 好像不舒服。
Nǐ zěnme le? Hǎoxiàng bù shūfu.

B: 我感冒了。我头疼发烧,
Wǒ gǎnmào le. Wǒ tóuténg fāshāo,

还有一点儿咳嗽。
háiyǒu yìdiǎr késòu.

A: 你看医生了没有?
Nǐ kàn yīshēng le méiyǒu?

B: 看了。我也吃药了。
Kàn le. Wǒ yě chīyào le.

可是还没有好呢。
Kěshì hái méiyǒu hǎo ne.

课文 Language in Use: 我感冒了 Wǒ gǎnmào le

唐志信： 欧阳迎，你吃饭了吗？
Ōuyáng Yíng, nǐ chīfàn le ma?

欧阳迎： 还没有呢。我不饿。
Hái méiyǒu ne. Wǒ bú è.

唐志信： 你怎么了？好像不舒服。
Nǐ zěnme le? Hǎoxiàng bù shūfu.

欧阳迎： 我感冒了。我头疼发烧，还有一点儿咳嗽。
Wǒ gǎnmào le. Wǒ tóuténg fāshāo, háiyǒu yìdiǎr késòu.

唐志信： 你怎么生病了呢？
Nǐ zěnme shēngbìng le ne?

欧阳迎： 这几天我有很多考试，每天都在复习，
Zhè jǐ tiān wǒ yǒu hěnduō kǎoshì, měitiān dōu zài fùxí,

睡觉睡得太少，所以就病了。
shuìjiào shuì de tàishǎo, suǒyǐ jiù bìng le.

唐志信： 你看医生了没有？
Nǐ kàn yīshēng le méiyǒu?

欧阳迎： 看了。我也吃药了。可是还没有好呢。
Kàn le. Wǒ yě chīyào le. Kěshì hái méiyǒu hǎo ne.

唐志信： 你应该在家好好地休息。不应该来上课。
Nǐ yīnggāi zàijiā hǎohǎo de xiūxi. Bù yīnggāi lái shàngkè.

欧阳迎： 你说得很对。可是我有很多考试。我得好好地准备。
Nǐ shuō de hěnduì. Kěshì wǒ yǒu hěnduō kǎoshì. Wǒ děi hǎohǎo de zhǔnbèi.

唐志信： 这是我上课的笔记，借给你看看。
Zhèshì wǒ shàngkè de bǐjì, jiè gěi nǐ kànkan.

欧阳迎： 非常感谢！好吧，我现在就回家休息。
Fēicháng gǎnxiè! Hǎo ba, wǒ xiànzài jiù huíjiā xiūxi.

唐志信： 好，我开车送你回去。你得好好地睡觉。
Hǎo, wǒ kāichē sòng nǐ huíqù. Nǐ děi hǎohǎo de shuìjiào.

注释 LANGUAGE NOTES

怎么了

怎么了 is a common phrase meaning "What happened?" "What's wrong?"

生病了

"I am sick" can be expressed by either 我病了 "I am sick" or 我生病了 (literally "I produced sickness").

地

地 [dì] can be a noun meaning "ground, earth" such as in 地图 and 地址. 地 [de] can also be attached to an adjective to transform the whole unit into an adverb, such as 慢慢地 (slowly).

语法 GRAMMAR

The Aspect Particle 了

The aspect particle 了 is usually used in the following situations:

A. Completion of an action: 了 is placed after a verb or at the end of a sentence to indicate the completion of an action.

了: indicate the completion of an action	Pattern	Example
(1) question	V._了吗, V._了没有	你看医生了吗? Did you go to see a doctor? 你看医生了没有? Did you go to see a doctor?
(2) Positive answer	V. 了, or sentence end 了	我看了医生。 I saw the doctor. 我看医生了。 I saw the doctor.
(3) Negative answer	(1) 没有 V. (to negate a completion aspect, indicating that an action didn't take place) (2) 还没有 ____ 呢 (to indicate a planned action)	我没有参加旅行。 I didn't go on the trip. 你们去旅行了吗? Have you gone on your trip yet? 我们还没有去旅行呢。 We haven't gone on our trip yet.

- 了 must **not** be regarded as a "past tense" marker. It is an aspect particle indicating action completion. In Chinese, to indicate the present, past, and future tenses, time words are often used, such as 去年, 现在, and 明天.
- Note that 了 is not used in negations in the completion of an action usage.
- Note that when 了 is followed by a quantified object, it is preferred to place 了 after the verb.

  e.g., 我看了两次医生。
  e.g., 我买了三本中文书。

B. New situation: 了 is also used at the end of a sentence to express a situation that has changed.

	Pattern	Example
了: new situation	Sentence end 了	你会开车了吗? Do you know how to drive? 我会开车了。 I can drive now.
	不... V. 了 (not doing V. any more)	他不吸烟 [xīyān] 了。 He does not smoke any more. 他不喝酒了。 He does not drink any more.

Note: When 了 is placed at the end of a sentence, it may be used to indicate the completion of an action or the change of a situation. For example, the sentence 他去北京了 can mean "He went to Beijing" (i.e., he did the action) or "He is in Beijing now", depending on the context.

的, 得, and 地

的, 得, and 地 are all pronounced as [de] but have different meanings and functions.

Pattern	Features	Examples
的 + N.	Possessive, structure 的	我的车 my car 上课的笔记 notes taken in class 他是一个认真的学生。 He is a conscientious student.
V. + 得 + Adv./Adj.	Used in a degree of complement sentences	他说中文说得很快。 He speaks Chinese very fast. 他写汉字写得很认真。 He writes the characters conscientiously.
Adj. + 地	Manner adverbial, combines with an adjective, similar to "-ly" in English, used before a verb to indicate the attitude or manner of an action	他慢慢地吃饭。 He eats slowly. 他认真地写汉字。 He writes the characters conscientiously.

Notes: 认真 [rènzhēn]: conscientious; serious
汉字 [hànzì]: Chinese characters

补充课文 SUPPLEMENTARY PRACTICE

This selection will help you test your comprehension of the grammar and vocabulary you have learned in this lesson. Be prepared to answer questions about the meaning of the passage.

欧阳迎是我中文班的同学。今天她好像有点儿不舒服，脸色很不好，中饭也没有吃，原来她感冒了。又是头疼又是发烧，还有一点儿咳嗽。

这几天她太忙了。这个学期她选了六门课，每门课都有很多功课，前几天刚写完了两个报告，还有几个考试。每天晚上她都要开夜车，复习到很晚，睡觉睡得太少，每天平均才睡四个小时。这两天天气也不太好，一会儿热，一会儿冷，又常常下雨，所以她感冒了。

我想送她去医院，她说前天她已经看了医生，也吃了点儿药。医生说她应该在家里好好地休息，多喝水，多睡觉。可是她得准备考试，没有时间休息，所以她的病好得很慢。我觉得她应该好好地睡一觉。我告诉她我有上课的笔记，可以借给她。然后我就开车送她回家了，我也给她买了一些吃的东西，她非常感激。

Notes: 脸色 [liǎnsè]: complexion
原来 [yuánlái]: It turned out that . . . ; apparently
报告 [bàogào]: report
开夜车 [kāiyèchē]: to burn the midnight oil
平均 [píngjūn]: on average
医院 [yīyuàn]: hospital
感激 [gǎnjī]: to appreciate

练习 ACTIVITIES

I. Pinyin Exercises

19-1 Listen to the instructor. Mark "√" if the Pinyin is correct, or write the correct Pinyin if it is incorrect.

1. gǎngmào ________	2. shūfù ________	3. tóuténg ________
4. késuò ________	5. kǒushì ________	6. shēngbìn ________
7. zhǔnbèi ________	8. yìshēng ________	9. xūxi ________
10. yánzhèng ________	11. chīyòu ________	12. suǒyǐ ________

19-2 Fill in each blank with the correct Pinyin:

1. 暖[和] ____	老师[和]学生 ____
2. [地]图 ____	好好[地]休息 ____
3. 睡[觉] ____	[觉]得 ____
4. [得]去接人 ____	游泳游[得]很快 ____
5. [教]中文 ____	篮球[教]练 ____

19-3 Read the following Chinese poem, paying special attention to the tones and rhythm:

Xún Yǐnzhě Bú Yù (Jiǎ Dǎo)	**寻隐者不遇** (贾岛)
Sōng xià wèn tóngzǐ,	松下问童子，
Yán shī cǎi yào qù.	言师采药去。
Zhǐ zài cǐ shān zhōng,	只在此山中，
Yún shēn bù zhī chù.	云深不知处。

Seeking the Hermit but Not Found
(Jia, Dao)

Beneath a pine tree I inquire of a young servant,
He says his master has gone to collect herbs.
"He is somewhere in the mountains,
But I can't tell where he is for the clouds are so deep."

II. Character Exercises

19-4 Read the following words, phrases, and sentences:

像	地
好像	好好地
好像病了	好好地休息
好像生病了	应该好好地休息
怎么好像生病了	应该在家好好地休息
怎么好像生病了呢	我觉得你应该在家好好地休息

Now try to use the following characters to make words, phrases, and then sentences:

1. 感 2. 饿 3. 舒 4. 疼 5. 烧 6. 咳
7. 病 8. 考 9. 所 10. 准 11. 医 12. 记

19-5 Write down the traditional forms for the following simplified characters.

1. 饿 ______ 2. 头 ______ 3. 发 ______ 4. 烧 ______
5. 复 ______ 6. 准 ______ 7. 备 ______ 8. 医 ______
9. 药 ______ 10. 笔 ______ 11. 还 ______ 12. 记 ______

III. Grammar Exercises

19-6 Substitution exercises:

1. 你吃饭了吗？
我还没有吃饭呢。

看球赛
跟朋友见面
坐火车去玩儿
去机场接妹妹
买衬衫
参加晚会

2. 你打电话了没有？
我打电话了。

知道	怎么去机场
看	电影
回	宿舍
打	篮球
包	饺子

3. 你会游泳了吗？
   我会游泳了。

说中文
骑自行车
做中国菜
用电脑
写汉字

Notes: 电脑 [diànnǎo]: computer
汉字 [hànzì]: Chinese characters

4. **A:** 你做作业了吗？
   B: 我做了。你呢？
   A: 我(还)没有做。

王老师	教第二十课	李老师
你爸爸	去北京	你哥哥
你的朋友	吃药	他的朋友
妈妈	吃饭	姐姐
妹妹	睡觉	弟弟

19-7 Fill in the blanks with 的, 得, or 地:

1. 那个穿红色裙子 _____ 人是我妹妹。
2. 他很快 _____ 吃了饭。
3. 这个公园 _____ 景色很美。
4. 我的德文说 _____ 不好。
5. 考试以后我要好好 _____ 玩玩。
6. 小文走路走 _____ 很慢。

19-8 Form pairs.

1. Take turns reading the following passage.
2. Take turns asking and answering the questions.

田进： 明明，你学开车了没有？
方明明： 我还没有学呢。你教我怎么样？
田进： 行，没问题。
方明明： 对了，昨天我给你打电话了，可是你不在。
田进： 我去参加晚会了。
方明明： 什么晚会？
田进： 中文课的中文晚会。
方明明： 我忘了！你们都做了什么？
田进： 我们吃饺子，唱歌，跳舞，还看了功夫表演。很有意思。
方明明： 你们唱中文歌了吗？
田进： 唱了，还是新的流行歌曲呢！

方明明： 你会唱中国歌了没有？
田进： 我会了。我们还看了一个叫《英雄》的中国电影。棒极了！
方明明： 你们喝啤酒了没有？
田进： 以前我喜欢喝啤酒，可是我女朋友不喜欢我喝酒，所以我现在已经不喝了。

Useful words:

忘 [wàng]: forget
唱歌 [chànggē]: to sing
跳舞 [tiàowǔ]: to dance
表演 [biǎoyǎn]: to perform
新 [xīn]: new
英雄 [yīngxióng]: hero
酒 [jiǔ]: wine, alcoholic beverage
功夫 [gōngfu]: martial arts
流行歌曲 [liúxíng gēqǔ]: popular songs
以前 [yǐqián]: before
已经 [yǐjīng]: already

Questions:

1. 他们是谁？
2. 方明明要田进教他什么？
3. 田进昨天为什么 [wèishénme] (why) 不在家？
4. 他们在中文晚会做了什么？
5. 田进会唱中国歌了吗？
6. 他们看了什么电影？
7. 电影怎么样？
8. 田进以前喜欢做什么？现在呢？为什么？

IV. Communicative Activities

19-9 Situational dialogues:

Situation 1:
Your roommate has just come back from a trip to China. Please chat with him/her about his/her experience.

Hints:
1. Topics to cover:
   - Greetings.
   - Discuss your roommate's impression of China.
   - Talk about your roommate's experience in China, including eating, seeing different scenic spots, shopping for clothes or gifts.

2. Words and expressions to use:

怎么样?		......了吗/了没有?
觉得	想	吃/参观/买...了

Situation 2:

Your classmate has been practicing for a basketball game for several days. Because the weather has been cold and he/she didn't wear warm clothes after practice, he/she caught a cold. Ask about your classmate's illness.

Hints:

1. Topics to cover:
   - Greetings.
   - Ask what is the matter when you see that your classmate doesn't look well.
   - Show your concern and give suggestions.

2. Words and expressions to use:

怎么了	是不是......	......了吗/了没有?	
打球......得	没有很快......穿	暖和 衣服	所以
药	医生	想......	应该......

Situation 3:

You return from a Chinese student's party, and your friend asks about it. Give your friend some information about the party.

Hints:

1. Topics to cover:
   - Greetings.
   - Tell him/her about your new Chinese friends.
   - Describe what you did at the party.

2. Words and expressions to use:

参加	介绍	中国学生	认识	中国朋友
中国菜	包	饺子	电影	了

文化知识 Culture Link

文化点滴 CULTURE NOTES

中医中药 [Zhōngyī Zhōngyào] Traditional Chinese Medicine and Pharmacology

Traditional Chinese medicine and pharmacology form a unique scientific system. In ancient times, traditional medicine and drugs were the only means to treat illnesses and protect the health of Chinese people. Today, many Chinese still have faith in traditional Chinese medicine and pharmacology, even though Western medicine has been practiced in China for years. Some believe that traditional Chinese medicine provides permanent cure for an illness, while Western medicine merely alleviates the symptoms.

Traditional Chinese medicine and pharmacology, taking the ancient Daoist ideas of 阴阳 [yīnyáng] (yin-yang) and 五行 [wǔxíng] (wu xing: the five elements) as a theoretical basis, strive to explain the various physiological and pathological phenomena and their interactions. Together, these ideas form a complete scientific system, unique in both theory and practice, containing interconnected elements of physiology, pathology, and pharmacology for the prevention, diagnosis, and treatment of diseases.

The Daoist 阴阳 concept has become the theoretical premise of traditional Chinese medicine. According to the 阴阳 concept, excitement suggests that the human body is in the state of 阳, while the state of 阴 inevitably results in depression. 阳 predominates during the day and turns into 阴 after dark. The human body is regarded as the universe in miniature. When the 阴 and 阳 elements in a person's body are well balanced, the person is in good health. A person falls sick when the balance is disrupted.

Like the 阴阳 concept, the concept of 五行 constitutes a fundamental theoretical premise of traditional Chinese medicine. Each vital organ of the human body is seen as belonging, by nature, to one of the five elements: earth, wood, metal, fire, and water. The five vital organs, the heart, the liver, the spleen, the lungs, and the kidneys are interlocked in a generative-subjugating relationship. It is believed that a pathological change in any of the vital organs will result in an abnormal function of other organs.

Street-side traditional Chinese pharmacies are common in China.
The concepts of 阴 [yīn], 阳 [yáng], and the balance of 气 [qì] are the essence of Chinese medicine.

Chinese herbal medicine is becoming popular outside Chinese communities.

The sea horse is an ingredient used in Chinese medicine.

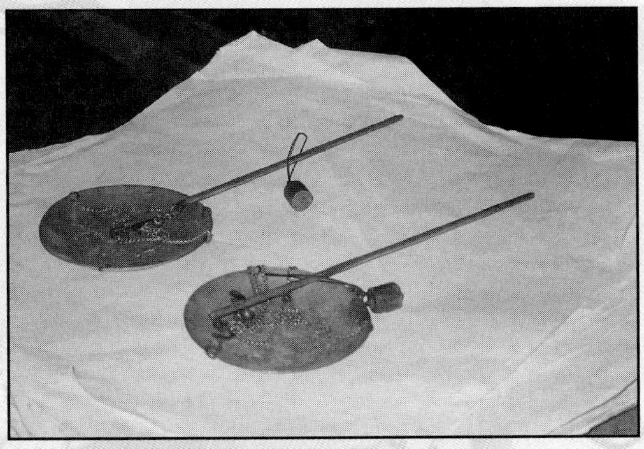

A tiny balancing scale is used to measure the herbal ingredients in Chinese medicine. The white square paper sheets are commonly used to wrap the ingredients after weighing.

A mortar and pestle are used to grind the medicine or mix the ingredients.

The traditional Chinese pharmacy consists mainly of natural medicinal materials — plants, animal parts, minerals of medicinal value, some chemical compounds, and biological drugs. For over 4,000 years, Chinese people have used herbal medicine to treat diseases. Hundreds of pharmacological works were compiled in ancient times and the most important is 本草纲目 [Běncǎogāngmù] (The Compendium of Material Medica) by 李时珍 [Lǐ Shízhēn] (Li, Shizhen) (1518–1593) of the Ming Dynasty. So far, specialists in traditional Chinese medicine have identified the therapeutic value of more than 8,000 medicinal materials, of which over 6,000 are plants.

Traditional Chinese medicine attaches great importance to the prevention of diseases, and Chinese people believe prevention of diseases is more important than treatment. To live a long, healthy life, Chinese people are faithful to traditional ways of maintaining physical and mental soundness by leading a regulated life, eating the type of diet that best fits their body conditions, and doing 气功 [qìgōng] (*qigong*), 太极拳 [tàijíquán] (*tai chi*), and 武术 [wǔshù] (*martial arts*) exercises. 气功 is a general term referring to different sets of regulated and controlled breathing exercises and is generally believed to allow the body and mind to regulate their functions in a completely natural state of relaxation and ease. 武术, or 功夫 [gōngfu] (*kung fu*) as it is better known in the West, was in fact a kind of martial art for hand-to-hand combat in ancient times. In modern times, however, people practice 武术 just for exercise. 武术 and 气功 are closely linked, hence the saying "without proper training in 气功, one will never master the art of 武术." A typical example of this combination is the Chinese shadow boxing known as 太极拳, which features high concentration of the mind and slow, regulated breathing accompanying rhythmical motions of the arms, legs, and body.

The other important way Chinese people keep fit is to cook food with herbs. This is sometimes called 食疗 [shíliáo] "treatment of diseases by food." For example, pears steamed with crystal rock sugar can cure bronchitis. Of course, acupuncture and moxibustion are also major ways of treating illnesses in traditional Chinese medicine.

Questions:

1. What's your opinion about the Daoist concept and traditional Chinese medicine?
2. Have you ever tried traditional Chinese medicine? Did it work?
3. Do you practice martial arts (kung fu) or any other hand-to-hand combat skill, e.g., boxing, karate, tae kwon do, tai chi, judo . . . ? Why?
4. Do you know any 食补 [shí bǔ] ("treatment of diseases by food") recipes?

趣味中文 FUN WITH CHINESE

良药苦口，忠言逆耳。

Good medicines are bitter, good advice is never pleasant to the ear.

liáng	yào	kǔ	kǒu,	zhōng	yán	nì	ěr.
良	药	苦	口，	忠	言	逆	耳。
good	medicine	bitter	mouth,	loyal	words	against	ear.

Question:

Do you believe "良药苦口，忠言逆耳"? Why or why not?

行动吧！ LET'S GO!

西瓜霜润喉片
Watermelon Frost Throat Lozenges

When 王中 visited his relatives in Beijing he got a sore throat. His aunt gave him some medicine. Let's study it.

Suggested procedure:

(1) Skim through to see how much of it you can understand.
(2) Study the useful words and expressions and then try to translate them into English.
(3) What are the spoken forms of items such as 良, 与, 服药, 含服, 至, etc.?
(4) Use your own words to retell the information. Try to use spoken forms instead of written forms.

Useful words and expressions:

西瓜 [xīguā]: watermelon
中药(中藥) [zhōngyào]: Chinese medicine
润喉片(潤喉片) [rùnhóu piàn]: throat lozenge
品种(品種) [pǐnzhǒng]: variety, assortment
咽喉 [yānhóu]: throat
良药(良藥) [liángyào]: good medicine
与 [yǔ]: (written form) and
双重(雙重) [shuāngchóng]: double
霜 [shuāng]: frost
名牌 [míngpái]: famous brand
产品(產品) [chǎnpǐn]: product
国家(國家) [guójiā]: country, nation
保护(保護) [bǎohù]: to protect
新一代 [xīnyídài]: new generation
口腔 [kǒuqiāng]: oral cavity
治疗(治療) [zhìliáo]: to treat, cure
预防(預防) [yùfáng]: to prevent
作用 [zuòyòng]: effect

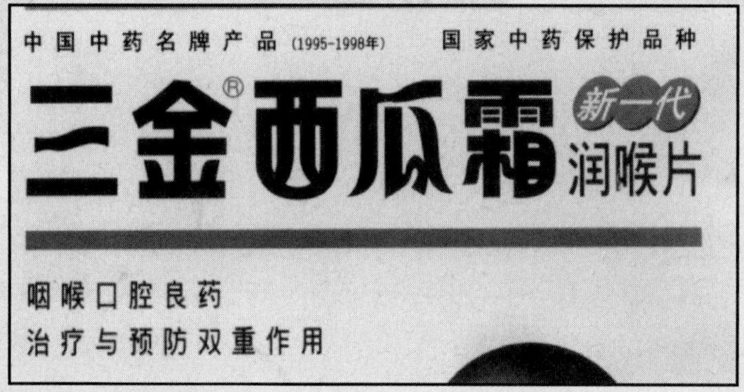

(5) Translate the information below into English:

New words:

主要 [zhǔyào]: main
薄荷脑(薄荷腦) [bòhenǎo]: menthol; peppermint camphor
利 [lì]: to benefit
消肿(消腫) [xiāozhǒng]: to reduce the swelling
嘶哑(嘶啞) [sīyǎ]: hoarse
用量 [yòngliàng]: dosage
服 [fú]: to take (medicine)
成分 [chéngfèn] ingredient
功能 [gōngnéng]: function
主治 [zhǔzhì]: main cure
咽 [yàn]: to swallow
止痛 [zhǐtòng]: to relieve pain
防治 [fángzhì]: to prevent
用法 [yòngfǎ]: usage
含 [hán]: to keep in the mouth

a. 主要成分：西瓜霜，冰片，薄荷脑等
b. 功能主治：清音利咽，消肿止痛，用于防治咽喉肿痛，声音嘶哑，喉咙痛等
c. 用法用量：含服，每小时含二至四片

第二十课
LESSON

20 我把小谢带来了...
I've Brought Xiao Xie Over . . .

教学目标 OBJECTIVES

- Rent an apartment
- Indicate the direction of a movement
- Describe an event and its cause

Safe and peaceful residence, special phone line: 9310278, apartment building management and maintenance company

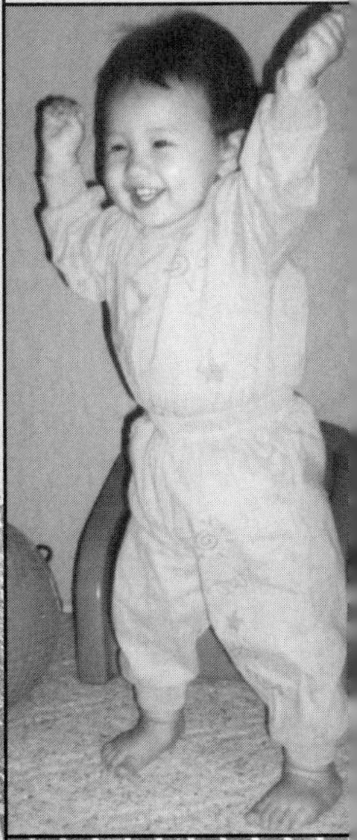

She wants to walk over.
她想走过去。*(走 [zǒu] to walk)*

Warm-up Exercises:
琳琳宝宝 [Línlin bǎobao] (Baby Linlin) on the move. You will learn to use directional complements (see grammar notes) to describe what 琳琳宝宝 can do or wants to do. Instructor may lead the students (use the grammar notes as a reference) to say these actions, then students may try on their own. For example, photo (1) 站: 她想站起来。

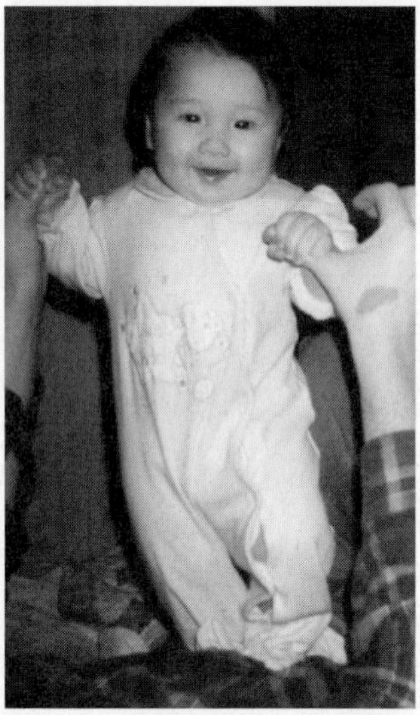

(1) Stand up (站 [zhàn] to stand)

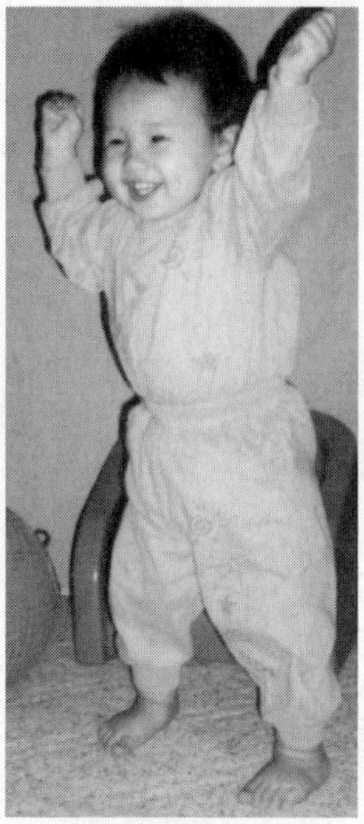

(2) Walk over (走 [zǒu] to walk)

(3) Crawl over (爬 [pá] to crawl)

(4) Slide down (滑 [huá] to slide)

(5) Crawl in and out (爬 [pá] to crawl)

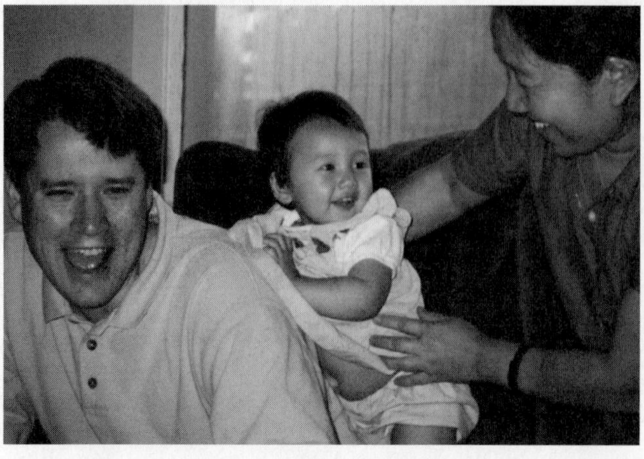

(6) Jump on (跳 [tiào] to jump)

(7) Run back and forth (跑 [pǎo] to run)

(8) It's such fun she doesn't want to come down.

Now try to use 把 [bǎ] and directional complements to describe what 琳琳宝宝 does below:

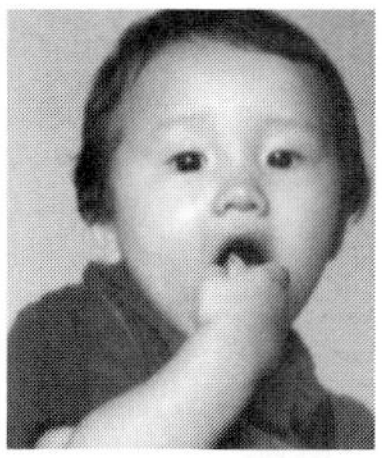

(9) Put stuff in her mouth (放 [fàng] to put)

(10) Pick up the shoes and put them on (捡 [jiǎn] to pick; 穿 [chuān] to put on)

(11) Hold the cup and drink the water (拿 [ná] to hold; 喝 [hē] to drink)

(12) Push little sister back and forth (推 [tuī] to push)

生词 VOCABULARY

核心词 Core Vocabulary

SIMPLIFIED	TRADITIONAL	PINYIN		
1. 把	把	bǎ	Prep.	(introduces the object of a verb)
2. 带来	帶來	dàilái	V.C.	to bring over
3. 啊	啊	a	Int.	(used at the end of a sentence to indicate surprise)
4. 进	進	jìn	V.	to enter
5. 搬	搬	bān	V.	to move
6. 出	出	chū	V.	to be out
7. 出去	出去	chūqù	V.C.	to go out
8. 过来	過來	guòlái	V.C.	to come over
9. 做饭	做飯	zuòfàn	V.O.	to cook
10. 吸烟	吸煙	xīyān	V.O.	to smoke
11. 没关系	沒關係	méiguānxi		no problem
12. 以前	以前	yǐqián	N.	before; previously
13. 但是	但是	dànshì	Conj.	but
14. 女朋友	女朋友	nǚpéngyou	N.	girlfriend
15. 必须	必須	bìxū	Aux.	must
16. 第一天	第一天	dìyītiān	N.	first day
17. 付	付	fù	V.	to pay
18. 房租	房租	fángzū	N.	rent
19. 楼上	樓上	lóushàng	N.	upstairs
20. 马上	馬上	mǎshàng	Adv.	immediately

专名 Proper Nouns

SIMPLIFIED	TRADITIONAL	PINYIN		
1. 常天	常天	Cháng Tiān	N.	(name) Tian Chang
2. 夏中明	夏中明	Xià Zhōngmíng	N.	(name) Zhongming Xia
3. 谢进学	謝進學	Xiè Jìnxué	N.	(name) Jinxue Xie

补充词 Supplementary Vocabulary

SIMPLIFIED	TRADITIONAL	PINYIN		
1. 房东	房東	fángdōng	N.	landlord
2. 房客	房客	fángkè	N.	tenant
3. 签约	簽約	qiānyuē	V.O.	to sign a contract
4. 租屋	租屋	zūwū	V.O.	to rent a house

语文知识 LANGUAGE LINK

The Sentence Patterns provide models that will help you with the Language in Use section. In both sections, pay attention to the grammar points, vocabulary, and expressions.

句型 Sentence Patterns

A: 我把我朋友带来了。
Wǒ bǎ wǒ péngyou dài lái le.

B: 快请他进来。
Kuài qǐng tā jìnlái.

A: 我们这儿有一个人搬出去了，
Wǒmen zhèr yǒu yíge rén bān chūqù le,
你要不要搬进来?
nǐ yàobuyào bān jìnlái?

B: 太好了！我可以先过去看看吗?
Tài hǎo le! Wǒ kěyǐ xiān guòqù kànkan ma?

A: 请你下来帮我把桌子
Qǐng nǐ xiàlái bāng wǒ bǎ zhuōzi
搬上去，好吗?
bān shàngqu, hǎo ma?

B: 好的，我马上下去。
Hǎo de, wǒ mǎshàng xiàqu.

课文 Language in Use: 我把小谢带来了. . . Wǒ bǎ Xiǎo Xiè dài lái le . . .

常天: 中明，我回来了。我把车开回来了，还把小谢也带来了。
Zhōngmíng, wǒ huílái le. Wǒ bǎ chē kāi huílái le, hái bǎ Xiǎo Xiè yě dàilái le.

夏中明: 是小谢啊! 快请他进来。
Shì Xiǎo Xiè a! Kuài qǐng tā jìnlái.

谢进学: 我听说你们这儿有一个人搬出去了，我想搬进来，
Wǒ tīngshuō nǐmen zhèr yǒu yíge rén bān chūqù le, wǒ xiǎng bān jìnlái,
所以过来看看。
suǒyǐ guòlái kànkan.

常天: 你不想住宿舍了，是不是?
Nǐ bù xiǎng zhù sùshè le, shìbushì?

谢进学: 是的。宿舍太小了，我想搬出来住。这儿可以不可以做饭?
Shì de. Sùshè tài xiǎo le, wǒ xiǎng bān chūlái zhù. Zhèr kěyǐbukěyǐ zuòfàn?

夏中明: 可以，我们有厨房。
Kěyǐ, wǒmen yǒu chúfáng.

谢进学: 太好了! 我很喜欢做饭。搬出来以后就可以常常
Tài hǎo le! Wǒ hěn xǐhuān zuòfàn. Bān chūlái yǐhòu jiù kěyǐ chángcháng
做饭了。
zuòfàn le.

夏中明: 你吸烟吗? 我们这儿不能吸烟。
Nǐ xīyān ma? Wǒmen zhèr bùnéng xīyān.

谢进学： 没关系。以前我吸烟，但是我女朋友说我不应该吸烟，
Méiguānxi. Yǐqián wǒ xīyān, dànshì wǒ nǚpéngyou shuō wǒ bù yīnggāi xīyān,

所以我现在不吸烟了。
suǒyǐ wǒ xiànzài bù xīyān le.

夏中明： 还有，我们必须在每个月的第一天付房租。
Háiyǒu, wǒmen bìxū zài měigeyuè de dìyītiān fù fángzū.

谢进学： 没问题！
Méi wèntí!

常天： 喂，小谢，我在楼上，你要不要上来看看？中明，
Wèi, Xiǎo Xiè, wǒ zài lóushàng, nǐ yàobuyào shànglái kànkan? Zhōngmíng,

你把小谢带上来看看吧。
nǐ bǎ Xiǎo Xiè dài shànglái kànkan ba.

夏中明： 常天，我们现在还不能上去。你得先下来帮我把
Chángtiān, wǒmen xiànzài hái bùnéng shàngqu. Nǐ děi xiān xiàlái bāng wǒ bǎ

这张桌子搬上去。
zhèzhāng zhuōzi bān shàngqu.

常天： 好的，我马上下去。
Hǎode, wǒ mǎshàng xiàqu.

注释 LANGUAGE NOTES

小谢

小谢 literally means "Little Xie." Here it refers to 谢进学.
In Mainland China, 老 (old) or 小 (young, little) + surname is a friendly and informal way to address familiar people who are older or younger than you.

吸烟

吸烟 [xīyān] and 抽烟 [chōuyān] are both common terms used for "smoke a cigarette."

但是 and 可是

Both 但是 and 可是 mean "but." 可是 is more colloquial than 但是.

必须

必须 is an optative verb meaning "must," "be required to."

序数

第 is used for ordinal numbers. For example, 第一 (the first), 第二 (the second), 第三 (the third), and 第一天 (the first day).

语法 GRAMMAR

Directional Complement 趋向补语 (DC)

A. The simple directional complement (simple DC)

来 and 去 are often attached to a verb to form a simple directional complement to indicate the direction of a motion. When the motion is towards the speaker, 来 is used. When the motion is away from the speaker, 去 is used. The following are some examples of simple directional complements.

Motion verbs + 来/去

Motion verbs	上 upward	下 downward	进 enter	出 outward	回 return	过 cross	起 up	搬 move	带 take with
来	上来	下来	进来	出来	回来	过来	起来	搬来	带来
去	上去	下去	进去	出去	回去	过去		搬去	带去

- 起 can only be combined with 来, forming 起来

Verb + Object (e.g., place, people) + 来/去

他回宿舍去了。
你们都进客厅去吧!
我带我女朋友来了。

B. Compound directional complement (Compound DC)
The simple directional complements 上来(去), 下来(去), 进来(去), 出来(去), 回来(去), 过来(去), and 起来 may be attached to other verbs to function as complements indicating the direction of movement. They are called compound directional complements.

Their combination possibilities are illustrated below:

Common action verbs:

走 [zǒu] to walk	跑 [pǎo] to run	跳 [tiào] to jump	坐 [zuò] to sit
站 [zhàn] to stand	搬 [bān] to move	带 [dài] to bring	
拿 [ná] to take	掉 [diào] to fall	捡 [jiǎn] to pick	

上来/上去:	坐上来	坐下去	跑上来	跑下去	
下来/下去:	走下来	走下去	跳下来	跳下去	掉下去
进来/进去:	走进来	走进去	拿进来	拿进去	
出来/出去:	搬出来	搬出去	带进来	带出去	
回来/回去:	跑回来	拿回来	跑回去	拿回去	
过来/过去:	带过来	搬过来	带过去	搬过去	
起来:	站起来	跳起来	拿起来	捡起来	

- The verbs such as 走, 跑, 跳, 拿 (walk, run, jump, pick) state the action.
- The simple directional complement indicates the direction of the action in relation to a location. It also can indicate the direction of the motion towards or away from the speaker.

Verb + Object (e.g., person, thing) + simple DC

他	要搬	桌子	过来。	
Subject	V.	Object	simple DC	
他	带	一瓶酒	回来	了。
	V.			

Note: 起来 has an idiomatic usage. Its object should be placed as below:

他拿起来一本书。
他拿起书来。

把 Sentences

把 sentences are used to stress the effects of an action upon its object. Their structure is illustrated below:

Subject + 把 + Object + Verb-complement

The following are some characteristics of 把 sentences:

- Used most often with action verbs.
- The object must be definite.
- The verb must incorporate a complement.
- Commonly occurs in imperative sentences. For example, 把饭吃了！(Eat your meal!); 把他带来！(Bring him over!); 把车开回来！(Drive the car back!)
- The common complements involved with 把 structures are:

  a. degree of complement 他把这个字写得很好。
  b. 了 may be used as complement for a 把 structure to indicate completion of an action. 我把汤喝了。
  c. directional complement 我要把那张桌子搬过去。
  d. resultative complement (will be introduced later) 他把我的杯子打破 [dǎpò] (break) 了。
  e. duration and frequency complements (will be introduced later) 他把这个汉字写了十遍。

把 Sentences and the Directional Complement

Group A	Group B
我带来我的室友了。	我把我室友带来了。
我搬来那张桌子了。	我把那张桌子搬来了。
我带我的手机过去了。	我把我的手机带过去了。

- With the directional complement, if there is a definite object of the action, the 把 structure (Group B) is preferred.
- The examples in Group A are not often used. They simply describe an event. However, the examples in Group B also imply that the location of the object has been changed due to (related to) the subject. That is, the subject is the cause of the change.

把 Construction

The 把 construction is also called a "disposal" construction. That is, the 把 sentence usually indicates that the object is disposed of, dealt with, or affected by the subject. Choosing a 把 construction or a non-把 construction is not an easy task. However, there are some guidelines listed below:

I. Situations in which the 把 construction is usually **preferred:**

1. The speaker wants to emphasize that an action has caused the object to change position or change from one state to another.

e.g., (a) 我吃了那包药。 I took that medicine.
(b) 我把那包药吃了。 I took that medicine.

Example (a) is a simple statement of fact. Example (b) emphasizes that the medicine has been taken by the subject and is gone.

2. If there is a long or complicated direct object, a 把 construction is preferred.

   e.g., 我把我妈妈昨天从药房买回来的那包药吃了。

3. The 把 construction is preferred in imperative sentences (commands).

   e.g., 把那包药吃了!

II. Situations in which the 把 construction is **obligatory** (there is no corresponding non-把 construction):

1. With some resultative complements (结果补语) (introduced in a later lesson).

   Subject 把 Object V. + 成 (into/to); V. + 做 (as); V. + 在; V. + 到

   e.g., 写成 [xiěchéng]: to write A as B
   他把那个故事写成小说了。 He wrote that story as a novel.

   e.g., 当做 [dàngzuò]: to treat as
   我把她当作自己的女儿。 I treated her as my own daughter.

   e.g., 停在 [tíngzài]: to park
   我把我的车停在河边。 I parked my car by the river.

   e.g., 放到 [fàngdào]: to put, place
   我把你的书放到桌上。 I placed your book on the desk.

2. If a sentence has a plural object and the adverb 都, the 把 construction must be used.

   e.g., 我把我们的书都卖 [mài] (to sell) 了。 I sold all our books.

III. Verbs that **cannot** be used in the 把 construction:

There are certain verbs that do not allow a "disposal" explanation. Therefore they cannot be used in the 把 construction. The following is a sample list of verbs that are incompatible with the 把 construction:

1. Intransitive verbs: 来 (to come), 去 (to go), 跑 (to run), 走 (to walk), 旅行 (to travel), 毕业 (to graduate), 工作 (to work), 站 (to stand), 坐 (to sit)
2. Existence verbs: 是 (to be), 在 (to be at), 有 (to have)
3. Emotion verbs: 喜欢 (to like), 爱 (to love), 怕 [pà] (to fear)
4. Sensory perception verbs: 会 (to be able to), 知道 (to know), 认识 (to recognize), 觉得 [juéde] (to think, to feel), 希望 [xīwàng] (to hope), 看见 [kànjiàn] (to see), 听见 [tīngjiàn] (to hear)
5. Others: 欢迎 (to welcome), 赞成 [zànchéng] (to approve)

补充课文 SUPPLEMENTARY PRACTICE

This selection will help you test your comprehension of the grammar and vocabulary you have learned in this lesson. Be prepared to answer questions about the meaning of the passage.

四月二十日 星期三 多云

今天常天开车把我带到他住的地方去了。他和夏中明一起住在校外的一个公寓楼里。前几天他们楼上有一个人搬出去了，昨天常天把这个消息告诉了我。我很想去看看，如果那儿很好，我也想搬过去。我不想住在宿舍里了。宿舍太小，又不能做饭。我喜欢自己做饭，我做饭也做得很好。

中明告诉我他们那儿有厨房，常天把我带上去看了一下，我觉得还不错，不大也不小，也很干净。中明还告诉我他们那儿不能吸烟。不过这对我来说没关系，因为我现在已经不吸烟了。其实吸烟真的很不好，我女朋友也说我不应该吸烟，所以我就把烟戒了。

常天说他们必须每个月的第一天付房租，这也没问题，我一定会按时付房租的。

我想明天给房东打电话，希望我能早一点儿搬过去。

Notes: 多云 [duōyún]: cloudy
对我来说 [duì wǒ lái shuō]: to me
没关系 [méiguānxi]: it doesn't matter
其实 [qíshí]: as a matter of fact
戒(烟) [jiè(yān)]: to quit (smoking)
按时 [ànshí]: on time, punctually
房东 [fángdōng]: landlord
希望 [xīwàng]: to hope

练习 ACTIVITIES

I. Pinyin Exercises

20-1 Listen to the instructor, then write the Pinyin for the following expressions:

1. 吸烟 ________	2. 没关系 ________	3. 必须 ________
4. 搬出去 ________	5. 付房租 ________	6. 走过来 ________

20-2 Listen to the instructor and fill in each blank with the correct Pinyin:

1. _____面_____雨了，我们进_____吧！
2. 我_____来了，我也_____晚饭_____回来了。
3. 我_____在_____饭呢，很好_____，你们_____来_____吧！
4. 我以_____很_____欢_____烟，_____是_____在不吸烟了。
5. 我们_____在_____个_____的_____一天_____房_____。

20-3 Read the following Chinese poem, paying special attention to the tones and rhythm:

Huí Xiāng ǒu Shū **(Hè Zhīzhāng)**	**回乡偶书** **(贺知章)**
Shào xiǎo lí jiā lǎo dà huí, Xiāngyīn wú gǎi bìnmáo shuāi. Értóng xiāngjiàn bù xiāngshí, Xiào wèn kè cóng hé chù lái.	少小离家老大回， 乡音无改鬓毛衰。 儿童相见不相识， 笑问客从何处来。

Returning Home
(He, Zhizhang)

I left home young, returned old,
My accent changed not, although my hair grew thin.
The youngsters see me, but don't know me,
With smiles they ask where I come from.

II. Character Exercises

20-4 Read the following words and phrases:

带	第
带来	第一
带回来	第一次出去
把朋友带回来	第一次搬出去
把朋友带回来了	我第一次搬出去
我把我朋友从学校带回来了	这是我第一次搬出去

Now try to use the following characters to make words, phrases, and then sentences:

1. 吸 2. 关 3. 但 4. 付 5. 租 6. 必
7. 进 8. 楼 9. 帮 10. 马 11. 搬 12. 出

20-5 Write down the traditional forms for the following simplified characters:

1. 带 ______ 2. 关 ______ 3. 系 ______ 4. 进 ______
5. 欢 ______ 6. 须 ______ 7. 楼 ______ 8. 马 ______

III. Grammar Exercises

20-6 Substitution exercises:

1. 你带了什么回来?
我带了一个蛋糕回来。

买	一瓶可乐	回来
借	两本书	回来
搬	一张桌子	进来
拿	一条裙子	上去
送	一张电影票	出去

2. 你要他做什么了?
我要他把那瓶药拿过来。

那碗饭	买回来
他写的信	寄出去
这个月的房租	付出去
那张桌子	搬过去
这碗汤	喝下去

Note: 寄 [jì]: to mail

20-7 Directional complement:

A. *访客 (A visitor)*: Fill in the blanks with 来 or 去

小花： 明明，这就是我的宿舍，外面有点儿冷，我们进_____吧！
小雪，我回_____了，我也把明明带_____了。
小雪： 我在楼上，我正在看电影呢，很有意思 [yǒuyìsi] (interesting)，你们一起上_____看看吧！
明明： 我们等一下再上_____。
小花： 对了，秋雨在她的房间，我去叫她。
秋雨，请出_____，明明来了。
秋雨： 我知道了，我正在打电话，我马上就出_____见她。
明明： 秋雨，我把你要的书带_____了。
秋雨： 太好了，谢谢。
小花： 小雪，我们都在楼下，请你下_____，好吗?
小雪： 好，我马上下_____。
小花： 啊！你最后[zuìhòu] (finally) 总算 [zǒngsuàn] (at long last) 下_____了。

B. Answer the following questions:

1. 小花回去的时候，小雪正在做什么?
2. 秋雨在哪儿? 她正在做什么? 她什么时候出来?
3. 明明把什么东西带去给秋雨了?
4. 小雪最后 [zuìhòu] (finally) 下去了吗?

20-8 Rewrite the following sentences using "把":

1. 我介绍我的老师给他了。
2. 我带来了我的中文书。
3. 他穿上那件衬衫了。
4. 小方带来了这盘炒面。
5. 爸爸给我了那张地图。
6. 她搬去了那张桌子。
7. 他带去了他的中文作业。
8. 我室友搬来了他的电脑。

20-9 Picture description: Form groups of three. Use 把 and directional complements to tell a story (at least ten sentences).

Useful words and expressions:

钓鱼 [diàoyú]: to go fishing
钓鱼竿 [diàoyúgān]: fishing pole
水桶 [shuǐtǒng]: bucket
取水 [qǔshuǐ]: to fetch water
石头 [shítou]: stone
树 [shù]: tree
滑 [huá]: to slide
爬 [pá]: to climb
跳 [tiào]: to jump
掉 [diào]: to fall
挖土 [wātǔ]: to dig the earth

上去　下去　过来　过去

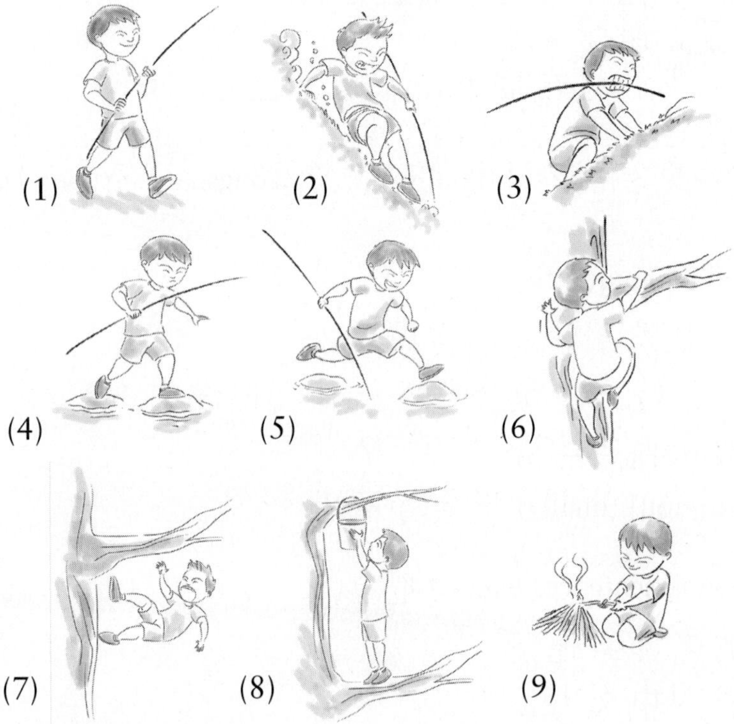

IV. Communicative Activities

20-10 Form pairs. Fill in the blanks with 把 and a directional complement:

A.1. 昨天我的好朋友要从纽约_____ _____看我，昨天下课以后，
(come over)

我从教室走_____ _____以后就_____宿舍_____了。
(go out) (return)

当 [dāng] (when) 我要开门_____ _____的时候，我的钥匙
(enter)

[yàoshi] (key) 不见了，我_____ _____ _____。
(cannot enter)

2. 我_____我的背包 [bēibāo] (backpack) _____ _____ _____
(pick up)
看看，还是没有。所以又_____ _____教室
(return to)
_____。我_____ _____ _____以后，_____桌子
(run and enter)

搬 _____ _____又搬_____ _____，我也_____书
(move the table back and forth)
_____ _____ _____看看，又_____ _____ _____，
(pick up the books) (put it down)
还是没找到 (cannot find it) 。

3. 后来 (later)，老师_____ _____了，她_____ _____
(enter) (come over)
问我怎么了？我告诉她我从宿舍
_____ _____ _____找我的钥匙 (key) 。
(run back)
老师_____她的书_____ _____ _____，里面有
(pick up her book)
一把钥匙(a key)

4. 那是我的钥匙 (key)，我高兴 [gāoxìng]
(happy) 地_____ _____ _____，原来 [yuánlái]
(jump up)
(adverb: indicating discovery of the truth) 我交 [jiāo]

(to submit) 作业的时候，不小心 (carelessness)_____
钥匙 (key) 也交_____ _____了。我说了谢谢，
(hand it in)
马上又 [yòu] (again) _____ _____宿舍_____了。
(run back)

B. Form pairs and act out the situation above.

20-11 Moving day! Classes will begin next week. There are a lot of students moving in and out around campus. You and your friends are chatting in the dorm. (Use the following hints to form your dialogue. Each person should contribute at least six sentences.)

A：明天我那儿有一个人要搬进来。
B：他要从哪儿搬来？
A：他要从纽约搬过来。
B：我的宿舍要搬走一个人。
A：他要搬到哪儿去...
B：...

从哪儿搬来： 芝加哥 [Zhījiāgē] (Chicago); 学校宿舍;
从哪儿搬走： 学校宿舍; 洛杉矶 [Luòshānjī] (Los Angeles)
搬到哪儿去： 三藩市 [Sānfānshì] (San Francisco); also called 旧金山 [Jiùjīnshān]
费城 [Fèichéng] (Philadelphia)

20-12 教练说 (The Coach Says . . .): You are a coach for a basketball team. The tournament is coming up soon. You are training your players. (Use 把 and the directional complement.)

For example,

比如： 把那个电视搬过来...
Hints: 桌子，椅子 [yǐzi] (chair)，三十本书，电脑，石头 [shítou] (stone)
跑 [pǎo] (to run) 上去(下来)，跳 [tiào] (to jump) 过去，
拿 [ná] (to take) 上去......

20-13 Potluck: You went to a potluck party at Teacher Wang's house. Every teacher brought a few dishes. You and your friends are chatting about the potluck party. (Form groups of three to make a dialogue. Each person should create at least five sentences. Try to use 把 sentences and the directional complement.)

Teachers	Dishes	Companion	Transportation
田 [Tián] 老师	蛋糕，绿茶	先生 [xiānsheng] (husband)	开车
黄老师	春卷 [chūnjuǎn] (spring roll)	孩子 [háizi] (child)	坐公车
吴老师	酸辣汤 [suān là tāng] (hot and sour soup)		走路
李老师	饺子	男朋友	骑自行车
梁 [Liáng] 老师	炒饭	太太 (wife)	走路
张老师	青岛啤酒 [Qīngdǎo píjiǔ] (Qingdao beer)		开车
方 [Fāng] 老师	不知道	孩子	骑自行车

For example,

田老师带了什么去?
田老师把谁带去了?
田老师是怎么过去的呢?
李老师呢?

20-14 Form groups of three. Use 把 and directional complements to describe the lesson pictures: *琳琳宝宝 on the move* (at least ten sentences).

文化知识 Culture Link

文化点滴 CULTURE NOTES

中国的住房改革 [Zhōngguó de zhùfáng gǎigé] Housing Reform in China

Ever since the founding of the People's Republic of China in 1949, China has practiced a policy of allocating houses to urban residents as a major part of their welfare benefits from the government or their work unit. Residents only pay a monthly fee for maintenance. In the late 1990s, China started to reform its housing system by implementing new policies on housing, taxation, and banking. More and more people in China now make it one of their lifetime goals to have their own home.

China has a huge population of 1.3 billion. To satisfy the housing needs of such a large population, many housing developers and realtors in Mainland China, Hong Kong, and Taiwan have seized this golden opportunity and jumped into China's housing market. They have focused on 公寓大楼 [gōngyù dàlóu] (apartment buildings) for the majority of residents in cities and towns, as well as 别墅 [biéshù] (mansions) on the outskirts of Beijing, Shanghai, Guangzhou, Shenzhen, and Zhuhai to meet the demands of high-income families, including those from other countries who are working in China. Statistics show that in the first ten months of 2001, over 95% of the apartment sales in Beijing went to individual buyers. From January to May, 2005, home sales in Beijing increased 40.6% over the same period in 2004.

According to a household survey, in the six cities of Beijing, Shanghai, Guangzhou, Dalian, Chengdu, and Xi'an, 28.2% of the residents bought apartments during 2000 and 2001 and 26.9% more planned to buy their own flats in the following two years. Moreover, a survey by the People's Bank of China in 2005 indicated that 19.1% of residents planned to purchase their own homes in the period of August to October 2005. These statistics illustrate that the demand for housing in China remains strong.

Funds for housing purchases are available to urban residents in China through various channels: 公积金 [gōngjījīn] (monetization of welfare housing allocation by work unit), 购房补贴 [gòufáng bǔtiē] (compensation for residents in redevelopment areas), and 房屋贷款 [fángwū dàikuǎn] (mortgages). A survey in Beijing found that most of the home buyers were 26–45 years old in the middle- and high-income groups, and the homes they purchased were mostly apartments with at least two bedrooms and a living room, with 81–150 square meters of living area.

The Chinese government has also made efforts to make housing easily available to low-income families. The government retrieves or purchases used apartments formerly occupied by government officials and staff, and rents them to low-income families at very low rents.

High-rise buildings in Hong Kong (left) and Shanghai (right).

Luxury homes in Taiwan.

A traditional study room.

A traditional bedroom.

A traditional living room.

China's housing market is still maturing and has quite a few problems, such as inflated prices, deceptive advertisements, arbitrarily enforced fees, and substandard management. However, the housing departments of the government have been taking measures to settle these problems and protect the legitimate rights and interests of the general public.

The per capita housing space in China in 2005 is less than 18 square meters. With the increase in people's incomes and the reform of the housing system, it is certain that more and more Chinese will have their own houses in the near future.

Questions:

1. Do you have any relatives or friends who live in China? Have you been to their homes? Are they different from homes in the U.S.?
2. Have you ever been to any other countries? What was the housing situation like?
3. Draw your dream house on the blackboard. Describe it to the class.

趣味中文 FUN WITH CHINESE

秀才不出门，能知天下事。
A learned person doesn't need to go out, but is able to know everything.

xiùcai	bù	chū	mén,	néng	zhī	tiānxià	shì.
秀才	不	出	门，	能	知	天下	事。
learned person	not	out	door,	can	know	world	matter.

Question:

Form groups of two to four. Have a conversation (in English) using "秀才不出门，能知天下事." Try to make it interesting or funny. Next try to speak several sentences in Chinese using what you've learned.

行动吧！ LET'S GO!

出租和出售房子
Houses for Rent and Houses for Sale

This is 明远's office. He is currently working intensively on two projects. Look at the signs below and then answer the following questions:

Useful words and expressions:

办公室(辦公室) [bàngōngshì]: office
租屋 [zūwū]: rental house
个案(個案) [gè'àn]: case, project
地产(地產) [dìchǎn]: real estate
案名 [ànmíng]: case title
价格(價格) [jiàgé]: price
万(萬) [wàn]: ten thousand
新第 [xīndì]: new house
特点(特點) [tèdiǎn]: features
日式 [rìshì]: Japanese style
豪宅 [háozhái]: luxury residential houses
接待中心 [jiēdài zhōngxīn]: receiving center

办公室

个案(1)

个案(2)

Questions:

1. 明远是做什么的？他的公司叫什么？电话号码是什么？
2. 个案(1)：案名：阳光新第，价格：390 万
   (Is the house for sale a new house or an old house? How much does it cost?)
3. 个案(2)：在卖什么样的房子，特点是什么？

复习 Review

LESSON 19 AND LESSON 20

Conversation

Make a phone call to invite your friend to your dorm to prepare for next week's exam. Your friend is sick and has to see a doctor. Try to include the following questions in the conversation:

1. 喂，请问……在吗？(You may refer to Lesson 9 "打电话" for phone manners)
2. ……去我宿舍一起复习准备考试好吗？
3. 我生病了(不舒服、头疼、发烧、感冒、咳嗽……)
4. 你怎么生病了呢？
5. 你看医生了没有？吃药了没有？

Situational Dialogues

You and your friends are chatting about your dorm. Try to include the following questions in the conversation:

1. 你住哪儿？离学校近不近？
2. 你的宿舍/公寓 [gōngyù] (apartment) 怎么样？好不好？你想搬出来吗？想搬到什么地方？
3. 你们每个月什么时候付房租？房东(landlord)怎么样？
4. 你喜欢做饭吗？

Simplified and Traditional Characters

Read each traditional character aloud. Then write the corresponding simplified character beside it. Finally make a phrase and a sentence using the character.

For example, 學 → 学 → 学生 → 我是学生。

L19: 頭 ( ) 發 ( ) 燒 ( ) 醫 ( ) 藥 ( ) 準 ( ) 備 ( ) 筆 ( )

L20: 帶 ( ) 進 ( ) 煙 ( ) 關 ( ) 係 ( ) 須 ( ) 樓 ( ) 馬 ( )

第二十一课
LESSON
21

暑假你要做什么？
What Will You Do During the Summer Vacation?

教学目标 OBJECTIVES

- Talk about plans
- Express blessings and wishes

Graduation day at a university.

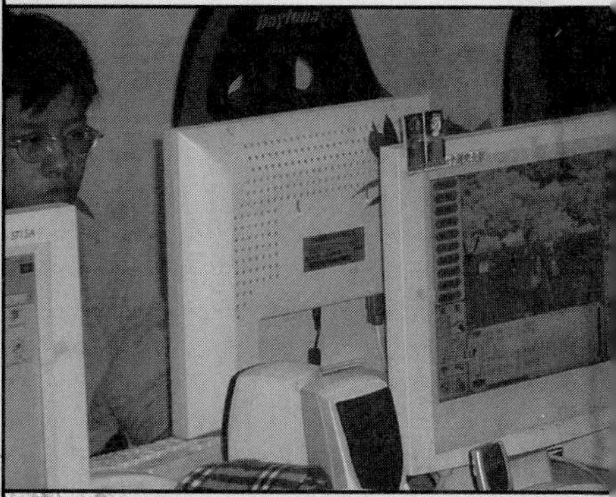

Computer company internships are popular.

College students find part-time jobs at places such as fast-food restaurants, coffee shops, and learning centers.

生词 VOCABULARY

核心词 Core Vocabulary

SIMPLIFIED	TRADITIONAL	PINYIN		
1. 暑假	暑假	shǔjià	N.	summer vacation
2. 毕业	畢業	bìyè	V.	to graduate
3. 决定	決定	juédìng	V.	to decide
4. 申请	申請	shēnqǐng	V.	to apply
5. 研究生院	研究生院	yánjiūshēngyuàn	N.	graduate school
6. 国外	國外	guówài	N.	overseas, abroad
7. 留学	留學	liúxué	V.O.	to study abroad
8. 找	找	zhǎo	V.	to seek; look for
9. 打工	打工	dǎgōng	V.O.	to work for others; to be employed
10. 家	家	jiā	M.W.	(measure word for company, enterprise, store, etc.)
11. 公司	公司	gōngsī	N.	company
12. 实习	實習	shíxí	N.	internship
13. 电脑	電腦	diànnǎo	N.	computer
14. 暑期	暑期	shǔqī	N.	summer
15. 班	班	bān	N.	class
16. 一面	一面	yímiàn	Adv.	at the same time
17. 有意思	有意思	yǒuyìsi	Adj.	interesting, enjoyable
18. 愉快	愉快	yúkuài	Adj.	happy
19. 一路平安	一路平安	yílùpíng'ān		have a pleasant journey
20. 好运	好運	hǎoyùn		good luck

专名 Proper Nouns

SIMPLIFIED	TRADITIONAL	PINYIN		
1. 程海华	程海華	Chéng Hǎihuá	N.	(name) Haihua Cheng
2. 白秋雨	白秋雨	Bái Qiūyǔ	N.	(name) Quiyu Bai
3. 加州	加州	Jiāzhōu	N.	California

补充词 Supplementary Vocabulary

SIMPLIFIED	TRADITIONAL	PINYIN		
1. 大学生	大學生	dàxuéshēng	N.	college students
2. 研究生	研究生	yánjiūshēng	N.	graduate students
3. 博士生	博士生	bóshìshēng	N.	doctoral students
4. 学位	學位	xuéwèi	N.	degree
5. 学士	學士	xuéshì	N.	bachelor's degree
6. 硕士	碩士	shuòshì	N.	master's degree
7. 博士	博士	bóshì	N.	doctoral degree
8. 简历 (履历表)	簡歷 (履歷表)	jiǎnlì (lǚlìbiǎo)	N.	resumé

语文知识 LANGUAGE LINK

The Sentence Patterns provide models that will help you with the Language in Use section. In both sections, pay attention to the grammar points, vocabulary, and expressions.

句型 Sentence Patterns

A: 毕业以后你想做什么?
Bìyè yǐhòu nǐ xiǎng zuò shénme?

B: 我想申请研究生院。
Wǒ xiǎng shēnqǐng yánjiūshēngyuàn.

A: 今年暑假你要做什么？
Jīnnián shǔjià nǐ yào zuò shénme?

B: 我要去一家公司做暑期实习。
Wǒ yào qù yìjiā gōngsī zuò shǔqī shíxí.

A: 你去中国做什么？
Nǐ qù Zhōngguó zuò shénme?

B: 我想在那儿一面旅行，
Wǒ xiǎng zài nàr yímiàn lǚxíng,

一面学中文。
yímiàn xué Zhōngwén.

A: 祝你工作愉快！
Zhù nǐ gōngzuò yúkuài!

B: 祝你一路平安！祝你好运！
Zhù nǐ yílùpíng'ān! Zhù nǐ hǎoyùn!

课文 Language in Use: 暑假你要做什么？Shǔjià nǐyào zuò shénme?

程海华： 秋雨，我问你，你明年就要毕业了，毕业以后你想做什么？
Qiūyǔ, wǒ wèn nǐ, nǐ míngnián jiùyào bìyè le, bìyè yǐhòu nǐ xiǎng zuò shénme?

白秋雨： 我还没有决定呢。可是我很喜欢学习，我可能会
Wǒ hái méiyǒu juédìng ne. Kěshì wǒ hěn xǐhuān xuéxí, wǒ kěnéng huì

申请研究生院，或者去国外留学。你呢？
shēnqǐng yánjiūshēngyuàn, huòzhě qù guówài liúxué. Nǐ ne?

你什么时候毕业？
Nǐ shénme shíhou bìyè?

程海华： 我还有两年才毕业呢。毕业以后我想去找工作。
Wǒ háiyǒu liǎngnián cái bìyè ne. Bìyè yǐhòu wǒ xiǎng qù zhǎo gōngzuò.

白秋雨：我们就要放暑假了，今年暑假你要做什么？
Wǒmen jiùyào fàng shǔjià le, jīnnián shǔjià nǐ yào zuò shénme?

程海华：我要去打工。我要去一家公司实习。
Wǒ yào qù dǎgōng. Wǒ yào qù yìjiā gōngsī shíxí.

白秋雨：在哪儿？是什么工作？
Zài nǎr? Shì shénme gōngzuò?

程海华：在加州，是一家电脑公司。你呢？暑假你要做什么？
Zài Jiāzhōu, shì yìjiā diànnǎo gōngsī. Nǐ ne? Shǔjià nǐ yào zuò shénme?

白秋雨：我要去中国，我申请了去上海的暑期班学习，
Wǒ yào qù Zhōngguó, wǒ shēnqǐng le qù Shànghǎi de shǔqībān xuéxí,

我想一面学中文，一面在中国旅行。
wǒ xiǎng yímiàn xué Zhōngwén, yímiàn zài Zhōngguó lǚxíng.

程海华：那一定很有意思。你什么时候去？
Nà yídìng hěn yǒuyìsi. Nǐ shénme shíhou qù?

白秋雨：下个星期。
Xiàge xīngqī.

程海华：这么快！你到中国以后要常常给我写电子邮件。
Zhème kuài! Nǐ dào Zhōngguó yǐhòu yào chángcháng gěi wǒ xiě diànzǐ yóujiàn.

白秋雨：没问题。我祝你工作愉快！
Méi wèntí. Wǒ zhù nǐ gōngzuò yúkuài!

程海华：我也祝你一路平安！祝你好运！
Wǒ yě zhù nǐ yílùpíng'ān! Zhù nǐ hǎoyùn!

注释 LANGUAGE NOTES

研究生院(研究所)

研究生 means "graduate students." To refer to "graduate school," 研究生院 is used in Mainland China, while 研究所 is used in Taiwan.

打工(工读) and 实习

打工 means "work study." 工读 is another common term meaning "work study." 实习 means "intern" or "internship." 暑期实习 means "summer internship."

语法 GRAMMAR

一面……一面……

一面……一面…… is a conjunction expressing simultaneous actions. For example,

他一面看电视，一面吸烟。
我想一面学中文，一面在中国旅行。

Similiarly, 一边……一边…… is also a conjunction used to indicate two actions that are carried out at the same time. For example,

他一边听音乐，一边看书。
我喜欢一边看书一边吃东西。

一 in 一边 can be omitted as in 边……边…… while 一 in 一面 has to be present. For example,

他常常边吃饭，边看电脑。

语法总复习 (1): Summary of the Aspects of Verbs

Chinese is a non-inflectional language. That means it generally does not change word endings to reflect person, gender, tense, number, or case. For example, the verb "work" in English can change to forms such as "worked," "is working," or "had worked" to indicate different aspects of the action. In Chinese, the time of an action (past, present, or future) is usually expressed by time words such as 去年, 现在, and 明天, rather than by changing the ending of the verb.

Moreover, the various aspects of an action (e.g., progressive, completion, continuous, about to happen, or showing past experience) are indicated by aspect particles, such as 了, 著, 过 (著 indicates the continuation of an action or state; 过 indicates the past experience. These aspects will be introduced in later lessons.); adverbs, such as 也, 很, 再, 又; optative verbs, such as 要, 想, 会, 可以, 能, 应该, or modal particles, such as 呢, 吧.

So far we have learned the following patterns to express different types of verbal aspects:

1. The progressive aspect of an action 在/正在 (Refer to Lesson 9).
The progressive aspect of an action indicates that someone is currently in the process of doing something. For example,

A: 你在看电视吗?
B: 我没有在看电视。我正在学习呢。

2. Imminent action expressed by 就要/快要...... 了 (Refer to Lesson 17).
Both 就要...了 and 快要...了 are patterns that are used to indicate that a certain action or event is about to take place. For example,

我就要毕业了。
我快要去中国了。

3. Completion of an action 了 (Refer to Lesson 19).
The aspect particle 了 is placed after a verb or at the end of a sentence to indicate the completion of an action. For example,

	Pattern	Example
Question	V._ 了吗 V._ 了没有	你去看医生了吗? 你去看医生了没有?
Positive answer	V._ 了 or sentence end	我去看了医生。 我去看医生了。
Negative answer	没有 V. 还没有____呢	我没有去看医生。 我还没有去看医生呢。

补充课文 SUPPLEMENTARY PRACTICE

This selection will help you test your comprehension of the grammar and vocabulary you have learned in this lesson. Be prepared to answer questions about the meaning of the passage.

白秋雨明年就要毕业了。他还没有最后决定毕业以后做什么。因为他很喜欢学习，毕业以后他可能会申请研究生院，或者去国外留学。

他的朋友程海华两年后才毕业，毕业以后他想找一份工作。今年暑假程海华要去加州的一家电脑公司实习。

白秋雨会去中国上海参加暑期班的学习。他想一面学中文，一面在中国旅行。他下个星期离开这里去中国。

秋雨和海华觉得暑假的时候应该常常给对方写电子邮件。最后他们祝对方愉快、平安和好运。

Notes: 最后 [zuìhòu]: finally
份 [fèn]: measure word for job
离开 [líkāi]: to depart
这里 [zhèlǐ]: here
对方 [duìfāng]: opposite side; the other part

练习 ACTIVITIES

I. Pinyin Exercises

21-1 Listen to the instructor, then write the Pinyin for the following expressions:

1. 暑假 ________　　2. 申请 ________　　3. 公司 ________
4. 实习 ________　　5. 有意思 ________　　6. 愉快 ________

21-2 Listen to the instructor and fill in each blank with the correct Pinyin:

1. 毕____以后你想____什么？
2. 我要去打____。是一____电____公司。
3. 我____有两年___毕业呢。
4. 你要____给我____电子邮____。

21-3 Read the following Chinese poem, paying special attention to the tones and rhythm:

Dēng Yōuzhōutái Gē **(Chén Zǐ'áng)**	**登幽州台歌** **(陈子昂)**
Qián bú jiàn gǔrén, Hòu bú jiàn láizhě. Niàn tiāndì zhī yōuyōu, Dú chuàngrán ér tì xià.	前不见古人， 后不见来者。 念天地之悠悠， 独怆然而涕下。

Ballad on Ascending Youzhou Tower
(Chen, Zi'ang)

Ahead, there is no sight of ancients,
Behind, those to come are unseen.
Pondering over the enormity of heaven and earth,
Alone and in sadness, tears fall.

II. Character Exercises

21-4 Read the following words, phrases, and sentences:

一面	留学
一面学中文	去留学
我想一面学中文	去国外留学
我想一面学中文，一面旅行	我想去国外留学
我想一面学中文，一面在中国旅行	今年夏天我们都想去国外留学

Now try to use the following characters to make words, phrases, and then sentences:

1. 毕	2. 决	3. 申	4. 研	5. 留	6. 司
7. 实	8. 脑	9. 班	10. 意	11. 愉	12. 运

21-5 Write down the simplified forms for the following traditional characters:

1. 畢 ______	2. 決 ______	3. 寫 ______	4. 電 ______
5. 實 ______	6. 請 ______	7. 國 ______	8. 運 ______

III. Grammar Exercises

21-6 Substitution exercises:

我喜欢一面吃饭一面看电视。你呢?
我也喜欢一面吃饭一面看电视。
or: 我不喜欢一面吃饭一面看电视。

看球赛	喝可乐
看书	听音乐
看电影	吃东西
洗澡	唱歌
打手机	上网
开车	听音乐
骑自行车	唱歌

Notes: 音乐 [yīnyuè]: music
唱歌 [chànggē]: to sing

21-7 Form pairs to ask and answer the following questions:

1. 你常一面上网一面打手机,是不是?
2. 昨天下午三点的时候,你正在做什么?
3. 你今年就要二十三岁了,是吗?
4. 第二十课的作业,你做了吗?
5. 你以前常常喝啤酒,现在不喝了,是不是?

IV. Communicative Activities

21-8 Form groups of four to perform the "What's your alibi?" scene:

Situation: A famous Chinese painting was reported stolen from the museum between 8:00 P.M. and 12:00 P.M. last night. The police officers are now cross-examining suspects.

Students 1 and 2: police officers
Students 3 and 4: suspects.

(use 一面...一面; 正在; 了 and 就要/快要...了)

e.g.: Police officer (1): 昨天晚上八点的时候,你正在做什么?
Suspect (1): 我正在一面看电视,一面打电话。
Police officer (1): 九点半呢?
Suspect (1): 我那时候正在...
Police officer (2): ...

21-9 That's what friends are for!
Form groups of two or three people to talk about Joe. Describe what he was like before and what he is like now. (Each person should say at least six sentences.)

<u>Situation</u>: Last year your friend Joe was making his New Year's resolutions and asked your advice. You suggested that he change some of his habits, and he did. See details below. (Useful words and expressions: 一面…一面；了；不…了；就要…了；正在…；得；想；要；会；应该；然后；觉得；以前；以后)

Joe's schedule last year:

11:00 A.M.	起床	12:00 noon	上课
2:00–4:00 A.M.	打电话	4:00–6:00 P.M.	跟朋友喝啤酒
6:00–8:00 P.M.	一面看电视一面做作业	9:00–11:00 P.M.	跳舞
12:00–2:00 A.M.	学习	4:00 A.M.	睡觉

<u>Other information</u>: Joe smokes two packs of cigarettes a day, drinks three bottles of beer a day, drinks five cups of coffee a day, gets no exercise, doesn't drink milk or orange juice.

Act out a conversation with Joe that happened last year.

Examples:
Friend 1: 你昨天做了什么？(你昨天做什么了？)
Joe: 我十一点起了床，然后去上课了。
Friend 1: 你起床起得太晚了，
你应该八点以前起床。
Friend 2: 你不应该一面看电视，一面做作业。
……

****

Joe's schedule now:

7:30–8:00 A.M.	起床	8:00–9:00 A.M.	跑步
9:00 A.M.–12:00 P.M.	上课	2:00–4:00 P.M.	去图书馆
4:00–6:00 P.M.	跟朋友一面打篮球一面练习中文		
8:00–11:00 P.M.	学习	11:00 P.M.	睡觉

Joe quit drinking and smoking. He is now very good at basketball.

Act out a conversation with Joe that occurred this year.

文化知识 Culture Link

文化点滴 CULTURE NOTES

中国的旅游业 [Zhōngguó de lǚyóu yè] Travel in China

The most popular seasons for travel in China are the two 黄金周 [Huángjīnzhōu] (Golden Weeks) and the Spring Festival. One Golden Week begins on May 1, Labor Day, and the other on October 1, National Day. Both weeks have ideal weather for traveling. Many companies arrange holiday tours for employees in appreciation of their hard work, and some families choose to travel together during the traditional Chinese festivals instead of having reunions at home. Chinese people also travel abroad in greater numbers, and Chinese faces can now be seen at tourist destinations all over the world.

People from other nations are also enthusiastic about visiting China. The number of foreign tourists has been increasing by millions each year. Many people know about 兵马俑 [Bīngmǎyǒng] (the terra cotta warriors), 紫禁城 [Zǐjìnchéng] (the Forbidden City), 天安门 [Tiān'ānmén] (the Gate of Heavenly Peace), 长城 [Chángchéng] (the Great Wall), the lovely and precious 熊猫 [xióngmāo] (giant panda), and the 丝绸之路 [Sīchóuzhīlù] (the Silk Road), but these are only a few of the vast natural and cultural resources of China. China has the longest continuous civilization on the planet. With a language-recorded history of over 4,000 years, China has a tremendously rich cultural heritage. A meaningful visit to China would not be limited to these well-known tourist sites, but would also include sampling of the many delicious cuisines, visiting ancient remote villages, listening to the unique Peking Opera, and appreciating the elegant traditional arts of China.

Tourism in China is booming and is one of its hottest industries. The country provides good transportation, accommodations, recreation, and catering services at reasonable prices. In many cities such as Beijing, Shanghai, Guangzhou, and Hong Kong, a foreigner can easily communicate in English. Of course, one can always amaze Chinese people by speaking even a few Chinese words.

Beijing streets.

A beautiful park in I-lan, in northeast Taiwan.

熊貓 [xióngmāo] (pandas).

The famous night market 夜市 [yèshì] in Taipei.

A good way to see Hong Kong.

Modern Hong Kong.

Attractions in China:

The Great Wall.

The Imperial Palace in Beijing.

A man selling things at the Great Wall.

Confucius's birthplace in Shandong Province in east China.

The Yellow Mountain, Anhui Province.

Questions:

1. Have you ever been to China?
2. If yes, where did you go? Share your experience with the class (something fun, or different, or that gave you a deep impression . . .)
3. If not, do you plan to go? Say something about your plans.
4. Which place in China do you want to visit most? Why?

趣味中文 FUN WITH CHINESE

活到老，学到老。
There is still much to learn after one has grown old.
The pursuit of knowledge is an endless effort.
No dog is too old to learn new tricks.

huó	dào	lǎo,	xué	dào	lǎo.
活	到	老，	学	到	老。
live	too	old,	learn	too	old.

Question:

Form groups of two to four. Role play a conversation (in English) using "活到老，学到老." Try to make it interesting or funny, and also try to speak several sentences in Chinese using what you've learned.

行动吧！ LET'S GO!

申请成绩单的发票
Receipt for Transcript Printing

小红现在是大四学生，她在广东外语学院念书。她明年就要毕业了，毕业以后她想申请去国外留学。她申请了她的大学成绩单，这是她的发票。回答以下的问题：

Useful words and expressions:

念书(念書) [niànshū]: to study
回答 [huídá]: answer
问题(問題) [wèntí]: question
广州市(廣州市) [Guǎngzhōu shì]: Guangzhou city
服务业(服務業) [fúwù yè]: service business
发票(發票) [fāpiào]: invoice; receipt
查询(查詢) [cháxún]: to check
报销 (報銷) [bàoxiāo]: reimbursement
名称(名稱) [míngchēng]: title
收款人 [shōukuǎn rén]: person who received the remittance
金额(金額) [jīn'é]: amount
付钱(付錢) [fùqián]: to pay
成绩单(成績單) [chéngjìdān/chéngjīdān]: transcript
以下 [yǐxià]: the following
广东省(廣東省) [Guǎngdōng shěng]: Guangdong Province in southern China
定额(定額) [dìng'é]: a fixed amount or number
发票联(發票聯) [fāpiào lián]: invoice; receipt
顾客(顧客) [gùkè]: customer
凭证(憑證) [píngzhèng]: proof
人民币(人民幣) [rénmínbì]: name of currency used in Mainland China
单位(單位) [dānwèi]: unit
营业(營業) [yíngyè]: business operation
查验(查驗) [cháyàn]: to examine
支票 [zhīpiào]: check

广东省广州市服务业定额发票
发票联
查询电话:(020)12366-3
地税监
440170123
查询号码: 534031191139
顾客名称:
人民币金额 壹佰元
收款人:
(顾客报销凭证)
20
发票专用章
使用范围:饮食业、娱乐业及其他服务业。

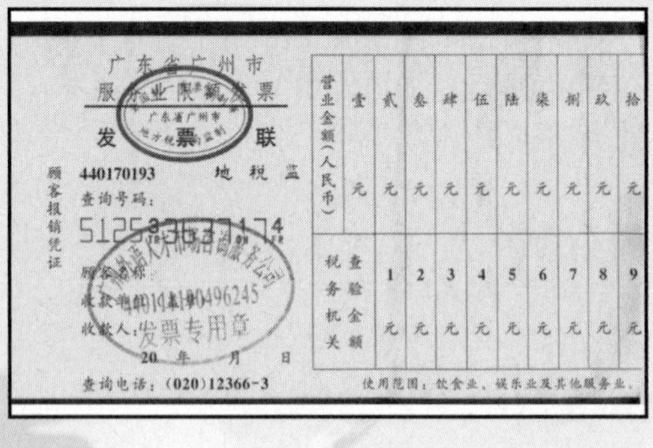
广东省广州市
服务业限额发票
发联
顾客报销凭证
440170193 地税监
查询号码:
发票专用章
收款人:
20 年 月 日
查询电话:(020)12366-3

营业金额(人民币)		壹元	贰元	叁元	肆元	伍元	陆元	柒元	捌元	玖元	拾元
税务机关	查验金额	1元	2元	3元	4元	5元	6元	7元	8元	9元	

使用范围:饮食业、娱乐业及其他服务业。

Questions:

1. 小红一共付了多少钱?
2. Translate the following sentence: 使用范围:饮食业,娱乐业及其他服务业.
3. What are the equivalent spoken forms for the written expressions: 金额, 收款人, and 及?
4. 小红's father wrote an amount on a check as 捌佰陆拾贰元. How much is that?

第二十二课
LESSON

22

我到上海了
I Have Arrived in Shanghai

教学目标 OBJECTIVES

- Exchange e-mails
- Describe your current situation

Several views of metropolitan Shanghai

小笼包 *[xiǎolóngbāo] Little steamed buns*

生词 VOCABULARY

核心词 Core Vocabulary

SIMPLIFIED	TRADITIONAL	PINYIN		
1. 对不起	對不起	duìbuqǐ		I'm sorry; Excuse me.
2. 因为	因為	yīnwèi	Conj.	because
3. 不过	不過	búguò	Conj.	but; however
4. 认真	認真	rènzhēn	Adj.	conscientious; serious
5. 已经	已經	yǐjīng	Adv.	already
6. 美丽	美麗	měilì	Adj.	beautiful
7. 城市	城市	chéngshì	N.	city
8. 到处	到處	dàochù	N.	everywhere
9. 新	新	xīn	Adj.	new
10. 大楼	大樓	dàlóu	N.	tall building
11. 地方	地方	dìfang	N.	place
12. 活动	活動	huódòng	N.	activity
13. 比如	比如	bǐrú	Conj.	for example
14. 京剧	京劇	jīngjù	N.	Peking Opera
15. 书法	書法	shūfǎ	N.	calligraphy
16. 东西	東西	dōngxi	N.	thing
17. 最	最	zuì	Adv.	most; the highest degree
18. 小笼包	小籠包	xiǎolóngbāo	N.	little steamed buns with stuffing
19. 机会	機會	jīhuì	N.	opportunity
20. 尝尝	嚐嚐	chángchang	V.	to have a taste
21. 开始	開始	kāishǐ	V.	to start; to begin
22. 高兴	高興	gāoxìng	Adj.	happy

SIMPLIFIED	TRADITIONAL	PINYIN		
23. 收到	收到	shōudào	V.C.	to receive
24. 看来	看來	kànlái		it seems
25. 开心	開心	kāixīn	Adj.	happy
26. 同事	同事	tóngshì	N.	colleague
27. 热心	熱心	rèxīn	Adj.	warm-hearted
28. 老板	老闆	lǎobǎn	N.	boss
29. 一些	一些	yìxiē	Adj.	some
30. 学到	學到	xuédào	V.C.	to learn and master
31. 来信	來信	láixìn	V.O.	to write a letter (to the speaker)
32. 保重	保重	bǎozhòng		take care

补充词 Supplementary Vocabulary

SIMPLIFIED	TRADITIONAL	PINYIN		
1. 心想事成	心想事成	xīnxiǎngshìchéng		Every wish comes true.
2. 健康	健康	jiànkāng	Adj.	healthy
3. 顺利	順利	shùnlì	Adj.	smooth

语文知识 LANGUAGE LINK

The Sentence Patterns provide models that will help you with the Language in Use section. In both sections, pay attention to the grammar points, vocabulary, and expressions.

句型 Sentence Patterns

A: 上海怎么样?
Shànghǎi zěnmeyàng?

B: 上海是一个非常美丽的
Shànghǎi shì yíge fēicháng měilìde
城市，到处都是新的大楼。
chéngshì, dàochù dōu shì xīnde dàlóu.

A: 你们在那儿做了什么？
Nǐmen zài nàr zuò le shénme?

B: 我们参加了一些活动，比如：
Wǒmen cānjiā le yìxiē huódòng, bǐrú:
看京剧、写书法等等。
kàn jīngjù, xiě shūfǎ děngděng.

A: 这儿的同事都很热心，常常
Zhèr de tóngshì dōu hěn rèxīn, chángcháng
教我很多东西，老板也不错。
jiāo wǒ hěnduō dōngxi, lǎobǎn yě búcuò.

B: 很好！你要认真地工作，
Hěn hǎo! Nǐ yào rènzhēn de gōngzuò,
才能学到一些东西。
cái néng xué dào yìxiē dōngxi.

课文 Language in Use: 我到上海了 Wǒ dào Shànghǎi le

海华：
Hǎihuá:

你好！今天是六月十五号，我一个星期以前就到上海了。
Nǐhǎo! Jīntiān shì liù yuè shíwǔ hào, wǒ yíge xīngqī yǐqián jiù dào Shànghǎi le.

对不起，因为太忙了，所以今天才给你写电子邮件。
Duìbuqǐ, yīnwèi tài máng le, suǒyǐ jīntiān cái gěi nǐ xiě diànzǐ yóujiàn.

我们每天都有很多课，功课也不少。不过老师教得很好，
Wǒmen měitiān dōu yǒu hěnduō kè, gōngkè yě bùshǎo. Búguò lǎoshī jiāode hěnhǎo,

也很认真。我们每天都说中文。我的中文进步得很快，
yě hěn rènzhēn. Wǒmen měitiān dōu shuō Zhōngwén. Wǒde Zhōngwén jìnbù de hěnkuài.

现在我已经能说很多中文了。
Xiànzài wǒ yǐjīng néng shuō hěnduō Zhōngwén le.

上海是一个非常美丽的城市，到处都是新的大楼。
Shànghǎi shì yíge fēicháng měilìde chéngshì, dàochù dōu shì xīnde dàlóu.

我们参观了一些地方，也参加了一些活动，比如：看京剧、
Wǒmen cānguān le yìxiē dìfang, yě cānjiā le yìxiē huódòng, bǐrú: kàn jīngjù,

写书法等等，都很有意思。还有，上海有很多好吃的东西，
xiě shūfǎ děngděng, dōu hěn yǒuyìsi. Háiyǒu, Shànghǎi yǒu hěnduō hǎochī de dōngxi,

其中我最喜欢吃的是小笼包，你有机会应该尝尝。
qízhōng wǒ zuì xǐhuān chī de shì xiǎolóngbāo. Nǐ yǒu jīhuì yīnggāi chángchang.

你开始实习了吗？忙不忙？有空请给我写电子邮件。
Nǐ kāishǐ shíxí le ma? Mángbumáng? Yǒukòng qǐng gěi wǒ xiě diànzǐ yóujiàn.

祝
Zhù

好！
Hǎo!

秋雨
Qiūyǔ

二〇〇四年六月十五日
Èr líng líng sì nián liù yuè shíwǔ rì

秋雨：
Qiūyǔ:

你好！很高兴收到你的电子邮件。看来你在上海过得很开心。
Nǐhǎo! Hěn gāoxìng shōudào nǐde diànzǐ yóujiàn. Kànlái nǐ zài Shànghǎi guòde hěn kāixīn.

我现在在洛杉矶，已经开始实习了。这儿的同事都很好，也很
Wǒ xiànzài zài Luòshānjī, yǐjīng kāishǐ shíxí le. Zhèr de tóngshì dōu hěnhǎo, yě hěn

热心，常常教我很多东西，老板也不错。我的工作有时候忙，
rèxīn, chángcháng jiāo wǒ hěnduō dōngxi, lǎobǎn yě búcuò. Wǒde gōngzuò yǒushíhou máng,

有时候不太忙，我想我得认真地工作，才能学到一些东西。
yǒushíhou bútàimáng. Wǒ xiǎng wǒ děi rènzhēn de gōngzuò, cái néng xué dào yìxiē dōngxi.

好了，不多写了。有空请多来信，多保重。
Hǎo le, bù duō xiě le. Yǒukòng qǐng duō lái xìn. Duō bǎozhòng.

祝
Zhù

好！
Hǎo!

海华
Hǎihuá

二〇〇四年六月十七日
Èr líng líng sì nián liù yuè shíqī rì

注释 LANGUAGE NOTES

等等

等等 means et cetera, and is usually used after a list of people or things. Sometimes one character 等 is used instead of two.

还有

还有 (and, also, in addition) is used to introduce additional information.

来信

来信 can be used as a noun to mean "a letter coming from . . ." 来 is used here to indicate that this is said from the speaker's point of view, which means the letter is coming to the speaker. If the letter is going away from the speaker, then 去信 should be used.

语法 GRAMMAR

比如

This is an expression equivalent to "for example" or "for instance" or "such as" in English. It is used to introduce specific examples. For example,

我们的晚会有很多活动，比如：唱歌、跳舞、写毛笔字等等。
他会说很多语言，比如：英文，中文，法文，西班牙文。

Summary of Measure Words in Chinese

In modern Chinese a numeral is never used immediately before a noun as in English. A measure word is always placed between a numeral or a demonstrative pronoun 这/那 and a noun. There are many measure words in Chinese, and different measure words are required for different nouns. The following is a list of the measure words we have learned so far:

Category	Measure word (Classifier)	Example
Measure words for people	个: used for all people 位: only used in a polite way	e.g., 六千多个学生 几位客人？两位，请进。
Measure words for things (definite)	个: the most commonly used measure word for things in general; used for cups, buildings, characters, etc.	e.g., 一个杯子，那个电话，三个专业 一个公园，一个图书馆， 五个汉字
	本: used for bound items (book-like things)	e.g., 这本汉英词典，两本中文书， 三本英文杂志

Category	Measure word (Classifier)	Example
	张: generally used for sheet-like things with a flat surface	e.g., 一张床，这张报纸，三张电影票，那张桌子
	只: generally used for animals	e.g., 一只狗，六只猫
	门: used for subjects and courses as well as special skills	e.g., 六门课 这门手艺 [shǒuyì] (skill)
	辆: used for vehicles	e.g., 这辆汽车，那辆公共汽车，三辆自行车
	家: used for a facility such as a company, a hospital, a factory, or a TV station	e.g., 一家公司， 这家电视台 [diànshìtái] (TV station), 一家医院 [yīyuàn] (hospital)
	点, 分, 秒 [miǎo] (second), 刻: used for time	e.g., 三点二十分 (3:20) 五点一刻 (5:15) 十二点三十分零 [líng] (zero) 六秒 [miǎo] (second) (12:30:06)
	元/块, 角/毛: used for money	e.g., 八十元七角三分 (¥80.73) 九块四毛六分 (¥9.46)
	件: used for clothing, especially for upper body clothing	e.g., 一件衬衫 (a shirt) 两件运动衫 [yùndòngshān] (sports wear)
	条: used for things of long and slim shape	e.g., 一条裤子 (a pair of pants) 三条裙子 (three skirts)
	双, 副 and 对: used for things in pairs	e.g., 一双运动鞋 (a pair of sports shoes) 一双手 (a pair of hands) 一双筷子 (a pair of chopsticks) 一双眼睛 [yǎnjīng] (a pair of eyes) 一副手套 [shǒutào] (a pair of gloves) 一副眼镜 [yǎnjìng] (a pair of eyeglasses) 一副耳环 [ěrhuán] (a pair of earrings) 一副手镯 [shǒuzhuó] (a pair of bracelets) 一对姐妹 [jiěmèi] (sisters) (two sisters) 一对夫妻 [fūqī] (a couple — husband and wife)
	碗, 盘, and, 杯: refer to containers, used for food or drinks	e.g., 一碗汤 (a bowl of soup) 两盘炒面 (two plates of fried noodles) 三杯啤酒 (three glasses of beer)

Category	Measure word (Classifier)	Example
Things (indefinite)	一点儿: means a little, used to indicate quantity (used before a noun) 一下儿, 一会儿: means a little, used to indicate a brief action (used after a verb)	e.g., A: 你会说中文吗? B: 我会说一点儿。 e.g., A: 你来一下儿，好吗? B: 好，我马上就来。 or: 请等一会儿。
Things (plural)	些	e.g., 我们参观了一些城市 他们收到了一些电子邮件。

Note: Measure words can be used in reduplication to indicate "each and every," but this usage is limited to single-syllable measure words only. For examples,

他们个个都是好学生。 (每个人)
这儿的书本本都很好看。 (每本)

Summary of Conjunctions in Chinese

Conjunctions are used to connect nouns/pronouns, verbs, adjectives, adverbs, numerals, and even clauses to indicate grammatical relationships. We have learned the following conjunctions so far:

Category	Conjunction	Example
和: – used to indicate a parallel relationship	– usually to connect two nouns, pronouns, and nominal phrases *Note:* 和 can never be used to connect two sentences/clauses.	e.g., 我爸爸和妈妈都是中国人。(N. 和 N.) 我们点一盘饺子和一碗汤吧。(NP. 和 NP.)
可是, 但是, 不过: – used to indicate transition, similar to "but," "however," "nevertheless." – can be used interchangeably	– usually used to introduce a clause that bears a meaning contrary to what might have been expected based on the previous clause, often used together with 虽然 [suīrán] (although) *Note:* While in English "although" and "so" are not used together, 虽然 and 但是/可是/不过 are often used together as a pair of conjunctions.	e.g., 中国文学不太难，<u>可是</u>功课不少。 我打球打得不太好，<u>但是</u>我很喜欢打球。 今天气温 [qìwēn] (temperature) 不太高，不过很舒服。 The temperature today is not very high, but very pleasant.

Category	Conjunction	Example
所以: – used to indicate causality, meaning "so" or "therefore" in English	– equivalent to "so" or "therefore" in English, often used together with 因为 as a pair of conjunctions *Note:* While in English "because" and "so" are never used together, in Chinese 因为 and 所以 can and often are used together in one sentence. Sometimes 因为 can be omitted if the cause-effect relationship between the first and the second clauses is very clear.	e.g., (因为)冬天太冷, 所以我不喜欢冬天。 (因为)她常常锻炼, 所以她的身体 [shēntǐ] (body) 很好。
还是, 或者: – used to indicate alternatives – can be translated as "or" in English	还是 is used in a question while 或者 is used in a statement	e.g., 你去体育馆还是健身房? 你每天走路还是坐公共汽车来学校? 我想明天或者后天搬过来。 今年暑假我想去北京或者上海暑期班学习。
然后: – used to indicate succession and order of things	– often used together with 先 and 再 *Note:* When using 先, 再, and 然后, 先 always comes first, but 再, and 然后 can be reversed.	e.g., 我想先回家, 再去洛杉矶看朋友, 然后去公司实习。 广东 [Guǎngdōng] (Canton, a province in southern China) 人都喜欢先喝汤, 然后吃饭。
一面……一面…… (一边…… 一边……): – used for simultaneous actions	– usually connects two verbs or verb phrases to indicate that two actions are happening at the same time	e.g., 他一面吃饭一面看电视。 我喜欢一面做功课一面听音乐 [tīng yīnyuè] (listen to music)。

补充课文 SUPPLEMENTARY PRACTICE

This selection will help you test your comprehension of the grammar and vocabulary you have learned in this lesson. Be prepared to answer questions about the meaning of the passage.

(打电话)

秋雨： 喂，你好！请问海华在吗？
海华： 我就是。你是秋雨吧？
秋雨： 对，是我。
海华： 你在哪儿？
秋雨： 我在上海。我一个星期以前就到了。对不起，因为太忙了，所以到现在才给你打电话。
海华： 没关系。你在那儿好吗？
秋雨： 很好，可是太忙了。我们每天都有很多课，功课也不少。
海华： 你们的老师怎么样？
秋雨： 老师很不错，教得很认真。
海华： 你现在中文一定进步得很快吧？
秋雨： 还不错，我们每天都说中文。我现在已经可以说很多了。
海华： 太好了。你觉得上海怎么样？
秋雨： 我很喜欢上海。上海非常漂亮。我们去了很多地方玩儿，还看了京剧，写了书法，参加了很多活动，很有意思。对了，这儿有很多好吃的东西。
海华： 真的？那你最喜欢吃什么？
秋雨： 我最喜欢吃小笼包。真的很好吃。有机会你一定要尝尝。
海华： 好的。看来你在上海过得很开心。
秋雨： 你呢？你在洛杉矶还好吗？
海华： 还可以。我已经开始实习了，老板还不错，同事们都很好，也很热心，还教了我不少东西。
秋雨： 工作忙不忙？
海华： 有时候忙，有时候不太忙。我想多学一些东西，所以得认真地工作。
秋雨： 有志者事竟成。祝你成功！
海华： 谢谢。好，就这样。请多保重。
秋雨： 我也要挂电话了。再见！
海华： 再见！

Notes: 漂亮 [piàoliang]: pretty
有志者事竟成。[Yǒuzhìzhě shì jìng chéng]: Where there is a will, there is a way.
成功 [chénggōng]: success
就这样 [jiùzhèyàng]: that's it; that's all
挂 [guà]: to hang up (the phone)

练习 ACTIVITIES

I. Pinyin Exercises

22-1 Listen to the instructor, then write out the Pinyin:

1. ____________________ 2. ____________________

3. ____________________ 4. ____________________

5. ____________________ 6. ____________________

22-2 Listen to the instructor and then write out the short dialogues in Pinyin:

1. ____

____

2. ____

____

3. ____

____

4. ____

____

5. ____

____

22-3 Read the following Chinese poem, paying special attention to the tones and rhythm:

Gŭyuán Căo **(Bái Jūyì)** Lílí yuán shàng căo, Yí suì yì kū róng. Yĕhuŏ shāo bú jìn, Chūnfēng chuī yòu shēng.	**古原草** **(白居易)** 离离原上草， 一岁一枯荣。 野火烧不尽， 春风吹又生。
Grass on the Old Grassland **(Bai, Juyi)** The grass is growing in full bloom on the grassland, Every year it withers and grows again. Wild fire will not burn it dead, It grows again with the coming of spring wind.	

II. Character Exercises

23-4 Read the following words, phrases, and sentences:

城	尝
城市	尝尝
大城市	尝尝小笼包
是一个大城市	应该尝尝小笼包
上海是一个大城市	有机会应该尝尝小笼包
上海是一个美丽的大城市	你有机会应该尝尝小笼包

Now try to use the following characters to make words, phrases, and then sentences:

1. 丽 2. 处 3. 新 4. 方 5. 比 6. 京
7. 东 8. 始 9. 高 10. 收 11. 板 12. 保

22-5 Group the following words according to their meanings (e.g., place, food, activity, adjective, verb, conjunction):

认真	保重	热心	不过	开心	同事	活动	书法
东西	高兴	小笼包	地方	上海	京剧	所以	收到
老板	美丽	来信	尝尝	城市	努力	吸烟	参观

Group 1: ______________________________

Group 2: ______________________________

Group 3: ______________________________

Group 4: ______________________________

Group 5: ______________________________

Group 6: ______________________________

Group 7: ______________________________

Group 8: ______________________________

Group 9: ______________________________

22-6 Circle the radicals of the following characters:

For example, 居(刂)

1. 认 2. 保 3. 笼 4. 丽 5. 理 6. 机 7. 愉 8. 体

III. Grammar Exercises

22-7 Fill in each blank with an appropriate measure word using to the clues:

1.  一 ___ 自行车

2.  一 ___ 皮鞋

3.  一 ___ 城市

4.  一 ___ 电脑公司

5.  一 ___ 茶
壶 [hú] (pot)

6.  一 ___ 酸辣汤
[suānlà tāng]
(hot and sour soup)

7.  一 ___ 书

8. 

一 ___ 报纸

22-8 Connect the sentences by using appropriate conjunctions:

因为……所以……，一面……一面……，可是，
先……再……然后……，还是

1. 方明正在看电脑。方明正在打手机。

___

2. 上海很美丽，我很想去上海看看。

___

3. 现在已经是四月了，天气还是很冷。

___

4. 你要去北京的暑期班吗？你要去公司实习吗？

___

5. 八点我起床，九点我上课，十点我去吃午饭。

___

22-9 Use 比如 to complete the following sentences with the help of the clues:

For example, 我们参加了很多活动……
(watch Peking Opera, practice calligraphy, etc.)
→ 我们参加了很多活动，比如：看京剧，写书法等等。

1. 我喜欢吃中国菜…… (hot and sour soup, fried rice, dumplings, etc.)

____

2. 我很想去中国看看，特别 [tèbié] (especially) 想去……
(big cities such as Beijing, Shanghai, and Hong Kong)

____

3. 我对很多活动有兴趣……
(swimming, playing basketball, bicycling, etc.)

____

IV. Communicative Activities

22-10 Situational dialogues:

Situation 1:
Your best friend 司马 [Sīmǎ] 学文 is now studying Chinese in Beijing, China, and you are doing an internship at a company in New York. This is your second week at work. You are talking with 学文 on the phone. Your conversation covers the following topics:

1. You ask 学文 about his life and studies in Beijing.
2. 学文 tells you about his classes and his teachers.
3. You tell him how you feel about your work at the company.
4. You encourage each other to do a good job in both studies and work.
5. You promise that you will e-mail each other as often as possible.

In your conversation you should use (but are not limited to) the following words and expressions:

对不起	因为	一个星期
功课	喜欢	开心
还是	每天	机会
参观	认真	虽然
常常	活动	参加
热心	比如	同事
一面……一面……		

文化知识 Culture Link

文化点滴 CULTURE NOTES

京剧; 书法
Peking Opera; Chinese Calligraphy

京剧 (Peking Opera)

京剧 originated in the 安徽 [Ānhuī] (Anhui) and 湖北 [Húběi] (Hubei) Provinces of China in the 18th century; it is now known as China's national opera. In fact, in Taiwan it is referred to as 国剧 [guójù] (national opera). 京剧 can be divided into two types, 文戏 [wénxì] (civil pieces), which are characterized by singing, and 武戏 [wǔxì] (martial pieces), which feature acrobatics and stunts. Some operas are a combination of both.

The repertoire of 京剧 includes historical subjects, comedic performances, tragedies, and farces. Two groups of musicians, a string section and a percussion section, accompany the singing. The 二胡 [èrhú], a two-stringed instrument played with a bow, is the backbone of the orchestra. The operatic dialogues and monologues are recited in Peking dialect, and some of the words are pronounced in a special fashion unique to Peking Opera.

Main instruments: Chinese fiddle, two-stringed violin, and pipa.

There are established movements in the opera that are used by the performers to portray emotions. Such movements include, for instance, smoothing of a beard, raising a foot, jerking a sleeve, or adjusting a hat.

In general there are four roles within the 京剧: 生 [shēng] (male), 旦 [dàn] (female), the 净 [jìng] (painted face), and 丑 [chǒu] (the clown). These roles are further classified by age and profession. The male role can be divided into three categories: old, young, and martial arts expert. The female role is divided into four categories: young or middle-aged, innocent or dissolute, martial arts expert, and old woman. The painted-face role represents open-minded men with brightly colored faces. The clown role is marked by white on the ridge of his nose. The clown can have a number of personalities, from a light-hearted, humorous character to an evil, crafty character. These personalities are revealed by the way each character sings and moves. For example, the personality of the painted-face character is indicated by the color his face is painted: red indicates uprightness and loyalty; white represents craftiness and cunning; blue represents vigor and courage; yellow represents intelligence; black represents honesty; and brown represents stubbornness.

Rehearsing before the show.

Costuming is a very extravagant part of the opera; all the costumes are based on Ming Dynasty dress. They are very colorful and very expensive in appearance. Props for the stage are relatively simple. Often there are just a table and a few chairs on the stage. Common props include a cloth wall, tents, parasols, a whip, paddles, and a few weapons. Someone holding a whip and walking around can represent a person riding a horse. A few soldiers may represent a huge army on stage. Performers also use their eyes and facial expressions to help convey more specific meanings.

Examples of costumes and stage props.

Since its birth 200 years ago, 京剧 survives today. There are a number of schools in China and Taiwan dedicated to training children to be future performers in the Peking Opera.

书法 (Calligraphy)

书法 is considered the highest form of art in China. Together with painting, it is the best embodiment of Chinese philosophy around the world. The Daoist theory of yin-yang is well integrated into the best works of calligraphy. Balance and harmony are essential for a masterpiece. Many calligraphers are at the same time scholars and artists. Very often they incorporate poems in their calligraphic art as well.

For a calligrapher, the most important tools are the 文房四宝 [wénfángsìbǎo] (the four treasures of the study room), an expression that refers to paper, writing brush, ink slab, and ink stick.

文房四宝 [wénfángsìbǎo] (the four treasures of the study room) paper, writing brush, ink slab, and ink stick. A calligraphy master writes Chinese lunar new year couplets by request.

Chinese calligraphy has five basic styles, the earliest being 篆书 [zhuànshū] (Seal Style). Later styles include 隶书 [lìshū] (Official Style), 楷书 [kǎishū] (Standard Style), 行书 [xíngshū] (Running Style) and 草书 [cǎoshū] (Grass/Cursive Style). Today, the most commonly used style for official documents is 楷书, and 行书 is used most by people in daily life.

Students being introduced to calligraphy.

Calligraphy is used for *Gualian* (couplets), mottos, and calligraphy paintings. These are common interior decorations for Chinese.

The following are examples by Yi Qing of the five major styles of Chinese calligraphy:

Zhuanshu (Seal Style)	Lishu (Official Style)	Kaishu (Regular Style)	Xingshu (Running Style)	Caoshu (Grass/Cursive Style)
				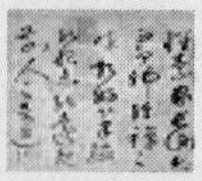

Questions:

1. Have you ever seen Peking Opera?
2. If yes, where, when, and what did you think of it?
3. If not, from what you learned from the textbook, do you think Peking Opera is similar to Western opera? Why or why not?
4. Do you know any other performing art? Introduce it to the class.
5. Have you ever tried calligraphy? Do you want to learn it?

趣味中文 FUN WITH CHINESE

心想事成
Whatever one wishes, it will come true.

xīn	xiǎng	shì	chéng
心	想	事	成
mind	think	matter	successful

Question:

Do you believe "心想事成"? Why or why not?

行动吧！ LET'S GO!

标语 Slogan

1. 小民 is studying in Beijing. He is also doing a work-study assignment at the new technology development area in 中关村. Below are several slogan posters he saw in 中关村. Translate the slogans into English.

Useful words and expressions:

海淀中关村(海淀中關村) [Hǎidiàn Zhōngguāncūn]: Zhongguan village in the Haidian area, famous for its devotion to developing advanced technology, similar to Silicon Valley in California.
人类(人類) [rénlèi]: human beings
必须 [bìxū]: must
增长(增長) [zēngzhǎng]: growth
资源(資源) [zīyuán]: resources
回收 [huíshōu]: to recycle
地球 [dìqiú]: the Earth
控制 [kòngzhì]: to control
环保(環保) [huánbǎo]: environmental protection

(1)

(2)

(3)

用你自己的话，说说标语(1) (2) (3)是什么意思？

2. 林荣圈 [Lín Róngquān] is a taxi driver for the 开心 taxi company in Taiwan. He is taking a passenger from the airport to Taipei. Below is the receipt he needs to fill out for his passenger. Use the following information to fill out the receipt:

Fare: NT $800, 开心车行, 电话: (02) 2675-8983

Useful words and expressions:

计程车(計程車) [jìchéngchē]: taxi
收据(收據) [shōujù]: receipt
车资(車資) [chēzī]: fare
车行(車行) [chēháng]: taxi company
驾驶人(駕駛人) [jiàshǐrén]: driver
拨(撥) [bō]: to dial
意见(意見) [yìjiàn]: opinion
下列 [xiàliè]: the following
监理处(監理處) [jiānlǐchù]: Department of Management and Supervision
市政府 [shìzhèngfǔ]: city government
警察局 [jǐngchájú]: police bureau
驾驶员(駕駛員) [jiàshǐyuán]: driver
新台币(新台幣) [xīntáibì]: name of currency used in Taiwan
搭乘 [dāchéng]: to take a vehicle
职业工会(職業工會) [zhíyè gōnghuì]: occupational association

計程車收據		謝謝您的搭乘，如有任何意見，請撥下列交通服務電話：
車資	新台幣 元	
車行名稱		台北市監理處 2767-8217
電話		台北市政府警察局 2394-9007 (日) 2321-9166 (夜)
車號	U4-190	台北區監理所 2688-6052
駕駛人姓名	林学[illegible]	基隆監理站 2451-7239 台北市汽車駕駛員職業工會 2659-9999

90. 5. 500,000

Translate the receipt:

____

____

____

____

复习 Review

LESSON 21 AND LESSON 22

Conversation

I. Form pairs. The semester will end in about two weeks. You and your roommate are discussing your plans for the summer. Remember, you will need to include the following topics in your conversation (Remember to use 了 as appropriate):

1. 去年夏天你原来 [yuánlái] (originally) 想做什么？后来你做了什么？
2. 今年暑假你想做什么？
3. 你要去哪儿实习/学习？

II. It is summer now. You are doing an internship at a company in New Jersey and your good friend 文华 is studying Chinese in Beijing, China. You are now talking to her over the phone and telling her about your internship. Include the following topics in your conversation:

1. 你在什么公司实习？你是不是很喜欢你实习的公司？
2. 你觉得你实习的工作有意思吗？
3. 你的老板怎么样？同事呢？
4. 实习完 [wán] (finish) 了以后你想做什么？

Hints: The following vocabulary items and conjunctions should be used:

实习，申请，决定，老板，同事
因为……所以……，虽然……不过/可是/但是……，还是，或者，
先……再……然后……，一面……一面……

III. You have just come back from your summer study in Shanghai. Your best friend 白雪 is also considering participating in a summer study abroad program next year. Therefore, you are talking to her about your experience in Shanghai. Remember to include the following:

1. 你是什么时候到上海的？你去上海做什么？
2. 你在上海忙吗？每天有什么活动？
3. 你觉得上海是一个什么样的城市？你喜欢不喜欢上海？为什么？
4. 你在中国旅行了吗？去了什么地方？

Hints: Please use the following vocabulary and conjunctions, and use 了 at appropriate places:

暑期班，星期，活动，最，参观，忙，城市，文化 [wénhuà] culture
因为……所以……，虽然……不过/可是/但是……，还是，或者，
先……再……然后……，一面……一面……

Measure Words

Fill in each blank with an appropriate measure word:

我到上海已经三________星期了。我们暑期班一共有三十六________学生。其中有十五________美国人，还有韩国人和日本人。

我们每天都很忙。上午有四________课，从八________上课到十一________三十________下课。下午有讲座 [jiǎngzuò] (lecture)，我有时候去听________，有时候我们一起坐公共汽车去参观上海的一些地方，或者去买东西。上________星期三我去了一________商店 [shāngdiàn] (store) 买了一________红衬衫，两________黑裙子和一________运动鞋[yùndòngxié] (sneaker)，很便宜，一共五十六________七________九________ (¥56.79)。

我们都住在外国学生宿舍。我的宿舍里有一________床，一________书桌。书桌上有很多书、几________字典 [zìdiǎn] (dictionary) 和一________电话。我还有两________玩具狗 [wánjù gǒu] (toy dog)。

学校里有三________校车 [xiàochē] (school bus)，很方便 [fāngbiàn] (convenient)。我们也有两________食堂 [shítáng] (cafeteria)，我们常常在那里吃饭。我常常点一________汤，一________菜，有时候我也喜欢喝一________中国茶。

我在上海过得很快乐。

Simplified and Traditional Characters

Circle the radical of each of the following characters and then match the character with its traditional form:

认　处　热　动　剧　实　观　丽

動　劇　觀　麗　處　認　實　熱

Small Report

Talk about your experiences such as work study, courses, or study abroad.

Useful words and expressions:

工作：公司，实习，申请，找工作，打工，履历表 [lǚlìbiǎo] (resume)，上班，老板，同事，机会

上课：留学，暑期班，功课，上课，教，活动，参观，进步，京剧，书法，新，地方，旅行

生词表 VOCABULARY LIST

Lesson 1

你	好	是	学生	学	吗	我	呢
也	他	不	老师				

Lesson 2

您	贵	姓	请问	请	问	的	英文
名字	中文	叫	什么	她	谁	同学	

专名

李文中　吴小美　于英

补充词

汉语　英语

Lesson 3

哪	国	人	很	对了	法国	美国	英国
中国	说	会	一点儿	儿	法文	和	

补充词

德国	德国人	德语(德文)	韩国	韩国人	韩语(韩文)
加拿大	加拿大人		泰国	泰国人	泰语(泰文)
日本	日本人	日语(日文)			
西班牙	西班牙人	西班牙语(西班牙文)			

Lesson 4

那	书	这	本	文学	工程	难	太
可是	功课	多	我们	们	少		

补充词

系	数学	计算机(电脑)		专业(主修)	辅修	容易
忙	累	作业	考试	有点儿	还好	

Lesson 5

朋友	来	介绍	一下	室友	有	几	两
个	他们	都	常	跟			

专名

王红　丁明　方小文

补充词

没有　女朋友　男朋友　认识

Lesson 6

家	大家	从	在	一	四	爸爸	妈妈
姐姐	工作	工程师	男	男朋友	没有	辆	车
只	狗	爱					

专名

纽约

补充词

自我介绍		自己	兄弟姐妹		哥哥	妹妹	弟弟
女	女朋友	孩子	宠物	猫			

Lesson 7

住	哪儿	宿舍	多少	号	房间	大	电话
小	号码	二	三	五	六	七	八
九	手机	校外					

专名

陈爱文　张友朋

补充词

校内　公寓　房子　十　○

Lesson 8

认识	去	上课	下课	以后	事儿	想	回
一起	吃	饭	吃饭	菜	今天	下次	怎么样
行	再见	再	见				

专名

韩国	日本

补充词

名片	休息	早饭	午饭(中饭)		晚饭	宵夜

Lesson 9

正在	打电话	喂	等一下儿		等	知道	了
谢谢	吧	对	忙	看	电视	做	上网
我就是	位	留言(留话)		对不起	时候	回来	晚上
要	给						

补充词

占线	打错了	小说	电影	网络(网路)		网吧(网咖)
网站	网页	聊天室	电脑游戏		在线游戏(线上游戏)	
病毒	软件(软体)		硬件(硬体)		发短信(送简信)	
通	休息	睡觉	不客气	不谢		

Lesson 10

每天	半	起床	大学	生活	学期	门	点
睡觉	就	才	刻	分	然后	图书馆	下午
喜欢	打球	写	信	电子邮件		地址	祝
年	月	日					

专名

小明	学文

补充词

点钟	钟头	小时	分钟	秒	过	差	早
晚	熬夜	刷牙	洗脸	洗澡			

Lesson 11

红	茶	还是	绿	服务员	坐	小姐	先生
先	喝	杯	冰	可乐	瓶	啤酒	面
饺子	盘	炒	十	碗	汤	双	筷子

专名

张正然　孙信美　杨欢

补充词

饭馆	餐厅	餐馆	饭店	菜单	白饭	饮料	果汁
橙汁	柳橙汁(柳丁汁)		咖啡	点菜	小费	买单	
结账(结帐)		酸	甜	苦	辣	咸	清淡
烫	凉						

Lesson 12

可以	借	明天	用	得	机场	接	妹妹
玩	飞机	到	手排挡(手排)		开	应该	问题
白	色	停	停车场	这次	练习	这样	就
能	进步						

专名

于影　王本乐　上海　洛杉矶

补充词

自动排挡(自排)

Lesson 13

买	件	衬衫	店员	条	裙子	或者	裤子
黄	不错	比较	穿	黑	试试	帮	好看
让	觉得	钱	块	张	电影	票	

专名

毛爱红　方子英

补充词

贵	便宜	卖	号	几号	特大	大	中
小	特小						

Lesson 14

岁	有空	星期	过	生日	为	舞会	参加
一定	做	蛋糕	送	棒	不客气	多大	地图

补充词

日历	月历	庆生	礼物	蜡烛	祝你生日快乐

Lesson 15

前边	参观	欢迎	里边	厨房	公用	旁边	客厅
走	对面	餐厅	洗澡间	卧室	中间	桌子	上边
后边	公园	真					

专名

田进	梁园生	包志中

补充词

左边	右边	门	书桌	窗户	椅子	衣橱	床
教室	杂志	乱	整齐	干净	脏	整理	

Lesson 16

篮球	得	俩	教练	教	游泳	非常	快
体育馆	游泳池	健身房	锻炼	现在	昨天	球赛	作业
包	慢						

补充词

社团	俱乐部	球季

Lesson 17

春天	久	时间	过	放	春假	气候	夏
秋	冬	其中	最	暖和	短	有时候	热
华氏	百	度	极	刮风	下雨	冷	雪
见面							

专名

小玲

补充词

天气　四季　放假　寒假　暑假　假期　摄氏　长
气温　上升　下降

Lesson 18

火车　旅行　离　学校　远　只要　分钟　骑
自行车　公共汽车　走路　近　西部　先　风景
船　南部　听说　海边　景色　一共　租

专名

季长风　白秋影　加拿大

补充词

海滩　东　北　旺季　淡季　单车(脚踏车)　汽车
机车(摩拖车)　出租汽车(计程车)　火车　公车(巴士)
面包车(包型车)　吉普车　跑车　大货车　四轮驱动(四轮传动)
越野车　车站　捷运　地铁　磁浮铁路　天桥　马路
地下道　隧道　码头　司机

Lesson 19

感冒　饿　好像　舒服　头疼　发烧　咳嗽　生病
考试　复习　所以　医生　吃药　地　休息　准备
笔记　感谢

专名

欧阳迎　唐志信

补充词

医务室(医护室)　打针　护士　医院　诊所　严重　厉害
体温　流感(流行性感冒)　预防针　流感疫苗

Lesson 20

把	带来	啊	进	搬	出	出去	过来
做饭	吸烟	没关系	以前	但是	女朋友	必须	第一天
付	房租	楼上	马上				

专名

常天 夏中明 谢进学

补充词

房东 房客 签约 租屋

Lesson 21

暑假	毕业	决定	申请	研究生院		国外	留学
找	打工	家	公司	实习	电脑	暑期	班
一面	有意思	愉快	一路平安		好运		

专名

程海华 白秋雨 加州

补充词

大学生 研究生 博士生 学位 学士 硕士 博士
简历(履历表)

Lesson 22

对不起	因为	不过	认真	已经	美丽	城市	到处
新	大楼	地方	活动	比如	京剧	书法	东西
最	小笼包	机会	尝尝	开始	高兴	收到	看来
开心	同事	热心	老板	一些	学到	来信	保重

补充词

心想事成 健康 顺利

简繁体字对照表
SIMPLIFIED/TRADITIONAL CHARACTER TABLE

简体字：[jiǎn tǐ zì] simplified character
繁体字：[fán tǐ zì] traditional character (or: complex character)

第一课 Lesson 1

简：	学	吗	师
繁：	學	嗎	師

第二课 Lesson 2

简：	贵	请	问	么	谁
繁：	貴	請	問	麼	誰

第三课 Lesson 3

简：	国	对	说	会	点	儿
繁：	國	對	說	會	點	兒

第四课 Lesson 4

简：	书	这	难	课	们
繁：	書	這	難	課	們

第五课 Lesson 5

简：	来	绍	几	两	个
繁：	來	紹	幾	兩	個

第六课 Lesson 6

简：	从	妈	没	辆	车	只	爱
繁：	從	媽	沒	輛	車	隻	愛

第七课 Lesson 7

简：	号	间	电	话	码	机
繁：	號	間	電	話	碼	機

第八课 Lesson 8

简：认 识 后 饭 样 见
繁：認 識 後 飯 樣 見

第九课 Lesson 9

简：谢 视 网 时 给
繁：謝 視 網 時 給

第十课 Lesson 10

简：门 觉 图 馆 欢 写 邮
繁：門 覺 圖 館 歡 寫 郵

第十一课 Lesson 11

简：红 还 绿 务 员 乐 面 饺 盘 汤 双
繁：紅 還 綠 務 員 樂 麵 餃 盤 湯 雙

第十二课 Lesson 12

简：场 飞 挡 开 应 该 题 练 习 进
繁：場 飛 擋 開 應 該 題 練 習 進

第十三课 Lesson 13

简：买 衬 条 裤 黄 错 较 试 帮 让 钱
繁：買 襯 條 褲 黃 錯 較 試 幫 讓 錢

简：块 张
繁：塊 張

第十四课 Lesson 14

简：岁 过 为 参 气
繁：歲 過 為 參 氣

第十五课 Lesson 15

简：边 观 里 厨 厅 卧 园
繁：邊 觀 裡 廚 廳 臥 園

第十六课 Lesson 16

简:	篮	俩	体	锻	炼	现	赛	业
繁:	籃	倆	體	鍛	煉	現	賽	業

第十七课 Lesson 17

简:	热	华	极	风
繁:	熱	華	極	風

第十八课 Lesson 18

简:	离	远	钟	骑	听
繁:	離	遠	鐘	騎	聽

第十九课 Lesson 19

简:	饿	头	发	烧	复	医	药	准	备	笔	记
繁:	餓	頭	發	燒	復	醫	藥	準	備	筆	記

第二十课 Lesson 20

简:	带	烟	关	系	须	楼	马
繁:	帶	煙	關	係	須	樓	馬

第二十一课 Lesson 21

简:	毕	决	实	脑	运
繁:	畢	決	實	腦	運

第二十二课 Lesson 22

简:	经	丽	处	动	剧	东	笼	尝	兴	板
繁:	經	麗	處	動	劇	東	籠	嚐	興	闆

课文 (简繁体字) (第一课至第二十二课)
LANGUAGE IN USE (SIMPLIFIED/TRADITIONAL CHARACTERS) (LESSONS 1–22)

第一课　你好!

Mary: 你好!
John: 你好!
Mary: 你是学生吗?
John: 我是学生。你呢?
Mary: 我也是学生。
John: 他呢? 他是学生吗?
Mary: 他不是学生。他是老师。

第一課　你好!

Mary: 你好!
John: 你好!
Mary: 你是學生嗎?
John: 我是學生。你呢?
Mary: 我也是學生。
John: 他呢? 他是學生嗎?
Mary: 他不是學生。他是老師。

第二课　您贵姓?

Mary: 你好! 请问您贵姓?
John: 我姓李，我的英文名字是 John Lee, 中文名字是李文中。你呢，请问你叫什么名字?
Mary: 我叫 Mary, 我的英文名字是 Mary Wood, 中文名字是吴小美。
John: 她呢? 她是谁?
Mary: 她是我的同学于英。

第二課　您貴姓?

Mary: 你好! 請問您貴姓?
John: 我姓李，我的英文名字是 John Lee, 中文名字是李文中。你呢，請問你叫什麼名字?
Mary: 我叫 Mary, 我的英文名字是 Mary Wood, 中文名字是吳小美。
John: 她呢? 她是誰?
Mary: 她是我的同學于英。

第三课　你是哪国人?

李文中：小美，你好吗?
吴小美：我很好。对了，文中，你是哪国人?
李文中：我是法国人，你呢? 你是美国人吗?
吴小美：不是，我不是美国人，我是英国人。
李文中：老师呢?
吴小美：他是中国人。他说中文。
李文中：你会说中文吗?
吴小美：我会说一点儿中文，我也会说法文和英文。

第三課　你是哪國人?

李文中：小美，你好嗎?
吳小美：我很好。對了，文中，你是哪國人?
李文中：我是法國人，你呢? 你是美國人嗎?
吳小美：不是，我不是美國人，我是英國人。
李文中：老師呢?
吳小美：他是中國人。他說中文。
李文中：你會說中文嗎?
吳小美：我會說一點兒中文，我也會說法文和英文。

第四课　你学什么?

吴小美：文中，那是你的书吗?
李文中：那是我的书。
吴小美：那是一本什么书?
李文中：那是一本英文书。
吴小美：这本呢? 这是一本什么书?
李文中：这是一本中文书。
吴小美：对了，你学什么?
李文中：我学英国文学，你呢?
吴小美：我学工程。
李文中：工程难吗?
吴小美：不太难，可是功课很多。
李文中：我们的功课也不少。

第四課　你學什麼?

吳小美: 文中，那是你的書嗎?
李文中: 那是我的書。
吳小美: 那是一本什麼書?
李文中: 那是一本英文書。
吳小美: 這本呢? 這是一本什麼書?
李文中: 這是一本中文書。
吳小美: 對了，你學什麼?
李文中: 我學英國文學，你呢?
吳小美: 我學工程。
李文中: 工程難嗎?
吳小美: 不太難，可是功課很多。
李文中: 我們的功課也不少。

第五课　这是我朋友

吴小美: 文中，来! 我来介绍一下。这是我室友，王红。这是我朋友，文中。
李文中: 你好!
王　红: 你好! 你有室友吗?
李文中: 有，我有室友。
王　红: 你有几个室友?
李文中: 我有两个室友。
王　红: 他们都是谁?
李文中: 他们是丁明和方小文。他们都是中国人。我常跟他们说中文。

第五課　這是我朋友

吳小美: 文中，來! 我來介紹一下。這是我室友，王紅。這是我朋友，文中。
李文中: 你好!
王　紅: 你好! 你有室友嗎?
李文中: 有，我有室友。
王　紅: 你有幾個室友?
李文中: 我有兩個室友。
王　紅: 他們都是誰?
李文中: 他們是丁明和方小文。他們都是中國人。我常跟他們說中文。

第六课　我的家

大家好！我叫吴小美。我是从纽约来的。我学工程。我来介绍一下我的家。我家在纽约，有四个人：爸爸、妈妈、姐姐和我。爸爸是英国人，妈妈是美国人，他们都在纽约工作。爸爸是工程师，妈妈是老师，我和姐姐都是学生。姐姐有男朋友，我没有。我们有两辆车，一只狗。我的家很好。我很爱我的家。

第六課　我的家

大家好！我叫吳小美。我是從紐約來的。我學工程。我來介紹一下我的家。我家在紐約，有四個人：爸爸、媽媽、姐姐和我。爸爸是英國人，媽媽是美國人，他們都在紐約工作。爸爸是工程師，媽媽是老師，我和姐姐都是學生。姐姐有男朋友，我沒有。我們有兩輛車，一隻狗。我的家很好。我很愛我的家。

第七课　你住哪儿?

陈爱文：友朋，你住在哪儿?
张友朋：我住宿舍。
陈爱文：多少号?
张友朋：三一四号。
陈爱文：你的房间大吗? 有没有电话?
张友朋：房间很小。有电话。
陈爱文：你的电话号码是多少?
张友朋：(一四二)二六八九三七五。
陈爱文：你有手机吗?
张友朋：有。号码是(一四二) 五一二六八三七。你也住宿舍吗?
陈爱文：不，我不住宿舍，我住校外。

第七課　你住哪兒?

陳愛文：友朋，你住在哪兒?
張友朋：我住宿舍。
陳愛文：多少號?
張友朋：三一四號。
陳愛文：你的房間大嗎? 有沒有電話?
張友朋：房間很小。有電話。
陳愛文：你的電話號碼是多少?
張友朋：(一四二)二六八九三七五。
陳愛文：你有手機嗎?
張友朋：有。號碼是(一四二) 五一二六八三七。你也住宿舍嗎?
陳愛文：不，我不住宿舍，我住校外。

第八课　你认识不认识他?

张友朋：爱文，你去哪儿?
陈爱文：是你，友朋，我去上课。你呢?
张友朋：我也去上课。下课以后你有事儿吗?
陈爱文：我没有事儿。我想回宿舍，有什么事儿吗?
张友朋：你认识不认识我的朋友小文?
陈爱文：我认识他。我们一起上英国文学课。
张友朋：下课以后我跟他一起去吃饭，你去不去?
陈爱文：太好了！去哪儿吃饭?
张友朋：你想不想吃韩国菜?
陈爱文：想。可是我也想吃日本菜。
张友朋：我们今天吃韩国菜，下次吃日本菜，怎么样?
陈爱文：行。下课以后再见。
张友朋：再见。

第八課　你認識不認識他?

張友朋：愛文，你去哪兒?
陳愛文：是你，友朋，我去上課。你呢?
張友朋：我也去上課。下課以後你有事兒嗎?
陳愛文：我沒有事兒。我想回宿舍，有什麼事兒嗎?
張友朋：你認識不認識我的朋友小文?
陳愛文：我認識他。我們一起上英國文學課。
張友朋：下課以後我跟他一起去吃飯，你去不去?
陳愛文：太好了！去哪兒吃飯?
張友朋：你想不想吃韓國菜?
陳愛文：想。可是我也想吃日本菜。
張友朋：我們今天吃韓國菜，下次吃日本菜，怎麼樣?
陳愛文：行。下課以後再見。
張友朋：再見。

第九课 他正在打电话

Situation 1: 在，请等一下儿

陈爱文：喂！我是爱文。请问友朋在吗？
方书程：在，他在他的房间。请等一下儿。喂！友朋！你的电话。
张友朋：知道了！谢谢！
张友朋：喂！我是友朋，你是爱文吧！
陈爱文：对，是我。你在忙吗？
张友朋：没有。我正在看电视呢。你在做什么？
陈爱文：我在上网。

Situation 2: 我就是

陈爱文：喂！
张友朋：喂！
陈爱文：请问友朋在吗？
张友朋：我就是。请问您是哪位？
陈爱文：我是爱文。

Situation 3: 不在，请留言

陈爱文：喂！请问友朋在吗？
丁　明：对不起，他不在。他在上课。
陈爱文：请问他什么时候回来？
丁　明：今天晚上。你要不要留言？
陈爱文：好的。我是爱文。我的电话是(一四二)二六八九七五三。请他回来以后给我打电话。谢谢！
丁　明：不谢。再见。

第九課　他正在打電話

Situation 1: 在，請等一下兒

陳愛文：喂！我是愛文。請問友朋在嗎？
方书程：在，他在他的房間。請等一下兒。喂！友朋！你的電話。
張友朋：知道了！謝謝！
張友朋：喂！我是友朋，你是愛文吧！
陳愛文：對，是我。你在忙嗎？
張友朋：沒有。我正在看電視呢。你在做什麼？
陳愛文：我在上網。

Situation 2: 我就是

陳愛文：喂！
張友朋：喂！
陳愛文：請問友朋在嗎？
張友朋：我就是。請問您是哪位？
陳愛文：我是愛文。

Situation 3: 不在，請留言

陳愛文：喂！請問友朋在嗎？
丁　明：對不起，他不在。他在上課。
陳愛文：請問他什麼時候回來？
丁　明：今天晚上。你要不要留言？
陳愛文：好的。我是愛文。我的電話是(一四二)二六八九七五三。請他回來以後給我打電話。謝謝！
丁　明：不謝。再見。

第十课　我每天七点半起床

小明：

你好！

这个学期我很忙，有五门课。你知道我每天几点起床、几点睡觉吗？我七点半就起床，晚上十二点半以后才睡觉。每天都很忙。九点一刻去上课，十点二十分下课。然后，我去图书馆看书。下午下课以后，我喜欢去打球。每天都有很多功课。

这是我的大学生活，你呢？给我写信吧。我的电子邮件地址是：xuewen376@zhongwen.edu

祝

好

学文

二〇〇三年十一月二十日

第十課　我每天七點半起床

小明：

你好！

這個學期我很忙，有五門課。你知道我每天幾點起床、幾點睡覺嗎？我七點半就起床，晚上十二點半以後才睡覺。每天都很忙。九點一刻去上課，十點二十分下課。然後，我去圖書館看書。下午下課以後，我喜歡去打球。每天都有很多功課。

這是我的大學生活，你呢？給我寫信吧。我的電子郵件地址是：xuewen376@zhongwen.edu

祝

好

學文

二〇〇三年十一月二十日

第十一课　你要红茶还是绿茶?

服务员：请问，几位?
张正然：三位。
服务员：好，请跟我来。请坐。
张正然，孙信美，杨欢：　谢谢!
服务员：小姐，先生，请问，你们想先喝点儿什么?
孙信美：我喜欢喝茶。
服务员：你要红茶还是绿茶?
孙信美：我要一杯冰红茶。
杨　欢：我要一杯可乐。
张正然：我要一瓶啤酒。
服务员：好，一杯冰红茶、一杯可乐、一瓶啤酒。请等一下。
张正然：对了，你们喜欢吃饭还是吃面?
孙信美：我都喜欢。
杨　欢：我想吃饺子。
服务员：这是您的冰红茶、可乐、还有啤酒。你们要点菜吗?
张正然：好，我们点一盘炒饭、一盘炒面和二十个饺子吧。
孙信美：我们还要三碗汤。对了，我们也要三双筷子，谢谢!

第十一課　你要紅茶還是綠茶?

服務員：請問，幾位?
張正然：三位。
服務員：好，請跟我來。請坐。
張正然，孫信美，楊歡：　謝謝!
服務員：小姐，先生，請問，你們想先喝點兒什麼?
孫信美：我喜歡喝茶。
服務員：你要紅茶還是綠茶?
孫信美：我要一杯冰紅茶。
楊　歡：我要一杯可樂。
張正然：我要一瓶啤酒。
服務員：好，一杯冰紅茶、一杯可樂、一瓶啤酒。請等一下。
張正然：對了，你們喜歡吃飯還是吃麵?
孫信美：我都喜歡。
楊　歡：我想吃餃子。
服務員：這是您的冰紅茶、可樂、還有啤酒。你們要點菜嗎?
張正然：好，我們點一盤炒飯、一盤炒麵和二十個餃子吧。
孫信美：我們還要三碗湯。對了，我們也要三雙筷子，謝謝!

第十二课　我可以借你的车吗？

于　影：本乐，明天下午你用不用车？
王本乐：我不用。你有什么事儿吗？
于　影：我得去机场接人，可以借你的车吗？
王本乐：可以。你要去接谁？
于　影：我妹妹和她男朋友。他们从上海坐飞机去洛杉矶玩儿，明天会到我这儿来。
王本乐：我的车是手排挡的，你会不会开？
于　影：应该没问题。我爸爸的车也是手排挡的，我常开他的车。
王本乐：我的车是白色的，车号是BD5730，停在五号停车场。
于　影：知道了。谢谢！
王本乐：不谢。你妹妹他们会说英文吗？
于　影：会一点儿，这次他们想多学习一点儿英文。
王本乐：太好了，我得跟他们多练习一点儿中文。这样，我的中文就能进步了。

第十二課　我可以借你的車嗎？

于　影：本樂，明天下午你用不用車？
王本樂：我不用。你有什麼事兒嗎？
于　影：我得去機場接人，可以借你的車嗎？
王本樂：可以。你要去接誰？
于　影：我妹妹和她男朋友。他們從上海坐飛機去洛杉磯玩兒，明天會到我這兒來。
王本樂：我的車是手排擋的，你會不會開？
于　影：應該沒問題。我爸爸的車也是手排擋的，我常開他的車。
王本樂：我的車是白色的，車號是BD5730，停在五號停車場。
于　影：知道了。謝謝！
王本樂：不謝。你妹妹他們會說英文嗎？
于　影：會一點兒，這次他們想多學習一點兒英文。
王本樂：太好了，我得跟他們多練習一點兒中文。這樣，我的中文就能進步了。

第十三课　我想买一件衬衫

店　员：两位小姐想买什么？
毛爱红：我想买一件衬衫。
方子英：我想买一条裙子或者裤子。
店　员：这件黄衬衫怎么样？
毛爱红：还不错。可是我比较喜欢穿黑色的，有没有黑色的？
店　员：有，在这儿，你试试！
方子英：爱红，来，你帮我看看，我穿裙子好看还是穿裤子好看？
毛爱红：你穿穿，让我看看。我觉得你穿这条裙子好看。
方子英：请问，这条裙子多少钱？
店　员：十五块。
方子英：好，我买了。
毛爱红：我要买这件黑衬衫。
店　员：对了，小姐，这张电影票是你的吗？
方子英：是的，这张电影票是我的。谢谢！我们等一下要去看电影。

第十三課　我想買一件襯衫

店　員：兩位小姐想買什麼？
毛愛紅：我想買一件襯衫。
方子英：我想買一條裙子或者褲子。
店　員：這件黃襯衫怎麼樣？
毛愛紅：還不錯。可是我比較喜歡穿黑色的，有沒有黑色的？
店　員：有，在這兒，你試試！
方子英：愛紅，來，你幫我看看，我穿裙子好看還是穿褲子好看？
毛愛紅：你穿穿，讓我看看。我覺得你穿這條裙子好看。
方子英：請問，這條裙子多少錢？
店　員：十五塊。
方子英：好，我買了。
毛愛紅：我要買這件黑襯衫。
店　員：對了，小姐，這張電影票是你的嗎？
方子英：是的，這張電影票是我的。謝謝！我們等一下要去看電影。

第十四课　我今年二十岁

方子英：爱红，二月十八日你有没有空？
毛爱红：二月十八日那天是星期几？
方子英：星期六。
毛爱红：我有空。有什么事儿吗？
方子英：那天我过生日，我男朋友要为我开一个生日舞会，我想请你参加。
毛爱红：谢谢你，我一定去。还有谁会去？
方子英：我们想请我们的同学和朋友都参加。
毛爱红：我会做蛋糕。我送你一个生日蛋糕，怎么样？
方子英：太棒了！谢谢你！
毛爱红：不客气。你今年多大？
方子英：我今年二十岁。你呢？你的生日是几月几号？
毛爱红：我的生日是十月三号，我今年二十二岁。你的舞会在哪儿开？
方子英：在我男朋友的家，这是他的地址。你知道怎么去吗？
毛爱红：没问题！我有地图。星期六下午五点见。
方子英：再见。

第十四課　我今年二十歲

方子英：愛紅，二月十八日你有沒有空？
毛愛紅：二月十八日那天是星期幾？
方子英：星期六。
毛愛紅：我有空。有什麼事兒嗎？
方子英：那天我過生日，我男朋友要為我開一個生日舞會，我想請你參加。
毛愛紅：謝謝你，我一定去。還有誰會去？
方子英：我們想請我們的同學和朋友都參加。
毛愛紅：我會做蛋糕。我送你一個生日蛋糕，怎麼樣？
方子英：太棒了！謝謝你！
毛愛紅：不客氣。你今年多大？
方子英：我今年二十歲。你呢？你的生日是幾月幾號？
毛愛紅：我的生日是十月三號，我今年二十二歲。你的舞會在哪兒開？
方子英：在我男朋友的家，這是他的地址。你知道怎麼去嗎？
毛愛紅：沒問題！我有地圖。星期六下午五點見。
方子英：再見。

第十五课　图书馆在宿舍前边

(<u>Situation:</u> 今天是宿舍参观日，在学生宿舍)

田　进：你们好！欢迎你们来看我的宿舍。请跟我来。
梁园生：田进，你的宿舍里边有没有厨房？
田　进：有厨房，是公用的。
包志中：你的房间在哪儿？
田　进：我的房间在旁边，从这儿走。来，请进。这是客厅，客厅的对面是一个餐厅。
梁园生：洗澡间呢？
田　进：洗澡间在客厅和卧室的中间。你看，这是我的卧室。
包志中：桌子上边的中文书都是你的吗？
田　进：有的是我的，有的是我朋友的。
包志中：你常在宿舍学习吗？
田　进：不，我不常在宿舍学习，我常去图书馆学习。
梁园生：图书馆在哪儿？
田　进：图书馆在宿舍前边。图书馆的后边还有一个公园。我常去那儿打球。
梁园生，包志中：你们的宿舍真不错。

第十五課　圖書館在宿舍前邊

(<u>Situation:</u> 今天是宿舍參觀日，在學生宿舍)

田　進：你們好！歡迎你們來看我的宿舍。請跟我來。
梁園生：田進，你的宿舍裡邊有沒有廚房？
田　進：有廚房，是公用的。
包志中：你的房間在哪兒？
田　進：我的房間在旁邊，從這兒走。來，請進。這是客廳，客廳的對面是一個餐廳。
梁園生：洗澡間呢？
田　進：洗澡間在客廳和臥室的中間。你看，這是我的臥室。
包志中：桌子上邊的中文書都是你的嗎？
田　進：有的是我的，有的是我朋友的。
包志中：你常在宿舍學習嗎？
田　進：不，我不常在宿舍學習，我常去圖書館學習。
梁園生：圖書館在哪兒？
田　進：圖書館在宿舍前邊。圖書館的後邊還有一個公園。我常去那兒打球。
梁園生，包志中：你們的宿舍真不錯。

第十六课 她打篮球打得很好

张正然：你们俩要去哪儿？
孙信美，杨欢： 我们去打篮球。
张正然：你们篮球打得怎么样？
孙信美：杨欢篮球打得很好。我还不太会打篮球，她是我的教练，她教得很好。
杨 欢：不行，我还打得不太好。
张正然：我不常打篮球，我常常和我室友去游泳，他游泳游得非常快。
杨 欢：你们常去哪儿游泳？
张正然：我们常去体育馆里边的游泳池游泳，我们也常去健身房锻炼。
孙信美：你现在要不要跟我们去打篮球？
张正然：现在不行。我昨天看球赛看得太晚了，今天起得很晚，现在得去做作业。
杨 欢：昨天我们那儿包饺子、做中国菜。你晚上到我们那儿吃饺子吧。
张正然：太好了！我很喜欢吃饺子。你们包饺子包得快不快？
孙信美：我们包得很慢。
杨 欢：信美很会做饭。她做饭做得很好。

第十六課 她打籃球打得很好

張正然：你們倆要去哪兒？
孫信美，楊歡： 我們去打籃球。
張正然：你們籃球打得怎麼樣？
孫信美：楊歡籃球打得很好。我還不太會打籃球，她是我的教練，她教得很好。
楊 歡：不行，我還打得不太好。
張正然：我不常打籃球，我常常和我室友去游泳，他游泳游得非常快。
楊 歡：你們常去哪兒游泳？
張正然：我們常去體育館裡邊的游泳池游泳，我們也常去健身房鍛煉。
孫信美：你現在要不要跟我們去打籃球？
張正然：現在不行。我昨天看球賽看得太晚了，今天起得很晚，現在得去做作業。
楊 歡：昨天我們那兒包餃子、做中國菜。你晚上到我們那兒吃餃子吧。
張正然：太好了！我很喜歡吃餃子。你們包餃子包得快不快？
孫信美：我們包得很慢。
楊 歡：信美很會做飯。她做飯做得很好。

第十七课 春天就要来了

小玲:

好久不见。

你现在怎么样? 时间过得真快, 春天就要来了, 我们也快要放春假了。

我们这儿的气候春夏秋冬都有。其中我最喜欢春天, 很暖和, 可是很短。夏天有时候很热, 最热的时候, 会到华氏一百度, 热极了。秋天有时候会刮风、下雨。这儿的冬天非常冷, 常常下雪。

放春假的时候我想去你那儿玩玩, 我们很快就要见面了!

祝

好!

大中

二〇〇四年三月十日

第十七課 春天就要來了

小玲:

好久不見。

你現在怎麼樣? 時間過得真快, 春天就要來了, 我們也快要放春假了。

我們這兒的氣候春夏秋冬都有。其中我最喜歡春天, 很暖和, 可是很短。夏天有時候很熱, 最熱的時候, 會到華氏一百度, 熱極了。秋天有時候會刮風、下雨。這兒的冬天非常冷, 常常下雪。

放春假的時候我想去你那兒玩玩, 我們很快就要見面了!

祝

好!

大中

二〇〇四年三月十日

第十八课 我们要坐火车去旅行

季长风：秋影，你住在校外吗？离学校远不远？
白秋影：不太远，开车只要五分钟。
季长风：你每天怎么来学校？
白秋影：我常骑自行车，下雨下雪的时候就坐公共汽车，有时候我也走路，可以锻炼锻炼。你呢？
季长风：我住在宿舍，离学校很近，我每天走路来学校。
白秋影：对了，这个春假你要做什么？
季长风：我要跟我的室友一起去西部旅行。
白秋影：你们怎么去？
季长风：我们想先坐火车去，路上看看风景。然后坐船去加拿大，再从加拿大坐飞机回来。你呢？
白秋影：我很想我爸爸、妈妈和妹妹，我要先回家。然后再跟朋友开车去玩儿。
季长风：你们要去哪儿玩儿？
白秋影：我们想去南部玩儿。听说那儿的海边景色很美。
季长风：你们有几个人去？
白秋影：我们一共有五个人去，我们想租一辆车。

第十八課 我們要坐火車去旅行

季長風：秋影，你住在校外嗎？離學校遠不遠？
白秋影：不太遠，開車只要五分鐘。
季長風：你每天怎麼來學校？
白秋影：我常騎自行車，下雨下雪的時候就坐公共汽車，有時候我也走路，可以鍛煉鍛煉。你呢？
季長風：我住在宿舍，離學校很近，我每天走路來學校。
白秋影：對了，這個春假你要做什麼？
季長風：我要跟我的室友一起去西部旅行。
白秋影：你們怎麼去？
季長風：我們想先坐火車去，路上看看風景。然後坐船去加拿大，再從加拿大坐飛機回來。你呢？
白秋影：我很想我爸爸、媽媽和妹妹，我要先回家。然後再跟朋友開車去玩兒。
季長風：你們要去哪兒玩兒？
白秋影：我們想去南部玩兒。聽說那兒的海邊景色很美。
季長風：你們有幾個人去？
白秋影：我們一共有五個人去，我們想租一輛車。

第十九课　我感冒了

唐志信：欧阳迎，你吃饭了吗？
欧阳迎：还没有呢。我不饿。
唐志信：你怎么了？好像不舒服。
欧阳迎：我感冒了。我头疼发烧，还有一点儿咳嗽。
唐志信：你怎么生病了呢？
欧阳迎：这几天我有很多考试，每天都在复习，睡觉睡得太少，所以就病了。
唐志信：你看医生了没有？
欧阳迎：看了。我也吃药了。可是还没有好呢。
唐志信：你应该在家好好地休息。不应该来上课。
欧阳迎：你说得很对，可是我有很多考试。我得好好地准备。
唐志信：这是我上课的笔记，借给你看看。
欧阳迎：非常感谢！好吧，我现在就回家休息。
唐志信：好，我开车送你回去。你得好好地睡觉。

第十九課　我感冒了

唐志信：歐陽迎，你吃飯了嗎？
歐陽迎：還沒有呢。我不餓。
唐志信：你怎麼了？好像不舒服。
歐陽迎：我感冒了。我頭疼發燒，還有一點兒咳嗽。
唐志信：你怎麼生病了呢？
歐陽迎：這幾天我有很多考試，每天都在復習，睡覺睡得太少，所以就病了。
唐志信：你看醫生了沒有？
歐陽迎：看了。我也吃藥了。可是還沒有好呢。
唐志信：你應該在家好好地休息。不應該來上課。
歐陽迎：你說得很對，可是我有很多考試。我得好好地準備。
唐志信：這是我上課的筆記，借給你看看。
歐陽迎：非常感謝！好吧，我現在就回家休息。
唐志信：好，我開車送你回去。你得好好地睡覺。

第二十课　我把小谢带来了 . . .

常　天：中明，我回来了。我把车开回来了，还把小谢也带来了。
夏中明：是小谢啊！快请他进来。
谢进学：我听说你们这儿有一个人搬出去了，我想搬进来，所以过来看看。
常　天：你不想住宿舍了，是不是？
谢进学：是的。宿舍太小了，我想搬出来住。这儿可以不可以做饭？
夏中明：可以，我们有厨房。
谢进学：太好了！我很喜欢做饭。搬出来以后就可以常常做饭了。
常　天：你吸烟吗？我们这儿不能吸烟。
谢进学：没关系。以前我吸烟，但是我女朋友说我不应该吸烟，所以我现在不吸烟了。
夏中明：还有，我们必须在每个月的第一天付房租。
谢进学：没问题！
常　天：喂，小谢，我在楼上，你要不要上来看看？中明，你把小谢带上来看看吧。
夏中明：常天，我们现在还不能上去，你得先下来帮我把这张桌子搬上去。
常　天：好的，我马上下去。

第二十課　我把小謝帶來了 . . .

常　天：中明，我回來了。我把車開回來了，還把小謝也帶來了。
夏中明：是小謝啊！快請他進來。
謝進學：我聽說你們這兒有一個人搬出去了，我想搬進來，所以過來看看。
常　天：你不想住宿舍了，是不是？
謝進學：是的。宿舍太小了，我想搬出來住。這兒可以不可以做飯？
夏中明：可以，我們有廚房。
謝進學：太好了！我很喜歡做飯。搬出來以後就可以常常做飯了。
常　天：你吸煙嗎？我們這兒不能吸煙。
謝進學：沒關係。以前我吸煙，但是我女朋友說我不應該吸煙，所以我現在不吸煙了。
夏中明：還有，我們必須在每個月的第一天付房租。
謝進學：沒問題！
常　天：喂，小謝，我在樓上，你要不要上來看看？中明，你把小謝帶上來看看吧。
夏中明：常天，我們現在還不能上去，你得先下來幫我把這張桌子搬上去。
常　天：好的，我馬上下去。

第二十一课 暑假你要做什么?

程海华: 秋雨, 我问你, 你明年就要毕业了, 毕业以后你想做什么?
白秋雨: 我还没有决定呢。可是我很喜欢学习, 我可能会申请研究生院, 或者去国外留学。你呢? 你什么时候毕业?
程海华: 我还有两年才毕业呢。毕业以后我想去找工作。
白秋雨: 我们就要放暑假了, 今年暑假你要做什么?
程海华: 我要去打工。我要去一家公司实习。
白秋雨: 在哪儿? 是什么工作?
程海华: 在加州, 是一家电脑公司。你呢? 暑假你要做什么?
白秋雨: 我要去中国, 我申请了去上海的暑期班学习, 我想一面学中文, 一面在中国旅行。
程海华: 那一定很有意思。你什么时候去?
白秋雨: 下个星期。
程海华: 这么快! 你到中国以后要常常给我写电子邮件。
白秋雨: 没问题。我祝你工作愉快!
程海华: 我也祝你一路平安! 祝你好运!

第二十一課 暑假你要做什麼?

程海華: 秋雨, 我問你, 你明年就要畢業了, 畢業以後你想做什麼?
白秋雨: 我還沒有決定呢。可是我很喜歡學習, 我可能會申請研究生院, 或者去國外留學。你呢? 你什麼時候畢業?
程海華: 我還有兩年才畢業呢。畢業以後我想去找工作。
白秋雨: 我們就要放暑假了, 今年暑假你要做什麼?
程海華: 我要去打工。我要去一家公司實習。
白秋雨: 在哪兒? 是什麼工作?
程海華: 在加州, 是一家電腦公司。你呢? 暑假你要做什麼?
白秋雨: 我要去中國, 我申請了去上海的暑期班學習, 我想一面學中文, 一面在中國旅行。
程海華: 那一定很有意思。你什麼時候去?
白秋雨: 下個星期。
程海華: 這麼快! 你到中國以後要常常給我寫電子郵件。
白秋雨: 沒問題。我祝你工作愉快!
程海華: 我也祝你一路平安! 祝你好運!

第二十二课　我到上海了

海华：

你好！今天是六月十五号，我一个星期以前就到上海了。对不起，因为太忙了，所以今天才给你写电子邮件。

我们每天都有很多课，功课也不少，不过老师教得很好，也很认真。我们每天都说中文，我的中文进步得很快，现在我已经能说很多中文了。

上海是一个非常美丽的城市，到处都是新的大楼。我们参观了一些地方，也参加了一些活动，比如：看京剧、写书法等等，都很有意思。还有，上海有很多好吃的东西，其中我最喜欢吃的是小笼包，你有机会应该尝尝。

你开始实习了吗？忙不忙？有空请给我写电子邮件。

祝

好！

秋雨

二〇〇四年六月十五日

秋雨：

你好！很高兴收到你的电子邮件。看来你在上海过得很开心。

我现在在洛杉矶，已经开始实习了。这儿的同事都很好，也很热心，常常教我很多东西，老板也不错。我的工作有时候忙，有时候不太忙，我想我得认真地工作，才能学到一些东西。

好了，不多写了。有空请多来信，多保重。

祝

好！

海华

二〇〇四年六月十七日

第二十二課　我到上海了

海華:

你好！今天是六月十五號，我一個星期以前就到上海了。對不起，因為太忙了，所以今天才給你寫電子郵件。

我們每天都有很多課，功課也不少，不過老師教得很好，也很認真。我們每天都說中文，我的中文進步得很快，現在我已經能說很多中文了。

上海是一個非常美麗的城市，到處都是新的大樓。我們參觀了一些地方，也參加了一些活動，比如：看京劇、寫書法等等，都很有意思。還有，上海有很多好吃的東西，其中我最喜歡吃的是小籠包，你有機會應該嚐嚐。

你開始實習了嗎？忙不忙？有空請給我寫電子郵件。

祝

好！

秋雨

二〇〇四年六月十五日

秋雨:

你好！很高興收到你的電子郵件。看來你在上海過得很開心。

我現在在洛杉磯，已經開始實習了。這兒的同事都很好，也很熱心，常常教我很多東西，老闆也不錯。我的工作有時候忙，有時候不太忙，我想我得認真地工作，才能學到一些東西。

好了，不多寫了。有空請多來信，多保重。

祝

好！

海華

二〇〇四年六月十七日

课文英文翻译 ENGLISH TRANSLATION OF LANGUAGE IN USE

Lesson 1 Hello!

Mary: Hello!
John: Hello!
Mary: Are you a student?
John: I'm a student. How about you?
Mary: I'm also a student.
John: How about him? Is he a student?
Mary: He is not a student. He is a teacher.

Lesson 2 What's Your Surname?

Mary: Hello. May I ask your surname?
John: My family name is Lee. My English name is John Lee. My Chinese name is Wenzhong Li. What's your name?
Mary: I'm Mary. My English name is Mary Wood. My Chinese name is Xiaomei Wu.
John: How about her? Who is she?
Mary: She is my classmate Ying Yu.

Lesson 3 Which Country Are You From?

Wenzhong Li: Xiaomei, how are you?
Xiaomei Wu: I'm fine. By the way, Wenzhong, which country are you from?
Wenzhong Li: I'm French. How about you? Are you American?
Xiaomei Wu: No, I'm not American. I'm British.
Wenzhong Li: How about the teacher?
Xiaomei Wu: He is Chinese. He speaks Chinese.
Wenzhong Li: Can you speak Chinese?
Xiaomei Wu: I can speak a little Chinese. I can also speak French and English.

Lesson 4 What Do You Study?

Xiaomei Wu: Wenzhong, is that your book?
Wenzhong Li: That is my book.
Xiaomei Wu: What book is that?
Wenzhong Li: That is an English book.
Xiaomei Wu: How about this book? What book is this?
Wenzhong Li: This is a Chinese book.
Xiaomei Wu: Well, what do you study?

Wenzhong Li: I study English literature. How about you?
Xiaomei Wu: I study engineering.
Wenzhong Li: Is engineering difficult?
Xiaomei Wu: Not very difficult. But there is a lot of homework.
Wenzhong Li: We have a lot of homework too.

Lesson 5 This Is My Friend

Xiaomei Wu: Wenzhong, come here! Let me introduce you. This is my roommate Hong Wang. This is my friend Wenzhong.
Wenzhong Li: Hello!
Hong Wang: Hello! Do you have roommates?
Wenzhong Li: Yes.
Hong Wang: How many roommates do you have?
Wenzhong Li: I have two roommates.
Hong Wang: Who are they?
Wenzhong Li: They are Ming Ding and Xiaowen Fang. They are both Chinese. I often speak with them in Chinese.

Lesson 6 My Family

Hi everybody! I'm Xiaomei Wu. I'm from New York. I study engineering. Let me introduce my family. My home is in New York. There are four people in my family: father, mother, elder sister, and I. My father is British. My mother is American. They both work in New York. My father is an engineer. My mother is a teacher. My elder sister and I are both students. She has a boyfriend; I don't. We have two cars and a dog. My family is very nice. I love my family.

Lesson 7 Where Do You Live?

Aiwen Chen: Youpeng, where do you live?
Youpeng Zhang: I live in the dorm.
Aiwen Chen: What's your room number?
Youpeng Zhang: No. 314.
Aiwen Chen: Is your room big? Is there a phone?
Youpeng Zhang: My room is very small. There is a phone.
Aiwen Chen: What's your phone number?
Youpeng Zhang: (142) 268-9375
Aiwen Chen: Do you have a cell phone?
Youpeng Zhang: Yes. My number is (142) 512-6037. Do you live in the dorm too?
Aiwen Chen: No, I don't live in the dorm. I live off campus.

Lesson 8 Do You Know Him?

Youpeng Zhang:	Aiwen, where are you going?
Aiwen Chen:	It's you, Youpeng. I'm going to class. How about you?
Youpeng Zhang:	I'm going to class too. Do you have any plans for after class?
Aiwen Chen:	No. I'd like to go back to the dorm. What's up?
Youpeng Zhang:	Do you know my friend Xiao Wen?
Aiwen Chen:	I know him. We take English literature together.
Youpeng Zhang:	I'm going to have dinner with him after class. Will you come?
Aiwen Chen:	Great! Where are we going?
Youpeng Zhang:	Do you want to have Korean food?
Aiwen Chen:	Yes. But I also want to have Japanese food.
Youpeng Zhang:	Let's have Korean food today. Next time we'll have Japanese food. How is that?
Aiwen Chen:	OK. See you after class.
Youpeng Zhang:	See you.

Lesson 9 He Is Making a Phone Call

Situation 1 Please Hold

Aiwen Chen:	Hello! This is Aiwen. Is Youpeng in now?
Shucheng Fang:	Yes, he is in his room. Please hold. Hey, Youpeng, the phone is for you.
Youpeng Zhang:	Got it! Thank you!
Youpeng Zhang:	Hello! This is Youpeng. You must be Aiwen!
Aiwen Chen:	Right, it's me. Are you busy?
Youpeng Zhang:	No. I'm watching TV. What are you doing?
Aiwen Chen:	I'm online.

Situation 2 Speaking

Aiwen Chen:	Hello!
Youpeng Zhang:	Hello!
Aiwen Chen:	Is Youpeng in?
Youpeng Zhang:	Speaking. May I ask who is calling?
Aiwen Chen:	It's Aiwen.

Situation 3 Please Leave a Message

Aiwen Chen:	Hello! Is Youpeng in?
Ding Ming:	Sorry, he is not here. He is in class.
Aiwen Chen:	When will he be back?
Ding Ming:	Tonight. Do you want to leave a message?
Aiwen Chen:	OK. I'm Aiwen. My phone number is (142) 268-9753. Please ask him to call back when he returns. Thank you!
Ding Ming:	My pleasure. Goodbye.

Lesson 10 I Get Up at 7:30 Every Day

Xiao Ming,

How are you?

I'm very busy this semester. I have five classes. Can you guess when I get up and go to bed every day? I get up at 7:30, and go to bed after 12:00. I'm very busy every day. I walk from the dorm to class at 9:15 every morning. Class is over at 10:20. Then I go to the library to study. In the afternoon after class, I like to play basketball. I have lots of homework every day.

This is my college life. How about you? Send me a letter. My e-mail address is xuewen376@zhongwen.edu.

Wish you all the best.

Xuewen
Nov. 20, 2003

Lesson 11 Do You Want Black Tea or Green Tea?

Waitress: How many?
Zhenran Zhang: Three.
Waitress: OK. Please follow me. Sit down, please.
Zhenran Zhang, Xinmei Sun, Huan Yang: Thank you.
Waitress: Miss, sir, what would you like to drink?
Xinmei Sun: I would like tea.
Waitress: Black tea or green tea?
Xinmei Sun: Iced black tea, please.
Huan Yang: Coke for me, please.
Zhenran Zhang: I'd like to have a bottle of beer.
Waitress: OK, iced tea, Coke, and a bottle of beer. Won't be a moment.
Zhenran Zhang: Well. Do you want to have rice or noodles?
Xinmei Sun: I like both.
Huan Yang: I want to have dumplings.
Waitress: These are your iced tea, Coke, and beer. Would you like to order food?
Zhenran Zhang: OK. Let's have one fried rice, one fried noodles, and twenty dumplings.
Xinmei Sun: We also want soup for three. And we would like to have three pairs of chopsticks too. Thanks.

Lesson 12 May I Borrow Your Car?

Xin Yu: Benle, will you use your car tomorrow afternoon?
Benle Wang: No. What's up?
Xin Yu: I need to go to the airport to pick somebody up. May I borrow your car?
Benle Wang: Sure. Who are you picking up?
Xin Yu: My younger sister and her boyfriend. They are flying to Los Angeles from Shanghai to do some sightseeing. They arrive tomorrow.

Benle Wang: My car has a manual transmission. Do you know how to drive it?
Xin Yu: There should be no problem. My dad's car also has a manual transmission. I often drove his car.
Benle Wang: My car is white. The plate number is BD5730, and it is parked at the parking lot No. 5.
Xin Yu: I see. Thanks!
Benle Wang: You are welcome. Does your sister speak English?
Xin Yu: A little bit. This time they want to learn some English.
Benle Wang: Great! I should practice some Chinese with them. That way, my Chinese will make progress.

Lesson 13 I Want to Buy a Shirt

Sales: What would you like to buy?
Aihong Mao: I want to buy a shirt.
Ziying Fang: I want to buy a skirt or pants.
Sales: How about this yellow shirt?
Aihong Mao: Good. But I like black better. Do you have black ones?
Sales: Yes, here. Have a try.
Ziying Fang: Aihong, come and have a look. Would I look good in this shirt or pants?
Aihong Mao: Put them on and let me have a look. I think you look good in this shirt.
Ziying Fang: How much is this shirt?
Sales: Fifteen dollars.
Ziying Fang: OK, I'll buy it.
Aihong Mao: I'll take this shirt too.
Sales: Well, miss, is this movie ticket yours?
Ziying Fang: Yes, thank you! The ticket is mine. We are going to see a movie later.

Lesson 14 I Am 20 This Year

Ziying Fang: Aihong, will you be free on February 18?
Aihong Mao: What day of the week is February 18?
Ziying Fang: It's a Saturday.
Aihong Mao: I'll be free. Do you have anything in mind?
Ziying Fang: It's my birthday. My boyfriend is having a party for me. I'd like to invite you.
Aihong Mao: Thank you. I'll definitely come. Who else is coming?
Ziying Fang: We want to invite all our classmates and friends.
Aihong Mao: I know how to make cake. I'll make a cake for you, how's that?
Ziying Fang: Great! Thank you!
Aihong Mao: You're welcome. How old are you?
Ziying Fang: I'll be twenty this year. How about you? When's your birthday?
Aihong Mao: My birthday is October 3. I'm twenty-two. Where will the party be held?
Ziying Fang: At my boyfriend's place. This is his address. Do you know how to get there?
Aihong Mao: No problem. I have a map. See you at 5:00 Saturday afternoon.
Ziying Fang: See you.

Lesson 15 The Library Is in Front of the Dorm

(At the students' dorm)

Jin Tian:	Hello! Welcome to my dorm. Please follow me.
Yuansheng Liang:	Jin Tian, is there a kitchen in your dorm?
Jin Tian:	Yes, it's shared.
Zhizhong Bao:	Where is your room?
Jin Tian:	My room is on that side. Go this way. Come, please come in! This is the living room. The dining room is on the opposite side.
Yuansheng Liang:	Where is the bathroom?
Jin Tian:	The bathroom is between the living room and the bedroom. Look, this is my bedroom.
Zhizhong Bao:	Are all the Chinese books on the table yours?
Jin Tian:	No. Some are mine, some are my friends'.
Zhizhong Bao:	Do you often study in your dorm?
Jin Tian:	No, I don't often study in the dorm. I usually go to study in the library.
Yuansheng Liang:	Where is the library?
Jin Tian:	The library is in front of the dorm. At the back of the library there is a park. I often go there to play ball.
Yuansheng Liang and Zhizhong Bao:	Your dorm is very nice.

Lesson 16 She Plays Basketball Very Well

Zhengran Zhang:	Where are you going?
Xinmei Sun and Huan Yang:	We are going to play basketball.
Zhengran Zhang:	Are you good at it?
Xinmei Sun:	Huan Yang plays very well. I'm not very good at it. She is my coach. She coaches me very well.
Huan Yang:	No, I don't play very well.
Zhengran Zhang:	I don't play basketball often. I usually go swimming with my roommate. He swims really fast!
Huan Yang:	Where do you usually go?
Zhengran Zhang:	The swimming pool in the gym. And we also exercise often in the gym.
Xinmei Sun:	Do you want to come to play basketball with us?
Zhengran Zhang:	Not now. I stayed up too late watching the game last night, so I got up very late this morning. Now I have to do homework.
Huan Yang:	Yesterday we made dumplings and Chinese food. Come to our place to eat dumplings tonight.
Zhengran Zhang:	Great. I like dumplings very much. Do you make dumplings quickly?
Xinme Sun:	No, we are very slow.
Huan Yang:	Xinmei is very good at cooking. She cooks very well.

Lesson 17 Spring Is Coming Soon

Xiao Ling:

Long time no see. How are you? Time is flying by. Spring is coming. And we will have spring break soon.

We have four seasons here. I like spring most. It's warm, but very short. In the summer, sometimes it's very hot. On the hottest days, the temperature usually reaches 100°F. So hot! In the fall, sometimes it is rainy and windy. Winter is very cold here, with lots of snow.

I plan to go to your place during spring break. We'll meet soon.

Best wishes.

Dazhong
Mar. 10, 2004

Lesson 18 We Are Going to Take a Train Trip

Ji Changfeng:	Qiuying, do you live off campus? Is it far from school?
Bai Qiuying:	Not too far. Only a five-minute drive.
Ji Changfeng:	How do you get to school each day?
Bai Qiuying:	I usually ride a bike. When it is raining or snowing, I take the bus. Sometimes I walk, which gives me some exercise. How about you?
Ji Changfeng:	I live in the dorm, which is very close to school. I walk to school every day.
Bai Qiuying:	Well, what will you do during the spring break?
Ji Changfeng:	I'll travel to the West with my roommates.
Bai Qiuying:	How will you go?
Ji Changfeng:	We want to go by train. We would like to do some sightseeing on the road. Then we'll go to Canada by boat. Finally, from Canada, we'll take a plane back home. How about you?
Bai Qiuying:	I miss my parents and sister very much. I'll go home first. Then I'll drive somewhere with my friends.
Ji Changfeng:	Where do you want to go?
Bai Qiuying:	We'd like to go to the South. It is said that the shore is beautiful there.
Ji Changfeng:	How many people will go with you?
Bai Qiuying:	There are five people. We want to rent a car.

Lesson 19 I Caught a Cold

Zhixin Tang:	Ouyang Ying, have you eaten yet?
Ouyang Ying:	Not yet. I'm not hungry.
Zhixin Tang:	What's wrong? You look sick.
Ouyang Ying:	I have a cold. I have a headache, a fever, and a bit of a cough.
Zhixin Tang:	How did you get sick?
Ouyang Ying:	I had lots of exams these past few days. Every day I revised a lot and didn't get enough sleep. So I'm sick.

Zhixin Tang: Did you see the doctor?
Ouyang Ying: Yes. I took pills. But it's not over yet.
Zhixin Tang: You should stay at home and get some rest. You shouldn't come to class.
Ouyang Ying: You are right. But I have lots of exams. I have to be well prepared.
Zhixin Tang: These are my class notes. You may borrow them.
Ouyang Ying: Thanks a lot. I'd better go home and get some rest.
Zhixin Tang: OK, I'll drive you home. You should sleep well.

Lesson 20 I've Brought Xiao Xie Over . . .

Tian Chang: Zhongming, I'm back. I drove the car back, and I also brought Xiao Xie over.
Zhongming Xia: Oh, it's Xiao Xie! Ask him to come in.
Jinxue Xie: I heard that one of your roommates moved out. I want to move in. So here I am to have a look.
Tian Chang: You don't want to live in the dorm any more, right?
Jinxue Xie: Yes. The dorm is too small. I want to move out. Can you cook here?
Zhongming Xia: Yes. We have a kitchen.
Jinxue Xie: Great. I like to cook. After moving out of the dorm, I could cook often.
Tian Chang: Do you smoke? It's non-smoking here.
Jinxue Xie: It's OK. I used to smoke, but my girlfriend said I shouldn't, so I quit.
Zhongming Xia: And, we have to pay the rent on the 1st of each month.
Jinxue Xie: No problem.
Tian Chang: Hi, Xiao Xie, I'm upstairs. Don't you want to come up to have a look? Zhongming, bring Xiao Xie up here.
Zhongming Xia: Tian Chang, we can't come up now. You'd better come down to help me move the table up first.
Tian Chang: OK. I will come down immediately.

Lesson 21 What Will You Do During the Summer Vacation?

Haihua Cheng: Qiuyu, let me ask you, you'll graduate next year. What will you do after graduation?
Qiuyu Bai: I haven't decided yet. But I love to study. I'll probably apply for graduate school, or go to study abroad. How about you? When will you graduate?
Haihua Cheng: I still have two more years to go. After graduation, I want to find a job.
Qiuyu Bai: We'll have summer vacation soon. What will you do this summer?
Haihua Cheng: I'll work. I have a summer internship with a company.
Qiuyu Bai: Where? What kind of job?
Haihua Cheng: In California, a computer company. How about you? What will you do this summer?
Qiuyu Bai: I'll go to China. I applied for a summer class in Shanghai. I want to learn some Chinese, and at the same time do some traveling in China.
Haihua Cheng: It must be very interesting. When will you leave?
Qiuyu Bai: Next week.

Haihua Cheng: So fast! E-mail me often after you arrive in China.
Qiuyu Bai: No problem. Have a good time working!
Haihua Cheng: Have a safe journey, and good luck!

Lesson 22 I Have Arrived in Shanghai

Haihua,

How are you? Today is June 15. I arrived in Shanghai a week ago. Sorry, I've been too busy to write you an e-mail before today.

We have many classes every day, and lots of homework too. The instructor is good and very conscientious. We speak Chinese every day. My Chinese has improved greatly. Now I can speak lots of Chinese.

Shanghai is a beautiful city, with new buildings everywhere. We visited some places, as well as attending some activities, including watching Peking Opera, writing calligraphy, etc. All very interesting! And, there is a lot of good food here. Of all the food, I love the little steamed buns the best. You should have a taste some time.

Have you begun your internship yet? Are you busy? When you have time, please e-mail me.

Best wishes.

Qiuyu
June 15, 2004

Qiuyu:

How are you? I was so glad to get your e-mail. It seems you are very happy in Shanghai.

I've begun my internship in Los Angeles. My colleagues here are all very nice and warmhearted. They are teaching me many things. The boss is nice too. I'm busy from time to time. I believe I will work hard to learn more things.

OK, I should stop here. Write to me more when you have time. Take care.

Best wishes.

Haihua
June 17, 2004

拼音索引 PINYIN INDEX

Each entry lists Pinyin, simplified character, traditional character, part of speech, English meaning, and lesson number.
Note: The letter "s" means that the entry occurs in the supplementary vocabulary to that lesson.

A

a	啊	啊	*Int.*	(used at the end of a sentence to indicate surprise)	20
āyí	阿姨	阿姨	*N.*	aunt (mother's sister)	6s
ài	爱	愛	*V.*	to love	6
áoyè	熬夜	熬夜	*V.O.*	to burn the midnight oil	10s

B

ba	吧	吧	*Part.*	(indicates an assumption or suggestion)	9
bā	八/捌	八/捌	*Num.*	eight	7
bǎ	把	把	*Prep.*	(introduces the object of a verb)	20
bàba	爸爸	爸爸	*N.*	father	6
bái	白	白	*Adj.*	white	12
báifàn	白饭	白飯	*N.*	steamed rice	11s
báisè	白色	白色	*Adj.*	white	13s
bǎi	百	百	*Num.*	hundred	17
bān	搬	搬	*V.*	to move	20
	班	班	*N.*	class	21
bàn	半	半	*Adj.*	half	10
bāng	帮	幫	*V.*	to help	13
bàng	棒	棒	*Adj.*	wonderful	14
bàngqiú	棒球	棒球	*N.*	baseball	16s
bāo	包	包	*V.*	to wrap	16
bǎozhòng	保重	保重		Take care.	22s
bēi	杯	杯	*M.W.*	cup	11
běi	北	北	*N.*	north	18s
bèixīn	背心	背心	*N.*	vest	13s
běn	本	本	*M.W.*	(measure word for book)	4
bǐjì	笔记	筆記	*N.*	notes	19
bǐjiào	比较	比較	*Adv.*	relatively	13
bǐrú	比如	比如	*Conj.*	for example	22
bìxū	必须	必須	*Aux.*	must	20

bìyè	毕业	畢業	*V.*	to graduate	21
biǎodì	表弟	表弟	*N.*	cousin (son of parents' sister or mother's brother) (younger than the speaker)	6s
biǎodìmèi	表弟妹	表弟妹	*N.*	cousin (wife of 表弟)	6s
biǎogē	表哥	表哥	*N.*	cousin (son of parents' sister or mother's brother) (older than the speaker)	6s
biǎojiě	表姐	表姐	*N.*	cousin (daughter of parents' sister or mother's brother) (older than the speaker)	6s
biǎojiěfu	表姐夫	表姐夫	*N.*	cousin (husband of 表姐)	6s
biǎomèi	表妹	表妹	*N.*	cousin (daughter of parents' sister or mother's brother) (younger than the speaker)	6s
biǎomèifu	表妹夫	表妹夫	*N.*	cousin (husband of 表妹)	6s
biǎosǎo	表嫂	表嫂	*N.*	cousin (wife of 表哥)	6s
bīng	冰	冰	*N.*	ice	11
bīngqiú	冰球	冰球	*N.*	ice hockey	16s
bǐnggān	饼干	餅乾	*N.*	cracker	11s
bìngdú	病毒	病毒	*N.*	virus	9s
bóbo	伯伯	伯伯	*N.*	uncle (father's elder brother)	6s
bómǔ	伯母	伯母	*N.*	aunt (wife of father's elder brother)	6s
bóshì	博士	博士	*N.*	doctoral degree	21s
bóshìshēng	博士生	博士生	*N.*	doctoral students	21s
bù	不	不	*Adv.*	not, no (used to form a negative)	1
búcuò	不错	不錯		not bad; pretty good	13
búguò	不过	不過	*Conj.*	but, however	22
búkèqi	不客气	不客氣		you're welcome; don't mention it (in reply to thank you)	9s, 14
búxiè	不谢	不謝		you're welcome; don't mention it (in reply to thank you)	9s

C

cái	才	才	*Adv.*	(used before a verb to indicate that something is rather late by general standards or something has just happened)	10
cǎisè	彩色	彩色	*Adj.*	multicolor	13s
cài	菜	菜	*N.*	dish	8
càidān	菜单	菜單	*N.*	menu	11s

cānguān	参观	參觀	*V.*	to visit	15
cānguǎn	餐馆	餐館	*N.*	restaurant	11s
cānjiā	参加	參加	*V.*	to participate, join	14
cāntīng	餐厅	餐廳	*N.*	restaurant, dining room	11s, 15
cǎoméi	草莓	草莓	*N.*	strawberry	11s
chá	茶	茶	*N.*	tea	11
chà	差	差	*V.*	to lack	10s
cháng	常	常	*Adv.*	often; frequently	5
	长	長	*Adj.*	long	17s
chángchang	尝尝	嚐嚐	*V.*	to have a try, taste	22
chángjiàn	常见	常見	*Adj.*	common	11s
chángkù	长裤	長褲	*N.*	long pants	13s
chǎo	炒	炒	*V.*	to stir fry	11
chē	车	車	*N.*	car	6
chēzhàn	车站	車站	*N.*	stop, station	18s
chènshān	衬衫	襯衫	*N.*	shirt	13
chēngwèi	称谓	稱謂	*N.*	form of address	6s
chéngsè (júsè)	橙色 (橘色)	橙色 (橘色)	*Adj.*	orange	13s
chéngshì	城市	城市	*N.*	city	22
chéngxùyuán (chéngshì shèjìshī)	程序员 (程式设计师)	程序員 (程式設計師)	*N.*	computer programmer	6s
chéngzhī	橙汁	橙汁	*N.*	orange juice	11s
chī	吃	吃	*V.*	to eat	8
chīfàn	吃饭	吃飯	*V.O.*	to eat, have a meal	8
chīyào	吃药	吃藥	*V.O.*	to take medicine	19
chǒngwù	宠物	寵物	*N.*	pet	6s
chū	出	出	*V.*	to be out	20
chūqù	出去	出去	*V.C.*	to go out	20
chūzūqìchē (jìchéngchē)	出租汽车 (计程车)	出租汽車 (計程車)	*N.*	taxi	18s
chúfáng	厨房	廚房	*N.*	kitchen	15
chuān	穿	穿	*V.*	to wear, put on (regular clothes)	13, 13s
chuānshàng	穿上	穿上	*V.C.*	to put on (regular clothes)	13s
chuán	船	船	*N.*	ship	18
chuānghu	窗户	窗戶	*N.*	window	15s
chuáng	床	床	*N.*	bed	15s
chūnjià	春假	春假	*N.*	spring break	17
chūnjuǎn	春卷	春捲	*N.*	spring roll	11s
chūntiān	春天	春天	*N.*	spring	17
cífú tiělù	磁浮铁路	磁浮鐵路	*N.*	magnetic railway	18s
cóng	从	從	*Prep.*	from	6

D

dǎ diànhuà	打电话	打電話	*V.O.*	to make a phone call	9
dǎcuòle	打错了	打錯了		to dial a wrong number	9s
dǎgōng	打工	打工	*V.O.*	to work for others, be employed	21
dǎqiú	打球	打球	*V.O.*	to play basketball/badminton/ tennis/table tennis	10
dǎzhēn	打针	打針	*V.O.*	to give or receive an injection	13s, 19s
dà	大	大	*Adj.*	big, large	7, 13s
dàhuòchē	大货车	大貨車	*N.*	truck	18s
dàjiā	大家	大家	*Pron.*	all, everybody	6
dàlóu	大楼	大樓	*N.*	tall building	22
dàxué	大学	大學	*N.*	college; university	10
dàxuéshēng	大学生	大學生	*N.*	college student(s)	6s, 21s
dàyī	大衣	大衣	*N.*	overcoat	13s
dài	戴	戴	*V.*	to wear, put on (accessories)	13s
dàilái	带来	帶來	*V.C.*	to bring over	20
dàishàng	戴上	戴上	*V.C.*	to put on (accessories)	13s
dānchē (jiǎotàchē)	单车 (脚踏车)	單車 (腳踏車)	*N.*	bicycle	18s
dàngāo	蛋糕	蛋糕	*N.*	cake	11s, 14
dànjì	淡季	淡季	*N.*	off-season	18s
dànshì	但是	但是	*Conj.*	but	20
dǎoyóu	导游	導遊	*N.*	tourist guide	6s
dào	到	到	*V.*	to arrive	12
dàochù	到处	到處	*Adv.*	everywhere	22
de	的	的	*Part.*	(a structural particle)	2
	得	得	*Part.*	(used between a verb or an adjective and its complement to indicate result, possibility or degree)	16
	地	地	*Part.*	(attached to an adjective to transform the whole unit into an adverb)	19
Déguó	德国	德國	*N.*	Germany	3s
Déguórén	德国人	德國人	*N.*	German (person)	3s
Déyǔ (Déwén)	德语 (德文)	德語 (德文)	*N.*	German (language)	3s
děi	得	得	*Aux.*	must; have to	12
děng	等	等	*V.*	to wait	9
děng yíxiàr	等一下儿	等一下兒		to wait for a moment	9
dìdi	弟弟	弟弟	*N.*	younger brother	6s

dìfang	地方	地方	*N.*	place	22
dìtú	地图	地圖	*N.*	map	14
dìtiě	地铁	地鐵	*N.*	subway	18s
dìxiàdào	地下道	地下道	*N.*	underground passage	18s
dìyītiān	第一天	第一天	*N.*	first day	20
dìzhǐ	地址	地址	*N.*	address	10
diǎn	点	點	*M.W.*	o'clock (point on clock)	10
diǎncài	点菜	點菜	*V.O.*	to order food	11s
diǎnzhōng	点钟	點鐘	*M.W.*	hour	10s
diànhuà	电话	電話	*N.*	phone	7
diànnǎo	电脑	電腦	*N.*	computer	21
diànnǎo yóuxì	电脑游戏	電腦遊戲	*N.*	computer game	9s
diànshì	电视	電視	*N.*	television	9
diànyǐng	电影	電影	*N.*	movie	9s, 13
diànyuán	店员	店員	*N.*	salesman; saleswoman	13
diànzǐ yóujiàn	电子邮件	電子郵件	*N.*	email	10
diàoyú	钓鱼	釣魚	*V.O.*	to fish	16s
dōng	冬	冬	*N.*	winter	17
	东	東	*N.*	east	18s
dōngxi	东西	東西	*N.*	thing	22
dòngzuò	动作	動作	*N.*	action	13s
dōu	都	都	*Adv.*	all; both	5
dòufu	豆腐	豆腐	*N.*	bean curd	11s
dù	度	度	*N.*	degree	17
duǎn	短	短	*Adj.*	short	17
duǎnkù	短裤	短褲	*N.*	shorts	13s
duànliàn	锻炼	鍛煉	*V.*	to exercise	16
duì	对	對	*Adj.*	correct, right	9
duìbuqǐ	对不起	對不起		sorry, I'm sorry; Excuse me.	9, 22
duìle	对了	對了		by the way (a phrase used to start a new topic)	3
duìmiàn	对面	對面	*N.*	opposite	15
duō	多	多	*Adj.*	many, much	4
duōdà	多大	多大		how old	14
duōshǎo	多少	多少	*Pron.*	how many, how much	7

E

è	饿	餓	*Adj.*	hungry	19
			V.	to starve	3
ér	儿	兒		(retroflex ending)	3
ěrhuán	耳环	耳環	*N.*	earrings	13s
èr	二/贰	二/貳	*Num.*	two	7

F

fā duǎnxìn (sòng jiǎnxùn)	发短信 (送简讯)	發短信 (送簡訊)	*V.O.*	to send a short (cell phone) message	9s
fāshāo	发烧	發燒	*V.O.*	to have a fever	19
Fǎguó	法国	法國	*N.*	France	3
Fǎwén	法文	法文	*N.*	French (language)	3
fàn	饭	飯	*N.*	cooked rice; meal	8
fàndiàn	饭店	飯店	*N.*	restaurant	11s
fànguǎn	饭馆	飯館	*N.*	restaurant	11s
fángdìchǎn gùwèn	房地产顾问	房地產顧問	*N.*	real estate agent	6s
fángdōng	房东	房東	*N.*	landlord	20s
fángjiān	房间	房間	*N.*	room	7
fángkè	房客	房客	*N.*	tenant	20s
fángzū	房租	房租	*N.*	rent	20
fángzi	房子	房子	*N.*	house; room	7s
fàng	放	放	*V.*	to have, start (a vacation)	17
fàngjià	放假	放假	*V.O.*	to have vacation	17s
fēicháng	非常	非常	*Adv.*	very	16
fēijī	飞机	飛機	*N.*	airplane	12
fēixíngyuán	飞行员	飛行員	*N.*	pilot	6s
fēn	分	分	*N.*	minute; 100 fen = 10 jiao/ 10 mao = 1 yuan/1 kuai	10, 13s
fēnzhōng	分钟	分鐘	*N.*	minute	10s, 18
fěnhóngsè	粉红色	粉紅色	*Adj.*	pink	13s
fēngjǐng	风景	風景	*N.*	scenery	18
fúwùyuán	服务员	服務員	*N.*	waiter/waitress	11
fǔxiū	辅修	輔修	*N.*	minor	4s
fù	付	付	*V.*	to pay	20
fùxí	复习	復習	*V.*	to review	19

G

gānjìng	干净	乾淨	*Adj.*	clean	15s
gǎnlǎnqiú	橄榄球	橄欖球	*N.*	football	16s
gǎnmào	感冒	感冒	*N.*	cold, flu	19
gǎnxiè	感谢	感謝	*V.*	to thank, be grateful	19
Gǎngbì	港币	港幣	*N.*	currency of Hong Kong	13s
gāo'ěrfūqiú	高尔夫球	高爾夫球	*N.*	golf	16s
gāoxìng	高兴	高興	*Adj.*	happy	22
gēge	哥哥	哥哥	*N.*	elder brother	6s
gè	个	個	*M.W.*	(the most commonly used measure word for cups, buildings, characters, etc.)	5

gěi	给	給	*Prep.*	for, to	9
			V.	to give	
gēn	跟	跟	*Prep.*	with	5
gōngchē	公车	公車	*N.*	bus	18s
(bāshì)	(巴士)	(巴士)			
gōngchéng	工程	工程	*N.*	engineering	4
gōngchéngshī	工程师	工程師	*N.*	engineer	6, 6s
gōnggòngqìchē	公共汽车	公共汽車	*N.*	bus	18
gōngkè	功课	功課	*N.*	homework; assignment	4
gōngsī	公司	公司	*N.*	company	21
gōngyù	公寓	公寓	*N.*	apartment	7s
gōngyòng	公用	公用	*Adj.*	for public use, communal	15
gōngyuán	公园	公園	*N.*	park	15
gōngzuò	工作	工作	*N.*	job	6
			V.	to work	6
gǒu	狗	狗	*N.*	dog	6
gūfù	姑父	姑父	*N.*	uncle (husband of father's sister)	6s
gūgu	姑姑	姑姑	*N.*	aunt (father's sister)	6s
gūmā	姑妈	姑媽	*N.*	aunt (father's sister)	6s
gūzhàng	姑丈	姑丈	*N.*	uncle (husband of father's sister)	6s
gùwèn	顾问	顧問	*N.*	consultant	6s
guāfēng	刮风	刮風	*V.O.*	to blow (wind)	17
guānyuán	官员	官員	*N.*	government official	6s
guì	贵	貴	*Adj.*	noble, honored; expensive	2, 13s
guó	国	國	*N.*	country	3
guówài	国外	國外	*N.*	overseas, abroad	21
guǒzhī	果汁	果汁	*N.*	juice	11s
guò	过	過	*V.*	to pass, to spend (life, time); celebrate (e.g., birthday)	10s, 14, 17
guòlái	过来	過來	*V.C.*	to come over	20

H

hái hǎo	还好	還好		not bad; okay	4s
háishì	还是	還是	*Conj.*	or	11
háizi	孩子	孩子	*N.*	child	6s
hǎibiān	海边	海邊	*N.*	seaside	18
hǎitān	海滩	海灘	*N.*	seashore	18s
hǎixiān	海鲜	海鮮	*N.*	seafood	11s
Hánguó	韩国	韓國	*N.*	Korea	3s, 8
Hánguórén	韩国人	韓國人	*N.*	Korean (person)	3s
hánjià	寒假	寒假	*N.*	winter vacation	17s
Hányǔ	韩语	韓語	*N.*	Korean (language)	3s
(Hánwén)	(韩文)	(韓文)			

Hànyǔ	汉语	漢語	*N.*	Chinese (language)	2s
hǎo	好	好	*Adj.*	good; well	1
hǎokàn	好看	好看	*Adj.*	good looking	13
hǎoxiàng	好像	好像	*V.*	to be like, seem	19
hǎoyùn	好运	好運		Good luck.	21
hào	号	號	*N.*	number, size	7, 13s
hàomǎ	号码	號碼	*N.*	number	7
hē	喝	喝	*V.*	to drink	11
hé	和	和	*Conj.*	and	3
hēi	黑	黑	*Adj.*	black	13
hēisè	黑色	黑色	*Adj.*	black	13s
hěn	很	很	*Adv.*	very, quite	3
hóng	红	紅	*Adj.*	red	11
hóngsè	红色	紅色	*Adj.*	red	13s
hòubiān	后边	後邊	*N.*	behind, at the back	15
hùshi	护士	護士	*N.*	nurse	6s, 19s
huábīng	滑冰	滑冰	*V.O.*	to skate	16s
huáchuán	划船	划船	*V.O.*	to row	16s
huáshì	华氏	華氏	*N.*	Fahrenheit	17
huáxuě	滑雪	滑雪	*V.O.*	to snow ski	16s
huānyíng	欢迎	歡迎	*V.*	to welcome	15
huáng	黄	黃	*Adj.*	yellow	13
huángsè	黄色	黃色	*Adj.*	yellow	13s
huīsè	灰色	灰色	*Adj.*	gray	13s
huí	回	回	*V.*	to return	8
huílai	回来	回來	*V.C.*	to return	9
huì	会	會	*Aux.*	can, be able to	3
húntun	馄饨	餛飩	*N.*	wonton	11s
huódòng	活动	活動	*N.*	activity	22
huǒchē	火车	火車	*N.*	train	18, 18s
huòbì	货币	貨幣	*N.*	currency	13s
huòzhě	或者	或者	*Conj.*	or; either . . . or . . .	13

J

jīchǎng	机场	機場	*N.*	airport	12
jīhuì	机会	機會	*N.*	opportunity	22
jīròu	鸡肉	雞肉	*N.*	chicken	11s
jí	极	極	*Adv.*	extremely	17
jípǔchē	吉普车	吉普車	*N.*	jeep	18s
jǐ	几	幾		how many	5
jǐ hào	几号	幾號		which size	13s
jìsuànjī (diànnǎo)	计算机 (电脑)	計算機 (電腦)	*N.*	computer	4s
jiā	家	家	*N.*	home; family	6

			M.W.	(measure word for company, enterprises, store, etc.)	21
Jiānádà	加拿大	加拿大	*N.*	Canada	3s
Jiānádàrén	加拿大人	加拿大人	*N.*	Canadian (person)	3s
jiātíng zhǔfù	家庭主妇	家庭主婦	*N.*	housewife	6s
Jiāzhōu	加州	加州	*N.*	California (state)	21
jiákèshān (jiákè)	夹克衫 (夹克)	夾克衫 (夾克)	*N.*	jacket	13s
jiàqī	假期	假期	*N.*	holiday	17s
jiǎnlì (lǚlìbiǎo)	简历 (履历表)	簡歷 (履歷表)	*N.*	resume	21s
jiàn	见	見	*V.*	to see	8
	件	件	*M.W.*	(measure word for clothes)	13
jiànkāng	健康	健康	*Adj.*	healthy	22s
jiànmiàn	见面	見面	*V.O.*	to meet each other	17
jiànshēnfáng	健身房	健身房	*N.*	gym	16
jiànzhùshī	建筑师	建築師	*N.*	architect	6s
jiāo	教	教	*V.*	to teach, coach	16
jiǎo	角	角	*N.*	(10 角 = 1 元)	13s
jiǎozi	饺子	餃子	*N.*	dumpling (crescent shaped)	11
jiào	叫	叫	*V.*	to call	2
jiàoliàn	教练	教練	*N.*	coach, trainer	16
jiàoshì	教室	教室	*N.*	classroom	15s
jiàoshòu	教授	教授	*N.*	professor	6s
jiàoyù gōngzuòzhě	教育工作者	教育工作者	*N.*	educator	6s
jiē	接	接	*V.*	to pick up	12
jiéyùn	捷运	捷運	*N.*	MRT (Mass Rapid Transportation) in Taiwan	18s
jiézhàng (jiézhàng)	结账 (结帐)	結賬 (結帳)	*V.O.*	to settle the account	11s
jiějie	姐姐	姐姐	*N.*	older sister	6
jiè	借	借	*V.*	to borrow	12
jièshào	介绍	介紹	*V.*	to introduce	5
			N.	introduction	5
jièzhi	戒指	戒指	*N.*	ring	13s
jīnhuángsè	金黄色	金黃色	*Adj.*	gold	13s
jīntiān	今天	今天	*N.*	today	8
jìn	近	近	*Adj.*	near	18
	进	進	*V.*	to enter	20
jìnbù	进步	進步	*V.*	to improve	12
jīngjìrén	经纪人	經紀人	*N.*	agent	6s
jīngjìshī	经济师	經濟師	*N.*	economist	6s
jīngjù	京剧	京劇	*N.*	Peking opera	22
jīnglǐ	经理	經理	*N.*	manager	6s
jǐngsè	景色	景色	*N.*	scenery; view	18

jiǔ	九/玖	九/玖	*Num.*	nine	7
	久	久	*Adj.*	for a long time	17
jiù	就	就	*Adv.*	as early as; already; therefore (connects two clauses, the first being the premise of the second)	10, 12
jiùjiu	舅舅	舅舅	*N.*	uncle (mother's brother)	6s
jiùmā	舅妈	舅媽	*N.*	aunt (wife of mother's brother)	6s
jǔzhòng	举重	舉重	*V.O.*	to lift weights	16s
jùlèbù	俱乐部	俱樂部	*N.*	club	16s
juéde	觉得	覺得	*V.*	to think, feel	13
juédìng	决定	決定	*V.*	to decide	21

K

kāfēi	咖啡	咖啡	*N.*	coffee	11s
kāi	开	開	*V.*	to drive	12
kāishǐ	开始	開始	*V.*	to start, begin	22
kāixīn	开心	開心	*Adj.*	happy	22
kàn	看	看	*V.*	to look at; see; watch	9
kànlái	看来	看來		it seems	22
kǎoshì	考试	考試	*N.*	exam	4s, 19
késòu	咳嗽	咳嗽	*V.*	to cough	19
kělè	可乐	可樂	*N.*	cola	11
kěshì	可是	可是	*Conj.*	but; yet; however	4
kěyǐ	可以	可以	*Aux.*	can, may	12
kè	刻	刻	*M.W.*	a quarter (of an hour)	10
kètīng	客厅	客廳	*N.*	living room	15
kǔ	苦	苦	*Adj.*	bitter	11s
kùzi	裤子	褲子	*N.*	pants	13
kuài	快	快	*Adj.*	fast	16
	块	塊	*N.*	dollar	13, 13s
kuàijìshī	会计师	會計師	*N.*	accountant	6s
kuàizi	筷子	筷子	*N.*	chopstick	11

L

là	辣	辣	*Adj.*	spicy	11s
làzhú	蜡烛	蠟燭	*N.*	candle	14s
lái	来	來	*V.*	to come (used before a verb to indicate that one is about to do something)	5
láixìn	来信	來信	*V.O.*	to write a letter (to the speaker)	22
lánqiú	篮球	籃球	*N.*	basketball	16, 16s
lánsè	蓝色	藍色	*Adj.*	blue	13s
lǎobǎn	老板	老闆	*N.*	boss	6s, 22

lǎolao	姥姥	姥姥	*N.*	maternal grandmother	6s
lǎoshī	老师	老師	*N.*	teacher	1, 6s
lǎoye	姥爷	老爺	*N.*	maternal grandfather	6s
le	了	了	*Part.*	(indicates assumption)	9
lèi	累	累	*Adj.*	tired	4s
lěng	冷	冷	*Adj.*	cold	17
lí	离	離	*V.*	to be off, away, from	18
lízi	梨子	梨子	*N.*	pear	11s
lǐbiān	里边	裡邊	*N.*	inside	15
lǐwù	礼物	禮物	*N.*	gift	14s
lìhài	厉害	厲害	*Adj.*	severely, very much	19s
liǎ	俩	倆		two people (colloquial)	16
liànxí	练习	練習	*V.*	to practice	12
liáotiānshì	聊天室	聊天室	*N.*	chat room	9s
liáng	凉	涼	*Adj.*	cool	11s
liángxié	凉鞋	涼鞋	*N.*	sandles	13s
liǎng	两	兩	*Num.*	two	5
liàng	辆	輛	*M.W.*	(measure word for vehicles)	6
líng	〇/零	〇/零	*Num.*	zero	7s
lǐngdài	领带	領帶	*N.*	necktie	13s
liúgǎn	流感	流感	*N.*	flu	19s
(liúxíngxìng gǎnmào)	(流行性感冒)	(流行性感冒)			
liúgǎn yìmiáo	流感疫苗	流感疫苗	*N.*	flu shot	19s
liú xuéshēng	留学生	留學生	*N.*	international students	6s
liúxué	留学	留學	*V.O.*	to study abroad	21
liúyán	留言	留言	*V.O.*	to leave a message	9
(liúhuà)	(留话)	(留話)			
liǔchéngzhī	柳橙汁	柳橙汁	*N.*	tangerine juice	11s
(liǔdīngzhī)	(柳丁汁)	(柳丁汁)			
liù	六/陆	六/陸	*Num.*	six	7
lóushàng	楼上	樓上	*N.*	upstairs	20
luàn	乱	亂	*Adj.*	messy	15s
lǚxíng	旅行	旅行	*V.*	to travel	18
lǜ	绿	綠	*Adj.*	green	11
lǜsè	绿色	綠色	*Adj.*	green	13s
lǜshī	律师	律師	*N.*	lawyer	6s

M

ma	吗	嗎	*Part.*	(used at the end of a sentence to transform it into a question)	1
māma	妈妈	媽媽	*N.*	mother	6
mǎlù	马路	馬路	*N.*	road, street	18s
mǎshàng	马上	馬上	*Adv.*	immediately	20

mǎtóu	码头	碼頭	*N.*	wharf, dock, pier	18s
mǎi	买	買	*V.*	to buy	13
mǎidān	买单	買單	*V.O.*	to pay the bill	11s
mài	卖	賣	*V.*	to sell	13s
màn	慢	慢	*Adj.*	slow	16
máng	忙	忙	*Adj.*	busy	4s, 9
māo	猫	貓	*N.*	cat	6s
máo	毛	毛	*N.*	(10 毛 = 1 块)	13s
máoyī	毛衣	毛衣	*N.*	sweater	13s
màozi	帽子	帽子	*N.*	hat	13s
méiguānxi	没关系	沒關係		No problem.	20
méiyǒu	没有	沒有	*V.*	to not have; be without	5s, 6
Měiguó	美国	美國	*N.*	the United States	3
Měijīn	美金	美金	*N.*	U.S. dollar	13s
měilì	美丽	美麗	*Adj.*	beautiful	22
měitiān	每天	每天	*N.*	every day	10
mèimei	妹妹	妹妹	*N.*	younger sister	6s, 12
men	们	們		(used after a personal pronoun or noun to show plural number)	4
mén	门	門	*M.W.*	(measure word for school course)	10
			N.	door	15s
mínǐqún	迷你裙	迷你裙	*N.*	miniskirt	13s
mìshū	秘书	祕書	*N.*	secretary	6s
miàn	面	麵	*N.*	noodle	11
miànbāo	面包	麵包	*N.*	bread	11s
miànbāochē (bāoxíngchē)	面包车 (包型车)	麵包車 (包型車)	*N.*	minibus, van	18s
miǎo	秒	秒	*N.*	second	10s
míngpiàn	名片	名片	*N.*	name card	8s
míngtiān	明天	明天	*N.*	tomorrow	12
míngzi	名字	名字	*N.*	name	2
mótuōchē (jīchē)	摩托车 (机车)	摩托車 (機車)	*N.*	scooter, motorcycle	18s

N

nǎ	哪	哪	*Pron.*	which	3
nà	那	那	*Pron.*	that	4
nǎinai	奶奶	奶奶	*N.*	grandmother	6s
nán	难	難	*Adj.*	difficult	4
	男	男	*N.*	male	6
nánbù	南部	南部	*N.*	south	18
nánpéngyou	男朋友	男朋友	*N.*	boyfriend	5s, 6
nǎr	哪儿	哪兒	*Pron.*	where	7

ne	呢	呢	*Part.*	(used at the end of an interrogative sentence)	1
nèikù	内裤	內褲	*N.*	underpants	13s
nèiyī	内衣	內衣	*N.*	underwear	13s
néng	能	能	*Aux.*	can	12
nǐ	你	你	*Pron.*	you	1
nián	年	年	*N.*	year	10
nín	您	您	*Pron.*	you (polite)	2
niúròu	牛肉	牛肉	*N.*	beef	11s
niúzǎikù	牛仔裤	牛仔褲	*N.*	jeans	13s
Niǔyuē	纽约	紐約	*N.*	New York	6
nuǎnhuo	暖和	暖和	*Adj.*	warm	17
nǚ	女	女	*N.*	female	6s
nǚpéngyou	女朋友	女朋友	*N.*	girlfriend	5s, 6s, 20

O

Ōuyuán	欧元	歐元	*N.*	Euro	13s

P

páshān	爬山	爬山	*N.* *V.O.*	mountain climbing to climb a mountain	16s
páiqiú	排球	排球	*N.*	volleyball	16s
pán	盘	盤	*M.W.*	plate	11
pángbiān	旁边	旁邊	*N.*	nearby	15
pǎobù	跑步	跑步	*V.O.*	to run	16s
pǎochē	跑车	跑車	*N.*	sports car	18s
péngyou	朋友	朋友	*N.*	friend	5
píjiǔ	啤酒	啤酒	*N.*	beer	11
píxié	皮鞋	皮鞋	*N.*	leather shoes	13s
piányi	便宜	便宜	*Adj.*	inexpensive	13s
piào	票	票	*N.*	ticket	13
píng	瓶	瓶	*M.W.*	bottle	11
píngguǒ	苹果	蘋果	*N.*	apple	11s
pútao	葡萄	葡萄	*N.*	grape	11s

Q

qī	七/柒	七/柒	*Num.*	seven	7
qí	骑	騎	*V.*	to ride	18
qí zìxíngchē	骑自行车	騎自行車	*V.O.*	to ride a bike	16s
qízhōng	其中	其中		among (whom, which)	17
qǐchuáng	起床	起床	*V.O.*	to get up	10
qìchē	汽车	汽車	*N.*	car	18s

qìhòu	气候	氣候	*N.*	climate	17
qìwēn	气温	氣溫	*N.*	temperature	17s
qiānyuē	签约	簽約	*V.O.*	to sign a contract	20s
qián	钱	錢	*N.*	money	13
qiánbiān	前边	前邊	*N.*	in front of	15
qiánshuǐ	潜水	潛水	*V.O.*	to dive	16s
qiǎnlǜsè	浅绿色	淺綠色	*Adj.*	light green	13s
qiǎnsè	浅色	淺色	*Adj.*	light	13s
qīnshǔ	亲属	親屬	*N.*	relatives	6s
qiū	秋	秋	*N.*	autumn	17
qiújì	球季	球季	*N.*	season (of a sport)	16s
qiúsài	球赛	球賽	*N.*	ball game, match	16
qiúxié	球鞋	球鞋	*N.*	sneakers	13s
qīngcài	青菜	青菜	*N.*	vegetable	11s
qīngdàn	清淡	清淡	*Adj.*	plain	11s
qìngshēng	庆生	慶生	*V.O.*	to celebrate a birthday	14s
qǐng	请	請		please (polite)	2
qǐng wèn	请问	請問		may I ask	2
qù	去	去	*V.*	to go	8
qúnzi	裙子	裙子	*N.*	skirt	13

R

ránhòu	然后	然後	*Adv.*	then; after that; afterwards	10
ràng	让	讓	*V.*	to let, allow	13
rè	热	熱	*Adj.*	hot	17
rèxīn	热心	熱心	*Adj.*	warm-hearted	22
rén	人	人	*N.*	person	3
Rénmínbì	人民币	人民幣	*N.*	currency of the People's Republic of China	13s
rènshi	认识	認識	*V.*	to know, recognize	5s, 8
rènzhēn	认真	認真	*Adj.*	conscientious; serious	22
rì	日	日	*N.*	day	10
Rìběn	日本	日本	*N.*	Japan	3s, 8
Rìběnrén	日本人	日本人	*N.*	Japanese (person)	3s
Rìyǔ	日语	日語	*N.*	Japanese (language)	3s
(Rìwén)	(日文)	(日文)			
róngyì	容易	容易	*Adj.*	easy	4s
ruǎnjiàn	软件	軟件	*N.*	sorftware	9s
(ruǎntǐ)	(软体)	(軟體)			

S

sān	三/叁	三/叁	*Num.*	three	7
sè	色	色	*N.*	color	12

shālā	沙拉	沙拉	*N.*	salad	11s
shǎo	少	少	*Adj.*	few, little	4
shāngrén	商人	商人	*N.*	businessman	6s
shàngbiān	上边	上邊	*N.*	on top of, above, over	15
shàngkè	上课	上課	*V.O.*	to begin class; attend class	8
shàngshēng	上升	上升	*V.C.*	to increase	17s
shàngwǎng	上网	上網	*V.O.*	to be online	9
shàngyī	上衣	上衣	*N.*	upper clothing	13s
shèshì	摄氏	攝氏	*N.*	Centigrade	17s
shètuán	社团	社團	*N.*	organization	16s
shéi	谁	誰	*Pron.*	who, whom	2
shēnlánsè	深蓝色	深藍色	*Adj.*	dark blue	13s
shēnqǐng	申请	申請	*V.*	to apply	21
shēnsè	深色	深色	*Adj.*	dark	13s
shénme	什么	什麼	*Pron.*	what	2
shěnshen	婶婶	嬸嬸	*N.*	aunt (wife of father's younger brother)	6s
shēngbìng	生病	生病	*V.O.*	to fall ill	19
shēnghuó	生活	生活	*N.*	life	10
shēngrì	生日	生日	*N.*	birthday	14
shèr	事儿	事兒	*N.*	matter, thing, business	8
shí	十/拾	十/拾	*Num.*	ten	7s, 11
shíhou	时候	時候	*N.*	time (the duration of time); (a point in)	9
shíjiān	时间	時間	*N.*	time	17
shípǐn	食品	食品	*N.*	food	11s
shíxí	实习	實習	*N.*	internship	21
shì	是	是	*V.*	to be; yes (affirmative answer)	1
shìpǐn	饰品	飾品	*N.*	accessory	13s
shìshi	试试	試試	*V.*	to try	13
shìyǒu	室友	室友	*N.*	roommate	5
shōudào	收到	收到	*V.C.*	to receive	22
shǒubiǎo	手表	手錶	*N.*	watch	13s
shǒujī	手机	手機	*N.*	cellular phone	7
shǒujuàn	手绢	手絹	*N.*	handkerchief	13s
shǒupáidǎng (shǒupái)	手排挡 (手排)	手排擋 (手排)	*N.*	manual transmission	12
shǒutào	手套	手套	*N.*	gloves	13s
shǒuzhuó	手镯	手鐲	*N.*	bracelet	13s
shū	书	書	*N.*	book	4
shūfǎ	书法	書法	*N.*	calligraphy	22
shūfu	舒服	舒服	*Adj.*	comfortable, be well	19
shūshu	叔叔	叔叔	*N.*	uncle (father's younger brother)	6s
shūzhuō	书桌	書桌	*N.*	desk	15s
shǔjià	暑假	暑假	*N.*	summer vacation	17s, 21
shǔqī	暑期	暑期	*N.*	summer	21

shùxué	数学	數學	*N.*	mathematics	4s
shuāyá	刷牙	刷牙	*V.O.*	to brush teeth	10s
shuāng	双	雙	*M.W.*	pair	11
shuìjiào	睡觉	睡覺	*V.O.*	to sleep; to go to bed	9s, 10
shùnlì	顺利	順利	*Adj.*	smooth	22s
shuō	说	說	*V.*	to speak	3
shuòshì	硕士	碩士	*N.*	master's degree	21s
sījī	司机	司機	*N.*	driver	18s
sījīn	丝巾	絲巾	*N.*	handkerchief	13s
sì	四/肆	四/肆	*Num.*	four	6
sìjì	四季	四季	*N.*	four seasons	17s
sìlúnqūdòng (sìlúnchuándòng)	四轮驱动 (四轮传动)	四輪驅動 (四輪傳動)	*N.*	four-wheel drive	18s
sòng	送	送	*V.*	to give as a present	14
sùshè	宿舍	宿舍	*N.*	dorm	7
suān	酸	酸	*Adj.*	sour	11s
suì	岁	歲	*N.*	age, years	14
suìdào	隧道	隧道	*N.*	tunnel	18s
suǒyǐ	所以	所以	*Conj.*	therefore, consequently	19

T

tā	他	他	*Pron.*	he, him	1
	她	她	*Pron.*	she, her	2
tāmen	他们	他們	*Pron.*	they, them	5
tài	太	太	*Adv.*	too	4
Tàiguó	泰国	泰國	*N.*	Thailand	3s
Tàiguórén	泰国人	泰國人	*N.*	Thai (person)	3s
Tàiyǔ (Tàiwén)	泰语 (泰文)	泰語 (泰文)	*N.*	Thai (language)	3s
tāng	汤	湯	*N.*	soup	11
tángdì	堂弟	堂弟	*N.*	cousin (son of father's brother) (younger than the speaker)	6s
tángdìmèi	堂弟妹	堂弟妹	*N.*	cousin (wife of 堂弟)	6s
tánggē	堂哥	堂哥	*N.*	cousin (son of father's brother) (older than the speaker)	6s
tángjiě	堂姐	堂姐	*N.*	cousin (daughter of father's brother) (older than the speaker)	6s
tángjiěfu	堂姐夫	堂姐夫	*N.*	cousin (husband of 堂姐)	6s
tángmèi	堂妹	堂妹	*N.*	cousin (daughter of father's brother) (younger than the speaker)	6s
tángmèifu	堂妹夫	堂妹夫	*N.*	cousin (husband of 堂妹)	6s
tángsǎo	堂嫂	堂嫂	*N.*	cousin (wife of 堂哥)	6s
tàng	烫	燙	*Adj.*	burning hot	11s

táozi	桃子	桃子	*N.*	peach	11s
tè dà	特大	特大	*Adj.*	extra large	13s
tè xiǎo	特小	特小	*Adj.*	extra small	13s
tiānqì	天气	天氣	*N.*	weather	17s
tiānqiáo	天桥	天橋	*N.*	overhead bridge	18s
tián	甜	甜	*Adj.*	sweet	11s
tiándiǎn	甜点	甜點	*N.*	dessert	11s
tiáo	条	條	*M.W.*	(measure word for skirt/pants)	13
tīxùshān	T-恤衫	T-恤衫	*N.*	T-shirt	13s
(tīxù)	(T-恤)	(T-恤)			
tǐwēn	体温	體溫	*N.*	body temperature	19s
tǐyùguǎn	体育馆	体育館	*N.*	gymnasium	16
tīngshuō	听说	聽說	*V.*	to be told; hear of; it is said	18
tíng	停	停	*V.*	to park	12
tíngchēchǎng	停车场	停車場	*N.*	parking lot	12
tōng	通	通	*M.W.*	(measure word for telephone conversation)	9s
tóngshì	同事	同事	*N.*	colleague	22
tóngxué	同学	同學	*N.*	classmate, student	2
tóuténg	头疼	頭疼	*V.*	to have a headache	19
túshūguǎn	图书馆	圖書館	*N.*	library	10
tuīxiāoyuán	推销员	推銷員	*N.*	salesman	6s
tuō	脱	脫	*V.*	to take off (regular clothes)	13s
tuōxià	脱下	脫下	*V.C.*	to take off (regular clothes)	13s
tuōxié	拖鞋	拖鞋	*N.*	slippers	13s

W

wàzi	袜子	襪子	*N.*	socks	13s
wàigōng	外公	外公	*N.*	maternal grandfather	6s
wàipó	外婆	外婆	*N.*	maternal grandmother	6s
wàisheng	外甥	外甥	*N.*	nephew (sister's son)	6s
wàishengnǚ	外甥女	外甥女	*N.*	niece (sister's daughter)	6s
wàitào	外套	外套	*N.*	coat	13s
wàizǔfù	外祖父	外祖父	*N.*	maternal grandfather	6s
wàizǔmǔ	外祖母	外祖母	*N.*	maternal grandmother	6s
wán	玩	玩	*V.*	to play, have fun	12
wǎn	晚	晚	*Adj.*	late	10s
	碗	碗	*M.W.*	bowl	11
wǎnfàn	晚饭	晚飯	*N.*	dinner	8s
wǎnshàng	晚上	晚上	*N.*	evening, night	9
wǎngbā	网吧	網吧	*N.*	Internet cafè	9s
(wǎngkā)	(网咖)	(網咖)			
wǎngluò	网络	網絡	*N.*	Internet	9s
(wǎnglù)	(网路)	(網路)			

wǎngqiú	网球	網球	*N.*	tennis	16s
wǎngyè	网页	網頁	*N.*	Web page	9s
wǎngzhàn	网站	網站	*N.*	Web site	9s
wàngjì	旺季	旺季	*N.*	busy season	18s
wéijīn	围巾	圍巾	*N.*	scarf	13s
wèi	位	位	*M.W.*	(polite form, measure word for people)	9
	为	為	*Prep.*	(indicates the object of one's act of service)	14
(wéi)	喂	喂	*Int.*	hello; hey (used in greeting or to attract attention)	9
wénxué	文学	文學	*N.*	literature	4
wèn	问	問	*V.*	to ask	2
wèntí	问题	問題	*N.*	problem, question	12
wǒ	我	我	*Pron.*	I, me	1
wǒjiùshì	我就是	我就是		this is he/she speaking (on the phone)	9
wǒmen	我们	我們	*Pron.*	we, us	4
wòshì	卧室	臥室	*N.*	bedroom	15
wǔ	五/伍	五/伍	*Num.*	five	7
wǔfàn	午饭	午飯	*N.*	lunch	8s
(zhōngfàn)	(中饭)	(中飯)			
wǔhuì	舞会	舞會	*N.*	dance party	14

X

xībù	西部	西部	*N.*	west	18
Xībānyá	西班牙	西班牙	*N.*	Spain	3s
Xībānyárén	西班牙人	西班牙人	*N.*	Spanish (person)	3s
Xībānyáyǔ	西班牙语	西班牙語	*N.*	Spanish (language)	3s
(Xībānyáwén)	(西班牙文)	(西班牙文)			
xīguā	西瓜	西瓜	*N.*	watermelon	11s
xīyān	吸烟	吸煙	*V.O.*	to smoke	20
xīzhuāng	西装	西裝	*N.*	suit	13s
xǐhuān	喜欢	喜歡	*V.*	to like	10
xǐliǎn	洗脸	洗臉	*V.O.*	to wash face	10s
xǐzǎo	洗澡	洗澡	*V.O.*	to take a bath	10s
xǐzǎojiān	洗澡间	洗澡間	*N.*	bathroom, restroom	15
xì	系	系	*N.*	department	4s
xiā	虾	蝦	*N.*	shrimp	11s
xià	夏	夏	*N.*	summer	17
xiàcì	下次	下次		next time	8
xiàjiàng	下降	下降	*V.C.*	to decrease	17s
xiàkè	下课	下課	*V.O.*	to end class	8
xiàwǔ	下午	下午	*N.*	afternoon	10

xiàyǔ	下雨	下雨	*V.O.*	to rain	17
xiān	先	先	*Adv.*	first	11, 18
xiānsheng	先生	先生	*N.*	mister	11
xián	咸	鹹	*Adj.*	salty	11s
xiànzài	现在	現在	*Adv.*	now	16
xiāngjiāo	香蕉	香蕉	*N.*	banana	11s
xiǎng	想	想	*V.*	to want	8
xiàngliàn	项链	項鏈	*N.*	necklace	13s
xiāoyè	宵夜	宵夜	*N.*	midnight snack	8s
xiǎo	小	小	*Adj.*	small	7, 13s
xiǎofèi	小费	小費	*N.*	tip	11s
xiǎojiě	小姐	小姐	*N.*	miss	11
xiǎolóngbāo	小笼包	小籠包	*N.*	little steamed buns with stuffing	22
xiǎoshí	小时	小時	*N.*	hour	10s
xiǎoshuō	小说	小說	*N.*	novel	9s
xiàonèi	校内	校內	*N.*	on campus	7s
xiàowài	校外	校外	*N.*	off campus	7
xiézi	鞋子	鞋子	*N.*	shoes	13s
xiě	写	寫	*V.*	to write	10
xièxie	谢谢	謝謝		thank you, thanks	9
xīn	新	新	*Adj.*	new	22
Xīntáibì	新台币	新台幣	*N.*	currency of Taiwan	13s
xīnxiǎngshìchéng	心想事成	心想事成		Every wish comes true.	22s
xìn	信	信	*N.*	letter	10
xīngqī	星期	星期	*N.*	week	14
xíng	行	行	*V.*	to be all right, okay	8
xìng	姓	姓	*N.*	surname, family	2
			V.	to be surnamed	2
xiōngdìjiěmèi	兄弟姐妹	兄弟姐妹	*N.*	siblings	6s
xiūxi	休息	休息	*V.*	to rest	8s, 9s, 19
xuēzi	靴子	靴子	*N.*	boots	13s
xué	学	學	*V.*	to study, learn	1
xuédào	学到	學到	*V.C.*	to learn and master	22
xuéqī	学期	學期	*N.*	semester	10
xuésheng	学生	學生	*N.*	student	1
xuéshì	学士	學士	*N.*	bachelor's degree	21s
xuéwèi	学位	學位	*N.*	degree	21s
xuéxiào	学校	學校	*N.*	school	18
xuě	雪	雪	*N.*	snow	17

Y

yánjiūshēng	研究生	研究生	*N.*	graduate students	21s
yánjiūshēngyuàn	研究生院	研究生院	*N.*	graduate school	21
yánsè	颜色	顏色	*N.*	color	13s

yánzhòng	严重	嚴重	*Adj.*	severe	19s
yǎnjìng	眼镜	眼鏡	*N.*	glasses	13s
yào	要	要	*V.*	to want, desire	9
yéye	爷爷	爺爺	*N.*	grandfather	6s
yě	也	也	*Adv.*	also, too	1
yī	一/壹	一/壹	*Num.*	one	6
yīchú	衣橱	衣櫥	*N.*	wardrobe	15s
yīfu	衣服	衣服	*N.*	clothes	13s
yīshēng	医生	醫生	*N.*	doctor	6s, 19
yīwùshì (yīhùshì)	医务室 (医护室)	醫務室 (醫護室)	*N.*	clinic	19s
yīyuàn	医院	醫院	*N.*	hospital	19s
yídìng	一定	一定	*Aux.*	certainly, surely	14
yífù	姨父	姨父	*N.*	uncle (husband of mother's sister)	6s
yígòng	一共	一共	*Adv.*	altogether; in all	18
yílùpíng'ān	一路平安	一路平安		Have a pleasant journey.	21
yímā	姨妈	姨媽	*N.*	aunt (mother's sister)	6s
yímiàn	一面	一面	*Adv.*	at the same time	21
yíxià	一下	一下		(used after a verb to indicate a brief action)	5
yízhàng	姨丈	姨丈	*N.*	uncle (husband of mother's sister)	6s
yǐhòu	以后	以後	*N.*	after; afterwards; later	8
yǐjīng	已经	已經	*Adv.*	already	22
yǐnliào	饮料	飲料	*N.*	drink	11s
yǐqián	以前	以前	*N.*	before; previously	20
yǐzi	椅子	椅子	*N.*	chair	15s
yìdiǎr	一点儿	一點兒		a little	3
yìqǐ	一起	一起	*Adv.*	together	8
yìxiē	一些	一些	*Adj.*	some	22
yīnwèi	因为	因為	*Conj.*	because	22
yínhuīsè	银灰色	銀灰色	*Adj.*	silver	13s
yīnggāi	应该	應該	*Aux.*	should	12
Yīngguó	英国	英國	*N.*	Britain	3
Yīngwén	英文	英文	*N.*	English (language)	2
Yīngyǔ	英语	英語	*N.*	English (language)	2s
yìngjiàn (yìngtǐ)	硬件 (硬体)	硬件 (硬體)	*N.*	hardware	9s
yòng	用	用	*V.*	to use	12
yóudìyuán (yóuchāi)	邮递员 (邮差)	郵遞員 (郵差)	*N.*	mailman	6s
yóuyǒng	游泳	游泳	*V.O.*	to swim	16
			N.	swimming	16s
yóuyǒngchí	游泳池	游泳池	*N.*	swimming pool	16

yǒu	有	有	*V.*	to have	5
yǒudiǎr	有点儿	有點兒	*Adv.*	a little	4s
yǒukòng	有空	有空	*V.O.*	to have free time	14
yǒushíhou	有时候	有時候	*Adv.*	sometimes	17
yǒuyìsi	有意思	有意思	*Adj.*	interesting, enjoyable	21
yòubiān	右边	右邊	*N.*	on the right	15s
yú	鱼	魚	*N.*	fish	11s
yúkuài	愉快	愉快	*Adj.*	happy	21
yǔmáoqiú	羽毛球	羽毛球	*N.*	badminton	16s
yùfángzhēn	预防针	預防針	*N.*	immunization shot	19s
yuán	元	元	*N.*	dollar	13s
yuǎn	远	遠	*Adj.*	far	18
yuǎnzú	远足	遠足	*N.*	hiking	16s
yuè	月	月	*N.*	month	10
yuèyěchē	越野车	越野車	*N.*	off-road vehicle	18s
yùndòng	运动	運動	*N.*	sports	16s

Z

zázhì	杂志	雜誌	*N.*	magazine	15s
zài	在	在	*V.*	to be at, be in	6
			Prep.	at, in	
zài	再	再	*Adv.*	again	8
zàijiàn	再见	再見		see you again; goodbye	8
zàixiàn yóuxì (xiànshàng yóuxì)	在线游戏 (线上游戏)	在線遊戲 (線上遊戲)	*N.*	on-line game	9s
zāng	脏	髒	*Adj.*	dirty	15s
zǎo	早	早	*Adj.*	early	10s
zǎofàn	早饭	早飯	*N.*	breakfast	8s
zěnmeyàng	怎么样	怎麼樣	*Pron.*	how (used as a predicative or complement)	8
zhāi	摘	摘	*V.*	to take off (accessories)	13s
zhāixià	摘下	摘下	*V.C.*	to take off (accessories)	13s
zhànxiàn	占线	佔線	*V.O.*	to occupy a (phone) line, the line is busy	9s
zhāng	张	張	*M.W.*	(measure word for piece of paper)	13
zhǎo	找	找	*V.*	to seek for, look for	21
zhè	这	這	*Pron.*	this	4
zhècì	这次	這次	*Pron.*	this time	12
zhèyàng	这样	這樣	*Pron.*	thus; in this way	12
zhēn	真	真	*Adv.*	really	15
zhěnsuǒ	诊所	診所	*N.*	clinic	19s
zhěnglǐ	整理	整理	*V.*	to arrange, put in order	15s

zhěngqí	整齐	整齊	*Adj.*	tidy	15s
zhèngzài	正在	正在	*Adv.*	in the process of; in the course of (to indicate an action in progress)	9
zhī	只	隻	*M.W.*	(measure word for certain animals, boats, or containers; or for one of a pair)	6
zhīdào	知道	知道	*V.*	to know; be aware of; realize	9
zhínǚ	侄女	姪女	*N.*	niece (brother's daughter)	6s
zhíyè	职业	職業	*N.*	occupation	6s
zhíyuán	职员	職員	*N.*	staff	6s
zhízi	侄子	姪子	*N.*	nephew (brother's son)	6s
zhǐyào	只要	只要	*Adv.*	only	18
zhōng	中	中	*Adj.*	medium	13s
zhōngjiān	中间	中間	*N.*	middle	15
zhōngtóu	钟头	鐘頭	*N.*	hour	10s
Zhōngguó	中国	中國	*N.*	China	3
Zhōngwén	中文	中文	*N.*	Chinese (language)	2
zhūròu	猪肉	豬肉	*N.*	pork	11s
zhù	住	住	*V.*	to live	7
	祝	祝	*V.*	to wish	10
Zhù nǐ shēngrì kuàilè.	祝你生日快乐	祝你生日快樂		Happy birthday to you.	14s
zhuānyè (zhǔxiū)	专业 (主修)	專業 (主修)	*N.*	major	4s
zhuōzi	桌子	桌子	*N.*	table	15
zhǔnbèi	准备	準備	*V.*	to prepare	19
zǐsè	紫色	紫色	*Adj.*	purple	13s
zìdòngpáidǎng (zìpái)	自动排挡 (自排)	自動排擋 (自排)	*Adj.*	automatic transmission	12s
zìjǐ	自己	自己	*N.*	oneself	6s
zìwǒjièshào	自我介绍	自我介紹	*N.* / *V.*	self-introduction / to introduce oneself	6s
zìxíngchē	自行车	自行車	*N.*	bicycle	18
zōngsè (kāfēisè)	棕色 (咖啡色)	棕色 (咖啡色)	*Adj.*	brown	13s
zǒu	走	走	*V.*	to walk	15
zǒulù	走路	走路	*V.O.*	to walk	18
zū	租	租	*V.*	to rent, hire, lease	18
zūwū	租屋	租屋	*V.O.*	to rent a house	20s
zúqiú	足球	足球	*N.*	soccer	16s
zǔfù	祖父	祖父	*N.*	grandfather	6s
zǔmǔ	祖母	祖母	*N.*	grandmother	6s
zuì	最	最	*Adv.*	most, the highest degree (indicates the superlative degree)	17, 22

英文索引 ENGLISH INDEX

Each entry lists English meaning, simplified character, traditional character, Pinyin, part of speech, and lesson number.

Note: The letter "s" means that the entry occurs in the supplementary vocabulary to that lesson.

Units of Measurement

10 jiao = 1 yuan	角	角	jiǎo	*N.*	13s
10 mao = 1 kuai	毛	毛	máo	*N.*	13s
100 fen = 10 jiao/10 mao = 1 yuan/1 kuai	分	分	fēn	*N.*	13s

Measure Words (Classifiers) for

books	本	本	běn	*M.W.*	4
certain animals, boats, or containers, or for one of a pair	只	隻	zhī	*M.W.*	6
clothes	件	件	jiàn	*M.W.*	13
company, enterprises, store, etc.	家	家	jiā	*M.W.*	21
cups, buildings, characters	个	個	gè	*M.W.*	5
people (polite form)	位	位	wèi	*M.W.*	9
a piece of paper	张	張	zhāng	*M.W.*	13
school courses	门	門	mén	*M.W.*	10
skirt/pants	条	條	tiáo	*M.W.*	13
telephone conversation	通	通	tōng	*M.W.*	9s
vehicles	辆	輛	liàng	*M.W.*	6

A

above, over, on top of	上边	上邊	shàngbiān	*N.*	15
accessory	饰品	飾品	shìpǐn	*N.*	13s
accountant	会计师	會計師	kuàijìshī	*N.*	6s
action	动作	動作	dòngzuò	*N.*	13s
activity	活动	活動	huódòng	*N.*	22
address	地址	地址	dìzhǐ	*N.*	10
after, afterwards, later	以后	以後	yǐhòu	*N.*	8
afternoon	下午	下午	xiàwǔ	*N.*	10
again	再	再	zài	*Adv.*	8
age, years old	岁	歲	suì	*N.*	14
agent	经纪人	經紀人	jīngjìrén	*N.*	6s
airplane	飞机	飛機	fēijī	*N.*	12

airport	机场	機場	jīchǎng	*N.*	12
all, everybody	大家	大家	dàjiā	*Pron.*	6
all, both	都	都	dōu	*Adv.*	5
already	已经	已經	yǐjīng	*Adv.*	22
already, as early as	就	就	jiù	*Adv.*	10
also, too	也	也	yě	*Adv.*	1
altogether, in all	一共	一共	yígòng	*Adv.*	18
among (whom, which)	其中	其中	qízhōng		17
and	和	和	hé	*Conj.*	3
apartment	公寓	公寓	gōngyù	*N.*	7s
apple	苹果	蘋果	píngguǒ	*N.*	11s
to apply	申请	申請	shēnqǐng	*V.*	21
architect	建筑师	建築師	jiànzhùshī	*N.*	6s
to arrange, put in order	整理	整理	zhěnglǐ	*V.*	15s
to arrive	到	到	dào	*V.*	12
to ask	问	問	wèn	*V.*	2
at, in	在	在	zài	*Prep.*	6
at the same time	同时	同時	tóngshí	*Adv.*	21
to attend classes, begin class	上课	上課	shàngkè	*V.O.*	8
aunt (father's sister)	姑妈	姑媽	gūmā	*N.*	6s
	姑姑	姑姑	gūgu	*N.*	6s
(mother's sister)	姨妈	姨媽	yímā	*N.*	6s
	阿姨	阿姨	āyí	*N.*	6s
(wife of father's elder brother)	伯母	伯母	bómǔ	*N.*	6s
(wife of father's younger brother)	婶婶	嬸嬸	shěnshen	*N.*	6s
(wife of mother's brother)	舅妈	舅媽	jiùmā	*N.*	6s
automatic transmission	自动排挡 (自排)	自動排擋 (自排)	zìdòngpáidǎng (zìpái)	*Adj.*	12s
autumn	秋	秋	qiū	*N.*	17

B

bachelor's degree	学士	學士	xuéshì	*N.*	21s
badminton	羽毛球	羽毛球	yǔmáoqiú	*N.*	16s
ball game, match	球赛	球賽	qiúsài	*N.*	16
banana	香蕉	香蕉	xiāngjiāo	*N.*	11s
baseball	棒球	棒球	bàngqiú	*N.*	16s
basketball	篮球	籃球	lánqiú	*N.*	16, 16s
to bathe, take a bath	洗澡	洗澡	xǐzǎo	*V.O.*	10s
bathroom, restroom	洗澡间	洗澡間	xǐzǎojiān	*N.*	15
to be all right, okay	行	行	xíng	*V.*	8
to be at, be in,	在	在	zài	*V.*	6
to be like, seem	好像	好像	hǎoxiàng	*V.*	19

bus	公共汽车	公共汽車	gōnggòngqìchē	*N.*	18
	公车	公車	gōngchē	*N.*	18s
	(巴士)	(巴士)	(bāshì)		
businessman	商人	商人	shāngrén	*N.*	6s
busy	忙	忙	máng	*Adj.*	4s, 9
busy season	旺季	旺季	wàngjì	*N.*	18s
but	但是	但是	dànshì	*Conj.*	20
but, however	不过	不過	búguò	*Conj.*	22
but, yet, however	可是	可是	kěshì	*Conj.*	4
to buy	买	買	mǎi	*V.*	13
by the way (a phrase used to start a new topic)	对了	對了	duìle	*Conj.*	3

C

cake	蛋糕	蛋糕	dàngāo	*N.*	11s, 14
California State	加州	加州	Jiāzhōu	*N.*	21
to call	叫	叫	jiào	*V.*	2
calligraphy	书法	書法	shūfǎ	*N.*	22
can	能	能	néng	*Aux.*	12
can, be able to	会	會	huì	*Aux.*	3
can, may	可以	可以	kěyǐ	*Aux.*	12
Canada	加拿大	加拿大	Jiānádà	*N.*	3s
Canadian (people)	加拿大人	加拿大人	Jiānádàrén	*N.*	3s
candle	蜡烛	蠟燭	làzhú	*N.*	14s
car	车	車	chē	*N.*	6
	汽车	汽車	qìchē	*N.*	18s
cat	猫	貓	māo	*N.*	6s
to celebrate a birthday	庆生	慶生	qìngshēng	*V.O.*	14s
cell phone	手机	手機	shǒujī	*N.*	7
Centigrade	摄氏	攝氏	shèshì	*N.*	17s
certainly, surely	一定	一定	yídìng	*Aux.*	14
chair	椅子	椅子	yǐzi	*N.*	15s
chat room	聊天室	聊天室	liáotiānshì	*N.*	9s
chicken	鸡肉	雞肉	jīròu	*N.*	11s
child	孩子	孩子	háizi	*N.*	6s
China	中国	中國	Zhōngguó	*N.*	3
Chinese (language)	中文	中文	Zhōngwén	*N.*	2
	汉语	漢語	Hànyǔ	*N.*	2s
chopstick	筷子	筷子	kuàizi	*N.*	11
city	城市	城市	chéngshì	*N.*	22
class	班	班	bān	*N.*	21
classmate, student	同学	同學	tóngxué	*N.*	2
classroom	教室	教室	jiàoshì	*N.*	15s

clean	干净	乾淨	gānjìng	*Adj.*	15s
climate	气候	氣候	qìhòu	*N.*	17
to climb a mountain	爬山	爬山	páshān	*V.O.*	16s
clinic	医务室	醫務室	yīwùshì	*N.*	19s
	(医护室)	(醫護室)	(yīhùshì)		
	诊所	診所	zhěnsuǒ	*N.*	19s
clothes	衣服	衣服	yīfu	*N.*	13s
clothing (for upper body)	上衣	上衣	shàngyī	*N.*	13s
club	俱乐部	俱樂部	jùlèbù	*N.*	16s
coach, trainer	教练	教練	jiàoliàn	*N.*	16
coat	外套	外套	wàitào	*N.*	13s
coffee	咖啡	咖啡	kāfēi	*N.*	11s
cola	可乐	可樂	kělè	*N.*	11
cold	冷	冷	lěng	*Adj.*	17
cold, flu	感冒	感冒	gǎnmào	*N.*	19
colleague	同事	同事	tóngshì	*N.*	22
college, university	大学	大學	dàxué	*N.*	10
college student(s)	大学生	大學生	dàxuéshēng	*N.*	6s, 21s
color	色	色	sè	*N.*	12
	颜色	顏色	yánsè	*N.*	13s
to come over	过来	過來	guòlái	*V.C.*	20
to come (used before a verb to indicate that one is about to do something)	来	來	lái	*V.*	5
comfortable	舒服	舒服	shūfu	*Adj.*	19
common	常见	常見	chángjiàn	*Adj.*	11s
company	公司	公司	gōngsī	*N.*	21
computer	计算机	計算機	jìsuànjī	*N.*	4s
	(电脑)	(電腦)	(diànnǎo)	*N.*	21
computer game	电脑游戏	電腦遊戲	diànnǎo yóuxì	*N.*	9s
computer programmer	程序员	程序員	chéngxùyuán	*N.*	6s
	(程式设计师)	(程式設計師)	(chéngshì shèjìshī)		
conscientious, serious	认真	認真	rènzhēn	*Adj.*	22
consultant	顾问	顧問	gùwèn	*N.*	6s
to cook	做饭	做飯	zuòfàn	*V.O.*	20
cool	凉	涼	liáng	*Adj.*	11s
correct, right	对	對	duì	*Adj.*	9
to cough	咳嗽	咳嗽	késòu	*V.*	19
country	国	國	guó	*N.*	3
cousin (daughter of father's brother)	堂姐	堂姐	tángjiě	*N.*	6s
	堂妹	堂妹	tángmèi	*N.*	6s
(daughter of parents' sister or mother's brother)	表姐	表姐	biǎojiě	*N.*	6s
	表妹	表妹	biǎomèi	*N.*	6s
(husband of 表姐)	表姐夫	表姐夫	biǎojiěfu	*N.*	6s

(husband of 表妹)	表妹夫	表妹夫	biǎomèifu	*N.*	6s
(husband of 堂姐)	堂姐夫	堂姐夫	tángjiěfu	*N.*	6s
(husband of 堂妹)	堂妹夫	堂妹夫	tángmèifu	*N.*	6s
(son of father's brother)	堂哥	堂哥	tánggē	*N.*	6s
	堂弟	堂弟	tángdì	*N.*	6s
(son of parents' sister or mother's brother)	表哥	表哥	biǎogē	*N.*	6s
	表弟	表弟	biǎodì	*N.*	6s
(wife of 表弟)	表弟妹	表弟妹	biǎodìmèi	*N.*	6s
(wife of 表哥)	表嫂	表嫂	biǎosǎo	*N.*	6s
(wife of 堂弟)	堂弟妹	堂弟妹	tángdìmèi	*N.*	6s
(wife of 堂哥)	堂嫂	堂嫂	tángsǎo	*N.*	6s
cracker	饼干	餅乾	bǐnggān	*N.*	11s
cup	杯	杯	bēi	*M.W.*	11
currency	货币	貨幣	huòbì	*N.*	13s
currency of Hong Kong	港币	港幣	Gǎngbì	*N.*	13s
currency of the People's Republic of China	人民币	人民幣	Rénmínbì	*N.*	13s
currency of Taiwan	新台币	新台幣	Xīntáibì	*N.*	13s
to cycle, to ride a bike	骑自行车	騎自行車	qí zìxíngchē	*V.O.*	16s

D

dance party	舞会	舞會	wǔhuì	*N.*	14
dark	深色	深色	shēnsè	*Adj.*	13s
dark blue	深蓝色	深藍色	shēnlánsè	*Adj.*	13s
day	日	日	rì	*N.*	10
to decide	决定	決定	juédìng	*V.*	21
to decrease	下降	下降	xiàjiàng	*V.C.*	17s
degree	度	度	dù	*N.*	17
	学位	學位	xuéwèi	*N.*	21s
department	系	系	xì	*N.*	4s
desk	书桌	書桌	shūzhuō	*N.*	15s
dessert	甜点	甜點	tiándiǎn	*N.*	11s
to dial a wrong number	打错了	打錯了	dǎcuòle		9s
difficult	难	難	nán	*Adj.*	4
dining room	餐厅	餐廳	cāntīng	*N.*	15
dinner	晚饭	晚飯	wǎnfàn	*N.*	8s
dirty	脏	髒	zāng	*Adj.*	15s
dish	菜	菜	cài	*N.*	8
to dive	潜水	潛水	qiánshuǐ	*V.O.*	16s
to do	做	做	zuò	*V.*	9
doctor	医生	醫生	yīshēng	*N.*	6s, 19
doctoral degree	博士	博士	bóshì	*N.*	21s
doctoral students	博士生	博士生	bóshìshēng	*N.*	21s
dog	狗	狗	gǒu	*N.*	6

dollar	块	塊	kuài	*N.*	13, 13s
	元	元	yuán	*N.*	13s
dollar (U.S.)	美金	美金	Měijīn	*N.*	13s
door	门	門	mén	*N.*	15s
dorm(itory)	宿舍	宿舍	sùshè	*N.*	7
drink	饮料	飲料	yǐnliào	*N.*	11s
to drink	喝	喝	hē	*V.*	11
to drive	开	開	kāi	*V.*	12
driver	司机	司機	sījī	*N.*	18s
dumpling (crescent-shaped)	饺子	餃子	jiǎozi	*N.*	11

E

early	早	早	zǎo	*Adj.*	10s
earrings	耳环	耳環	ěrhuán	*N.*	13s
east	东	東	dōng	*N.*	18s
easy	容易	容易	róngyì	*Adj.*	4s
to eat	吃	吃	chī	*V.*	8
to eat, have a meal	吃饭	吃飯	chīfàn	*V.O.*	8
economist	经济师	經濟師	jīngjìshī	*N.*	6s
educator	教育工作者	教育工作者	jiàoyù gōngzuòzhě	*N.*	6s
eight	八/捌	八/捌	bā	*Num.*	7
elder brother	哥哥	哥哥	gēge	*N.*	6s
elder sister	姐姐	姐姐	jiějie	*N.*	6
e-mail	电子邮件	電子郵件	diànzǐ yóujiàn	*N.*	10
to end class	下课	下課	xiàkè	*V.O.*	8
engineer	工程师	工程師	gōngchéngshī	*N.*	6, 6s
engineering	工程	工程	gōngchéng	*N.*	4
English (language)	英文	英文	Yīngwén	*N.*	2
	英语	英語	Yīngyǔ	*N.*	2s
to enter	进	進	jìn	*V.*	20
Euro	欧元	歐元	Ōuyuán	*N.*	13s
evening, night	晚上	晚上	wǎnshàng	*N.*	9
every day	每天	每天	měitiān	*N.*	10
Every wish comes true.	心想事成	心想事成	xīnxiǎngshìchéng		22s
everywhere	到处	到處	dàochù	*Adv.*	22
exam	考试	考試	kǎoshì	*N.*	4s, 19
Excuse me, I'm sorry.	对不起	對不起	duìbuqǐ		22
to exercise	锻炼	鍛煉	duànliàn	*V.*	16
expensive	贵	貴	guì	*Adj.*	13s
extra large	特大	特大	tè dà	*Adj.*	13s
extra small	特小	特小	tè xiǎo	*Adj.*	13s
extremely	极	極	jí	*Adv.*	17

F

Fahrenheit	华氏	華氏	huáshì	*N.*	17
to fall ill	生病	生病	shēngbìng	*V.O.*	19
far	远	遠	yuǎn	*Adj.*	18
fast	快	快	kuài	*Adj.*	16
father	爸爸	爸爸	bàba	*N.*	6
female	女	女	nǚ	*N.*	6s
fen (RMB unit)	分	分	fēn	*N.*	13s
few, little	少	少	shǎo	*Adj.*	4
first	先	先	xiān	*Adv.*	11, 18
first day	第一天	第一天	dìyītiān	*N.*	20
fish	鱼	魚	yú	*N.*	11s
to fish	钓鱼	釣魚	diàoyú	*V.O.*	16s
five	五/伍	五/伍	wǔ	*Num.*	7
flu	流感 (流行性感冒)	流感 (流行性感冒)	liúgǎn (liúxíngxìng gǎnmào)	*N.*	19s
flu shot	流感疫苗	流感疫苗	liúgǎn yìmiáo	*N.*	19s
food	食品	食品	shípǐn	*N.*	11s
football	橄榄球	橄欖球	gǎnlǎnqiú	*N.*	16s
for a long time	久	久	jiǔ	*Adj.*	17
for example	比如	比如	bǐrú	*Conj.*	22
for public use, communal	公用	公用	gōngyòng	*Adj.*	15
for, to	给	給	gěi	*Prep.*	9
form of address	称谓	稱謂	chēngwèi	*N.*	6s
four	四/肆	四/肆	sì	*Num.*	6
four seasons	四季	四季	sìjì	*N.*	17s
four-wheel drive	四轮驱动 (四轮传动)	四輪驅動 (四輪傳動)	sìlúnqūdòng (sìlúnchuándòng)	*N.*	18s
France	法国	法國	Fǎguó	*N.*	3
French (language)	法文	法文	Fǎwén	*N.*	3
friend	朋友	朋友	péngyou	*N.*	5
from	从	從	cóng	*Prep.*	6

G

German (language)	德语 (德文)	德語 (德文)	Déyǔ (Déwén)	*N.*	3s
(people)	德国人	德國人	Déguórén	*N.*	3s
Germany	德国	德國	Déguó	*N.*	3s
to get up	起床	起床	qǐchuáng	*V.O.*	10
gift	礼物	禮物	lǐwù	*N.*	14s
girlfriend	女朋友	女朋友	nǚpéngyou	*N.*	5s, 6s, 20

to give (as a present)	送(礼)	送(禮)	sòng(lǐ)	*V.O.*	14
give or receive an injection	打针	打針	dǎzhēn	*V.O.*	19s
glasses	眼镜	眼鏡	yǎnjìng	*N.*	13s
gloves	手套	手套	shǒutào	*N.*	13s
to go	去	去	qù	*V.*	8
to go to bed, sleep	睡觉	睡覺	shuìjiào	*V.O.*	9s, 10
to go out	出去	出去	chūqù	*V.C.*	20
gold	金黄色	金黃色	jīnhuángsè	*Adj.*	13s
golf	高尔夫球	高爾夫球	gāo'ěrfūqiú	*N.*	16s
good-looking	好看	好看	hǎokàn	*Adj.*	13
Good luck.	好运	好運	hǎoyùn		21
good, well	好	好	hǎo	*Adj.*	1
goodbye, see you again	再见	再见	zàijiàn		8
government official	官员	官員	guānyuán	*N.*	6s
to graduate	毕业	畢業	bìyè	*V.*	21
graduate school	研究生院	研究生院	yánjiūshēngyuàn	*N.*	21
graduate student	研究生	研究生	yánjiūshēng	*N.*	21s
grandfather	爷爷	爺爺	yéye	*N.*	6s
	祖父	祖父	zǔfù	*N.*	6s
grandmother	奶奶	奶奶	nǎinai	*N.*	6s
	祖母	祖母	zǔmǔ	*N.*	6s
grape	葡萄	葡萄	pútao	*N.*	11s
gray	灰色	灰色	huīsè	*Adj.*	13s
green	绿	綠	lǜ	*Adj.*	11
	绿色	綠色	lǜsè	*Adj.*	13s
gym	健身房	健身房	jiànshēnfáng	*N.*	16
gymnasium	体育馆	體育館	tǐyùguǎn	*N.*	16

H

half	半	半	bàn	*Adj.*	10
handkerchief	手绢	手絹	shǒujuàn	*N.*	13s
happy	愉快	愉快	yúkuài	*Adj.*	21
	高兴	高興	gāoxìng	*Adj.*	22
	开心	開心	kāixīn	*Adj.*	22
Happy birthday to you.	祝你生日快乐	祝你生日快樂	Zhù nǐ shēngrì kuàilè.		14s
hardware	硬件 (硬体)	硬件 (硬體)	yìngjiàn (yìngtǐ)	*N.*	9s
hat	帽子	帽子	màozi	*N.*	13s
to have	有	有	yǒu	*V.*	5
to have a fever	发烧	發燒	fāshāo	*V.O.*	19
to have a headache	头疼	頭疼	tóuténg	*V.*	19
Have a pleasant journey.	一路平安	一路平安	yílùpíng'ān		21

to have a try, taste	尝尝	嚐嚐	chángchang	*V.*	22
to have free time	有空	有空	yǒukòng	*V.O.*	14
to have or start (a vacation)	放假	放假	fàngjià	*V.O.*	17
he, him	他	他	tā	*Pron.*	1
healthy	健康	健康	jiànkāng	*Adj.*	22s
hello, hey (used in greetings or to attract attention)	喂	喂	wèi (wéi)	*Int.*	9
to help	帮	幫	bāng	*V.*	13
hiking	远足	遠足	yuǎnzú	*N.*	16s
home, family	家	家	jiā	*N.*	6
homework	作业	作業	zuòyè	*N.*	16
homework, assignment	作业	作業	zuòyè	*N.*	4s
	功课	功課	gōngkè	*N.*	4
hospital	医院	醫院	yīyuàn	*N.*	19s
hot	热	熱	rè	*Adj.*	17
hour	点钟	點鐘	diǎnzhōng	*N.*	10s
	钟头	鐘頭	zhōngtóu	*M.W.*	10s
	小时	小時	xiǎoshí	*N.*	10s
house, room	房子	房子	fángzi	*N.*	7s
housewife	家庭主妇	家庭主婦	jiātíng zhǔfù	*N.*	6s
how (used as a predicative or complement)	怎么样	怎麼樣	zěnmeyàng	*Pron.*	8
how many	几	幾	jǐ		5
how many, how much	多少	多少	duōshǎo	*Pron.*	7
how old	多大	多大	duōdà		14
hundred	百	百	bǎi	*Num.*	17
hungry	饿	餓	è	*Adj.*	19

I

I, me	我	我	wǒ	*Pron.*	1
ice	冰	冰	bīng	*N.*	11
ice hockey	冰球	冰球	bīngqiú	*N.*	16s
immediately	马上	馬上	mǎshàng	*Adv.*	20
immunization shot	预防针	預防針	yùfángzhēn	*N.*	19s
to improve	进步	進步	jìnbù	*V.*	12
in front of	前边	前邊	qiánbiān	*N.*	15
in the process of, in the course of (to indicate an action in progress)	正在	正在	zhèngzài	*Adv.*	9
to increase	上升	上升	shàngshēng	*V.C.*	17s
(indicates assumption)	了	了	le	*Part.*	9
(indicates one's act of service)	为	為	wèi	*Prep.*	14
(indicates the superlative degree)	最	最	zuì	*Adv.*	17

inexpensive	便宜	便宜	piányi	*Adj.*	13s
inside	里边	裡邊	lǐbiān	*N.*	15
interesting, enjoyable	有意思	有意思	yǒuyìsi	*Adj.*	21
international students	留学生	留學生	liúxuéshēng	*N.*	6s
Internet	网络 (网路)	網絡 (網路)	wǎngluò (wǎnglù)	*N.*	9s
Internet café	网吧 (网咖)	網吧 (網咖)	wǎngbā (wǎngkā)	*N.*	9s
internship	实习	實習	shíxí	*N.*	21
to introduce	介绍	介紹	jièshào	*V.*	5
to introduce oneself; self-introduction	自我介绍	自我介紹	zìwǒjièshào	*V./N.*	6s
(introduces the object of a verb)	把	把	bǎ	*Prep.*	20
introduction	介绍	介紹	jièshào	*N.*	5
it seems	看来	看來	kànlái		22

J

jacket	夹克衫 (夹克)	夾克衫 (夾克)	jiákèshān (jiákè)	*N.*	13s
Japan	日本	日本	Rìběn	*N.*	3s, 8
Japanese (language)	日语 (日文)	日語 (日文)	Rìyǔ (Rìwén)	*N.*	3s
(people)	日本人	日本人	Rìběnrén	*N.*	3s
jeans	牛仔裤	牛仔褲	niúzǎikù	*N.*	13s
jeep	吉普车	吉普車	jípǔchē	*N.*	18s
jiao (RMB unit of 10 cents) 10 fen	角	角	jiǎo	*N.*	13s
job, to work	工作	工作	gōngzuò	*N./V.*	6
juice	果汁	果汁	guǒzhī	*N.*	11s

K

kitchen	厨房	廚房	chúfáng	*N.*	15
to know	认识	認識	rènshi	*V.*	5s
to know, recognize	认识	認識	rènshi	*V.*	8
to know, be aware of, realize	知道	知道	zhīdào	*V.*	9
Korea	韩国	韓國	Hánguó	*N.*	3s, 8
Korean (language)	韩语 (韩文)	韓語 (韓文)	Hányǔ (Hánwén)	*N.*	3s
(people)	韩国人	韓國人	Hánguórén	*N.*	3s

L

to lack	差	差	chà	*V.*	10s
landlord	房东	房東	fángdōng	*N.*	20s
large	大	大	dà	*Adj.*	13s
late	晚	晚	wǎn	*Adj.*	10s
lawyer	律师	律師	lǜshī	*N.*	6s
to learn, to master	学到	學到	xuédào	*V.C.*	22
leather shoes	皮鞋	皮鞋	píxié	*N.*	13s
to leave a message	留言 (留话)	留言 (留話)	liúyán (liúhuà)	*V.O.*	9
to let, allow	让	讓	ràng	*V.*	13
letter	信	信	xìn	*N.*	10
library	图书馆	圖書館	túshūguǎn	*N.*	10
life	生活	生活	shēnghuó	*N.*	10
to lift weights	举重	舉重	jǔzhòng	*V.O.*	16s
light	浅色	淺色	qiǎnsè	*Adj.*	13s
light green	浅绿色	淺綠色	qiǎnlǜsè	*Adj.*	13s
to like	喜欢	喜歡	xǐhuān	*V.*	10
literature	文学	文學	wénxué	*N.*	4
little, a	一点儿	一點兒	yìdiǎr		3
	有点儿	有點兒	yǒudiǎr	*Adv.*	4s
little steamed buns with stuffing	小笼包	小籠包	xiǎolóngbāo	*N.*	22
to live	住	住	zhù	*V.*	7
living room	客厅	客廳	kètīng	*N.*	15
to look at, see, watch	看	看	kàn	*V.*	9
long	长	長	cháng	*Adj.*	17s
long pants	长裤	長褲	chángkù	*N.*	13s
to love	爱	愛	ài	*V.*	6
lunch	午饭 (中饭)	午飯 (中飯)	wǔfàn (zhōngfàn)	*N.*	8s

M

magazine	杂志	雜誌	zázhì	*N.*	15s
magnetic railway	磁浮铁路	磁浮鐵路	cífú tiělù	*N.*	18s
mailman	邮递员 (邮差)	郵遞員 (郵差)	yóudìyuán (yóuchāi)	*N.*	6s
major	专业 (主修)	專業 (主修)	zhuānyè (zhǔxiū)	*N.*	4s
to make a phone call	打电话	打電話	dǎ diànhuà	*V.O.*	9
to make, do	做	做	zuò	*V.*	14
male	男	男	nán	*N.*	6
manager	经理	經理	jīnglǐ	*N.*	6s

manual transmission	手排挡 (手排)	手排擋 (手排)	shǒupáidǎng (shǒupái)	*N.*	12
many, much	多	多	duō	*Adj.*	4
mao (the RMB unit of 10 cents) 1/10 of yuan	毛	毛	máo	*N.*	13s
map	地图	地圖	dìtú	*N.*	14
master's degree	硕士	碩士	shuòshì	*N.*	21s
maternal grandfather	外公	外公	wàigōng	*N.*	6s
	外祖父	外祖父	wàizǔfù	*N.*	6s
	姥爷	老爺	lǎoye	*N.*	6s
maternal grandmother	外婆	外婆	wàipó	*N.*	6s
	外祖母	外祖母	wàizǔmǔ	*N.*	6s
	姥姥	姥姥	lǎolao	*N.*	6s
mathematics	数学	數學	shùxué	*N.*	4s
matter, thing, business	事儿	事兒	shèr	*N.*	8
may I ask	请问	請問	qǐng wèn		2
medium	中	中	zhōng	*Adj.*	13s
to meet each other	见面	見面	jiànmiàn	*V.O.*	17
menu	菜单	菜單	càidān	*N.*	11s
messy	乱	亂	luàn	*Adj.*	15s
middle	中间	中間	zhōngjiān	*N.*	15
midnight snack	宵夜	宵夜	xiāoyè	*N.*	8s
minibus, van	面包车 (包型车)	麵包車 (包型車)	miànbāochē (bāoxíngchē)	*N.*	18s
miniskirt	迷你裙	迷你裙	míníqún	*N.*	13s
minor	辅修	輔修	fǔxiū	*N.*	4s
minute	分	分	fēn	*N.*	10
	分钟	分鐘	fēnzhōng	*N.*	10s, 18
miss	小姐	小姐	xiǎojiě	*N.*	11
mister	先生	先生	xiānsheng	*N.*	11
money	钱	錢	qián	*N.*	13
month	月	月	yuè	*N.*	10
most, the superlative degree	最	最	zuì	*Adv.*	22
mother	妈妈	媽媽	māma	*N.*	6
to move	搬	搬	bān	*V.*	20
movie	电影	電影	diànyǐng	*N.*	9s, 13
MRT (Mass Rapid Transportation) in Taiwan	捷运	捷運	jiéyùn	*N.*	18s
multicolor	彩色	彩色	cǎisè	*Adj.*	13s
must	必须	必須	bìxū	*Aux.*	20
must, have to	得	得	děi	*Aux.*	12

N

name	名字	名字	míngzi	*N.*	2
name card	名片	名片	míngpiàn	*N.*	8s
near	近	近	jìn	*Adj.*	18
nearby	旁边	旁邊	pángbiān	*N.*	15
necklace	项链	項鏈	xiàngliàn	*N.*	13s
necktie	领带	領帶	lǐngdài	*N.*	13s
nephew (brother's son)	侄子	姪子	zhízi	*N.*	6s
(sister's son)	外甥	外甥	wàisheng	*N.*	6s
new	新	新	xīn	*Adj.*	22
New York	纽约	紐約	Niǔyuē	*N.*	6
next time	下次	下次	xiàcì		8
niece (brother's daughter)	侄女	姪女	zhínǚ	*N.*	6s
(sister's daughter)	外甥女	外甥女	wàishengnǚ	*N.*	6s
nine	九/玖	九/玖	jiǔ	*Num.*	7
No problem	没关系	沒關係	méiguānxi		20
noble, honored; expensive	贵	貴	guì	*Adj.*	2
noodle	面	麵	miàn	*N.*	11
north	北	北	běi	*N.*	18s
not bad, okay	还好	還好	hái hǎo		4s
not bad, pretty good	不错	不錯	búcuò		13
not, no (used to form negation)	不	不	bù	*Adv.*	1
notes	笔记	筆記	bǐjì	*N.*	19
novel	小说	小說	xiǎoshuō	*N.*	9s
now	现在	現在	xiànzài	*Adv.*	16
number	号	號	hào	*N.*	7
	号码	號碼	hàomǎ	*N.*	7
nurse	护士	護士	hùshi	*N.*	6s, 19s

O

occupation	职业	職業	zhíyè	*N.*	6s
to occupy a (phone) line, the line is busy	占线	佔線	zhànxiàn	*V.O.*	9s
o'clock	点	點	diǎn	*M.W.*	10
off campus	校外	校外	xiàowài	*N.*	7
off-road vehicle, jeep	越野车	越野車	yuèyěchē	*N.*	18s
off-season	淡季	淡季	dànjì	*N.*	18s
often, frequently	常	常	cháng	*Adv.*	5
on campus	校内	校內	xiàonèi	*N.*	7s
on the left	左边	左邊	zuǒbiān	*N.*	15s
on the right	右边	右邊	yòubiān	*N.*	15s
one	一/壹	一/壹	yī	*Num.*	6

P

please (polite)	请	請	qǐng		2
pork	猪肉	豬肉	zhūròu	*N.*	11s
to practice	练习	練習	liànxí	*V.*	12
to prepare	准备	準備	zhǔnbèi	*V.*	19
problem, question	问题	問題	wèntí	*N.*	12
professor	教授	教授	jiàoshòu	*N.*	6s
purple	紫色	紫色	zǐsè	*Adj.*	13s
to put on (accessories)	戴上	戴上	dàishàng	*V.C.*	13s
(clothes)	穿上	穿上	chuānshàng	*V.C.*	13s

Q

quarter (of an hour)	刻	刻	kè	*M.W.*	10

R

to rain	下雨	下雨	xiàyǔ	*V.O.*	17
real estate agent	房地产顾问	房地產顧問	fángdìchǎn gùwèn	*N.*	6s
really	真	真	zhēn	*Adv.*	15
to receive	收到	收到	shōudào	*V.C.*	22
red	红	紅	hóng	*Adj.*	11
	红色	紅色	hóngsè	*Adj.*	13s
relatively	比较	比較	bǐjiào	*Adv.*	13
relatives	亲属	親屬	qīnshǔ	*N.*	6s
rent	房租	房租	fángzū	*N.*	20
to rent a house	租屋	租屋	zū wū	*V.O.*	20s
to rent, hire, lease	租	租	zū	*V.*	18
to rest	休息	休息	xiūxi	*V.*	8s, 9s, 19
restaurant	饭馆	飯館	fànguǎn	*N.*	11s
	餐厅	餐廳	cāntīng	*N.*	11s
	餐馆	餐館	cānguǎn	*N.*	11s
	饭店	飯店	fàndiàn	*N.*	11s
resume	简历	簡歷	jiǎnlì	*N.*	21s
	(履历表)	(履歷表)	(lǚlìbiǎo)		
(retroflex ending)	儿	兒	ér		3
to return	回	回	huí	*V.*	8
	回来	回來	huílai	*V.C.*	9
to review	复习	復習	fùxí	*V.*	19
rice, meal	饭	飯	fàn	*N.*	8
to ride	骑	騎	qí	*V.*	18
ring	戒指	戒指	jièzhi	*N.*	13s
road, street	马路	馬路	mǎlù	*N.*	18s
room	房间	房間	fángjiān	*N.*	7
roommate	室友	室友	shìyǒu	*N.*	5

to row a boat	划船	划船	huáchuán	*V.O.*	16s
to run	跑步	跑步	pǎobù	*V.O.*	16s

S

salad	沙拉	沙拉	shālā	*N.*	11s
salesman	推销员	推銷員	tuīxiāoyuán	*N.*	6s
salesman, saleswoman	店员	店員	diànyuán	*N.*	13
salty	咸	鹹	xián	*Adj.*	11s
sandals	凉鞋	涼鞋	liángxié	*N.*	13s
scarf	围巾	圍巾	wéijīn	*N.*	13s
scenery	风景	風景	fēngjǐng	*N.*	18
scenery, view	景色	景色	jǐngsè	*N.*	18
school	学校	學校	xuéxiào	*N.*	18
scooter, motorcycle	摩托车 (机车)	摩托車 (機車)	mótuōchē (jīchē)	*N.*	18s
seafood	海鲜	海鮮	hǎixiān	*N.*	11s
seashore	海滩	海灘	hǎitān	*N.*	18s
seaside	海边	海邊	hǎibiān	*N.*	18
season (of sports)	球季	球季	qiújì	*N.*	16s
second	秒	秒	miǎo	*N.*	10s
secretary	秘书	祕書	mìshū	*N.*	6s
to see	见	見	jiàn	*V.*	8
to seek for, to look for	找	找	zhǎo	*V.*	21
to sell	卖	賣	mài	*V.*	13s
to send a short (cell phone) message	发短信 (送简讯)	發短信 (送簡訊)	fā duǎnxìn (sòng jiǎnxùn)	*V.O.*	9s
semester	学期	學期	xuéqī	*N.*	10
to settle the account	结账 (结帐)	結賬 (結帳)	jiézhàng (jiézhàng)	*V.O.*	11s
seven	七/柒	七/柒	qī	*Num.*	7
severe	严重	嚴重	yánzhòng	*Adj.*	19s
severely, very much	厉害	厲害	lìhai	*Adj.*	19s
she, her	她	她	tā	*Pron.*	2
ship	船	船	chuán	*N.*	18
shirt	衬衫	襯衫	chènshān	*N.*	13
shoes	鞋子	鞋子	xiézi	*N.*	13s
short	短	短	duǎn	*Adj.*	17
short pants	短裤	短褲	duǎnkù	*N.*	13s
should	应该	應該	yīnggāi	*Aux.*	12
shrimp	虾	蝦	xiā	*N.*	11s
siblings	兄弟姐妹	兄弟姐妹	xiōngdìjiěmèi	*N.*	6s
to sign a contract	签约	簽約	qiānyuē	*V.O.*	20s

stop, station	车站	車站	chēzhàn	*N.*	18s
strawberry	草莓	草莓	cǎoméi	*N.*	11s
structural particle	的	的	de	*Part.*	2
student	学生	學生	xuésheng	*N.*	1
to study abroad	留学	留學	liúxué	*V.O.*	21
to study, to learn	学	學	xué	*V.*	1
subway	地铁	地鐵	dìtiě	*N.*	18s
suit	西装	西裝	xīzhuāng	*N.*	13s
summer	夏	夏	xià	*N.*	17
	暑期	暑期	shǔqī	*N.*	21
summer vacation	暑假	暑假	shǔjià	*N.*	17s, 21
surname, family name	姓	姓	xìng	*N.*	2
sweater	毛衣	毛衣	máoyī	*N.*	13s
sweet	甜	甜	tián	*Adj.*	11s
to swim; swimming	游泳	游泳	yóuyǒng	*V.O./N.*	16
swimming pool	游泳池	游泳池	yóuyǒngchí	*N.*	16

T

table	桌子	桌子	zhuōzi	*N.*	15
to take medicine	吃药	吃藥	chīyào	*V.O.*	19
Take care	保重	保重	bǎozhòng		22s
to take off (accessories)	摘	摘	zhāi	*V.*	13s
	摘下	摘下	zhāixià	*V.C.*	13s
(clothes)	脱	脱	tuō	*V.*	13s
	脱下	脱下	tuōxià	*V.C.*	13s
tall building	大楼	大樓	dàlóu	*N.*	22
tangerine juice	柳橙汁 (柳丁汁)	柳橙汁 (柳丁汁)	liǔchéngzhī (liǔdīngzhī)	*N.*	11s
taxi	出租汽车 (计程车)	出租汽車 (計程車)	chūzūqìchē (jìchéngchē)	*N.*	18s
tea	茶	茶	chá	*N.*	11
to teach, coach	教	教	jiāo	*V.*	16
teacher	老师	老師	lǎoshī	*N.*	1, 6s
T-shirt	T-恤衫 (T-恤)	T-恤衫 (T-恤)	tīxùshān (tīxù)	*N.*	13s
television	电视	電視	diànshì	*N.*	9
temperature	气温	氣溫	qìwēn	*N.*	17s
ten	十/拾	十/拾	shí	*Num.*	7s, 11
tenant	房客	房客	fángkè	*N.*	20s
tennis	网球	網球	wǎngqiú	*N.*	16s
Thai (language)	泰语 (泰文)	泰語 (泰文)	Tàiyǔ (Tàiwén)	*N.*	3s
(people)	泰国人	泰國人	Tàiguórén	*N.*	3s

Thailand	泰国	泰國	Tàiguó	*N.*	3s
to thank, be grateful for	感谢	感謝	gǎnxiè	*V.*	19
Thank you, Thanks.	谢谢	謝謝	xièxie		9
that	那	那	nà	*Pron.*	4
then, after that, afterwards	然后	然後	ránhòu	*Adv.*	10
therefore	就	就	jiù	*Adv.*	12
therefore, consequently	所以	所以	suǒyǐ	*Conj.*	19
they, them	他们	他們	tāmen	*Pron.*	5
thing	东西	東西	dōngxi	*N.*	22
to think, feel	觉得	覺得	juéde	*V.*	13
this	这	這	zhè	*Pron.*	4
this time	这次	這次	zhècì	*Pron.*	12
three	三/叁	三/叁	sān	*Num.*	7
thus, in this way	这样	這樣	zhèyàng	*Pron.*	12
ticket	票	票	piào	*N.*	13
tidy	整齐	整齊	zhěngqí	*Adj.*	15s
time	时间	時間	shíjiān	*N.*	17
(duration of point in)	时候	時候	shíhou	*N.*	9
tip	小费	小費	xiǎofèi	*N.*	11s
tired	累	累	lèi	*Adj.*	4s
today	今天	今天	jīntiān	*N.*	8
together	一起	一起	yìqǐ	*Adv.*	8
tomorrow	明天	明天	míngtiān	*N.*	12
too	太	太	tài	*Adv.*	4
tourist guide	导游	導遊	dǎoyóu	*N.*	6s
train	火车	火車	huǒchē	*N.*	18, 18s
to travel	旅行	旅行	lǚxíng	*V.*	18
truck	大货车	大貨車	dàhuòchē	*N.*	18s
to try	试试	試試	shìshi	*V.*	13
tunnel	隧道	隧道	suìdào	*N.*	18s
two	两	兩	liǎng	*Num.*	5
	二/贰	二/貳	èr	*Num.*	7
two people (colloquial)	俩	倆	liǎ		16

U

uncle (father's elder brother)	伯伯	伯伯	bóbo	*N.*	6s
(father's younger brother)	叔叔	叔叔	shūshu	*N.*	6s
(husband of father's	姑父	姑父	gūfù	*N.*	6s
sister)	姑丈	姑丈	gūzhàng	*N.*	6s
(husband of mother's	姨丈	姨丈	yízhàng	*N.*	6s
sister)	姨父	姨父	yífù	*N.*	6s
(mother's brother)	舅舅	舅舅	jiùjiu	*N.*	6s

underground passage	地下道	地下道	dìxiàdào	*N.*	18s
underpants	内裤	內褲	nèikù	*N.*	13s
underwear	内衣	內衣	nèiyī	*N.*	13s
United States of America, the	美国	美國	Měiguó	*N.*	3
upstairs	楼上	樓上	lóushàng	*N.*	20
to use	用	用	yòng	*V.*	12
(used after a personal pronoun or noun to show plural number)	们	們	men		4
(used after a verb to indicate a brief action)	一下	一下	yíxià		5
(used at the end of a sentence to indicate surprise)	啊	啊	a	*Int.*	20
(used at the end of a sentence to transform it into a question)	吗	嗎	ma	*Part.*	1
(used at the end of an interrogative sentence)	呢	呢	ne	*Part.*	1
(to indicate an assumption or a suggestion)	吧	吧	ba	*Part.*	9
(used before a verb to indicate that something is rather late)	才	才	cái	*Adv.*	10
(used between a verb or an adjective and its complement to indicate result, possibility or degree)	得	得	de	*Part.*	16

V

vacation	假期	假期	jiàqī	*N.*	17s
vegetable	青菜	青菜	qīngcài	*N.*	11s
very	非常	非常	fēicháng	*Adv.*	16
very, quite	很	很	hěn	*Adv.*	3
vest	背心	背心	bèixīn	*N.*	13s
virus	病毒	病毒	bìngdú	*N.*	9s
to visit	参观	參觀	cānguān	*V.*	15
volleyball	排球	排球	páiqiú	*N.*	16s

W

to wait	等	等	děng	*V.*	9
to wait for a moment	等一下儿	等一下兒	děng yíxiàr		9
waiter/waitress	服务员	服務員	fúwùyuán	*N.*	11
to walk	走	走	zǒu	*V.*	15
	走路	走路	zǒulù	*V.O.*	18
to want	想	想	xiǎng	*V.*	8
to want, desire	要	要	yào	*V.*	9
wardrobe	衣橱	衣櫥	yīchú	*N.*	15s
warm	暖和	暖和	nuǎnhuo	*Adj.*	17
warmhearted	热心	熱心	rèxīn	*Adj.*	22
to wash one's face	洗脸	洗臉	xǐliǎn	*V.O.*	10s
watch	手表	手錶	shǒubiǎo	*N.*	13s
watermelon	西瓜	西瓜	xīguā	*N.*	11s
we, us	我们	我們	wǒmen	*Pron.*	4
wear, put on (accessories)	戴	戴	dài	*V.*	13s
(clothes)	穿	穿	chuān	*V.*	13s
to wear	穿	穿	chuān	*V.*	13
weather	天气	天氣	tiānqì	*N.*	17s
Web page	网页	網頁	wǎngyè	*N.*	9s
Web site	网站	網站	wǎngzhàn	*N.*	9s
week	星期	星期	xīngqī	*N.*	14
to welcome	欢迎	歡迎	huānyíng	*V.*	15
west	西部	西部	xībù	*N.*	18
wharf, dock, pier	码头	碼頭	mǎtóu	*N.*	18s
what	什么	什麼	shénme	*Pron.*	2
where	哪儿	哪兒	nǎr	*Pron.*	7
which	哪	哪	nǎ	*Pron.*	3
what size	几号	幾號	jǐ hào		13s
white	白	白	bái	*Adj.*	12
	白色	白色	báisè	*Adj.*	13s
who, whom	谁	誰	shéi	*Pron.*	2
window	窗户	窗戶	chuānghu	*N.*	15s
winter	冬	冬	dōng	*N.*	17
winter vacation	寒假	寒假	hánjià	*N.*	17s
to wish	祝	祝	zhù	*V.*	10
with	跟	跟	gēn	*Prep.*	5
wonderful	棒	棒	bàng	*Adj.*	14
wonton	馄饨	餛飩	húntun	*N.*	11s
to work for others	打工	打工	dǎgōng	*V.O.*	21
to wrap	包	包	bāo	*V.*	16
to write	写	寫	xiě	*V.*	10
to write a letter (to the speaker)	来信	來信	láixìn	*V.O.*	22

Y

year	年	年	nián	*N.*	10
yellow	黄	黄	huáng	*Adj.*	13
	黄色	黄色	huángsè	*Adj.*	13s
yesterday	昨天	昨天	zuótiān	*N.*	16
you	你	你	nǐ	*Pron.*	1
you (polite)	您	您	nín	*Pron.*	2
You're welcome.	不客气	不客氣	Búkèqi		9s, 14
(in reply to thank you)	不谢	不謝	Búxiè		9s
younger brother	弟弟	弟弟	dìdi	*N.*	6s
younger sister	妹妹	妹妹	mèimei	*N.*	6s, 12

Z

zero	〇/零	〇/零	líng	*Num.*	7s

写字簿的生字 CHARACTERS IN THE CHARACTER BOOK

The following list shows the 432 characters that appear in the Character Book, grouped by the lesson in which they are first introduced. Students are required to memorize how to read and write these key characters to build up their literacy skills. The number of new characters introduced in each lesson is carefully controlled, and is provided in the list.

(1) 第一课 你好! (13 characters)

你 好 是 学 生 吗 我 呢 也 他 不 老 师

(2) 第二课 您贵姓? (17 characters)

您 贵 姓 请 问 的 英 文 名 字 中 叫 什 么 她 谁 同

(3) 第三课 你是哪国人? (14 characters)

哪 国 人 很 对 了 法 美 说 会 一 点 儿 和

(4) 第四课 你学什么? (14 characters)

那 书 这 本 工 程 难 太 可 功 课 多 们 少

(5) 第五课 这是我朋友 (14 characters)

朋 友 来 介 绍 下 室 有 几 两 个 都 常 跟

(6) 第六课 我的家 (16 characters)

家 大 从 在 四 爸 妈 姐 作 男 没 辆 车 只 狗 爱

(7) 第七课 你住哪儿? (21 characters)

住 宿 舍 号 房 间 电 话 小 码 二 三 五 六 七 八 九 手 机 校 外

(8) 第八课 你认识不认识他? (21 characters)

认 识 去 上 以 后 事 想 回 起 吃 饭 菜 今 天 次 怎 样 行 再 见

(9) 第九课 他正在打电话 (22 characters)

打 喂 等 知 道 谢 吧 忙 正 看 视 做 网 就 位 留 言 时 候 晚 要 给

(10) 第十课 我每天七点半起床 (29 characters)

活 期 门 每 床 睡 觉 半 才 刻 分 然 图 馆 午 喜 欢 球 写 信 子 邮 件 地 址 祝 年 月 日

(11) 第十一课 你要红茶还是绿茶? (25 characters)

红 茶 还 绿 服 务 员 坐 先 喝 杯 冰 乐 瓶 啤 酒 面 饺 盘 炒 十 碗 汤 双 筷

(12) 第十二课　我可以借你的车吗？(25 characters)

借 明 用 得 场 接 妹 飞 玩 到 排 挡 开 应 该 题 白 色 停 到 习 练 能 进 步

(13) 第十三课　我想买一件衬衫 (23 characters)

买 衬 衫 店 条 裙 或 者 裤 黄 错 比 较 穿 黑 试 帮 让 钱 块 张 影 票

(14) 第十四课　我今年二十岁 (15 characters)

岁 空 星 过 为 舞 参 加 定 蛋 糕 送 棒 客 气

(15) 第十五课　图书馆在宿舍前边 (18 characters)

前 边 迎 观 里 厨 公 旁 走 厅 面 餐 洗 澡 卧 桌 园 真

(16) 第十六课　她打篮球打得很好 (20 characters)

篮 俩 教 游 泳 非 快 体 育 池 健 身 锻 炼 现 昨 赛 业 包 慢

(17) 第十七课　春天就要来了 (22 characters)

春 久 放 假 夏 秋 冬 其 最 暖 短 热 华 氏 百 度 极 刮 风 雨 冷 雪

(18) 第十八课　我们要坐火车去旅行 (20 characters)

火 旅 离 远 只 钟 骑 自 共 汽 路 近 西 部 景 船 南 听 海 租

(19) 第十九课　我感冒了 (23 characters)

感 冒 饿 像 舒 头 疼 发 烧 咳 嗽 病 考 复 所 医 药 休 息 准 备 笔 记

(20) 第二十课　我把小谢带来了 . . . (17 characters)

把 带 啊 搬 出 吸 烟 关 系 但 女 必 须 第 付 楼 马

(21) 第二十一课　暑假你要做什么？(18 characters)

暑 毕 决 申 研 究 院 找 司 实 脑 班 意 思 愉 平 安 运

(22) 第二十二课　我到上海了 (25 characters)

因 已 经 丽 城 市 处 新 些 方 动 如 京 剧 东 笼 尝 始 高 兴 收 心 板 保 重